AGE ESTIMATION OF THE HUMAN SKELETON

Edited by

KRISTA E. LATHAM, PH.D.

and

MICHAEL FINNEGAN, PH.D., D-ABFA

With a Foreword by

Stanley Rhine, PH.D., D-ABFA

University of New Mexico

CHARLES C THOMAS • PUBLISHER, LTD.
Springfield • Illinois • U.S.A.

Published and Distributed Throughout the World by

CHARLES C THOMAS • PUBLISHER, LTD.
2600 South First Street
Springfield, Illinois 62794-9265

© 2010 by CHARLES C THOMAS • PUBLISHER, LTD.

ISBN 978-0-398-07949-9 (hard)
ISBN 978-0-398-07950-5 (paper)

Library of Congress Catalog Card Number: 2010016116

With THOMAS BOOKS *careful attention is given to all details of manufacturing
and design. It is the Publisher's desire to present books that are satisfactory as to their
physical qualities and artistic possibilities and appropriate for their particular use.*
THOMAS BOOKS *will be true to those laws of quality that assure a good name
and good will.*

Printed in the United States of America
MM-R-3

Library of Congress Cataloging in Publication Data

Age estimation of the human skeleton / edited by Krista E. Latham, Ph.D. &
Michael Finnegan, Ph.D., D-ABFA, with a foreword by Jane E. Buikstra,
Ph.D., D-ABFA and Stanley J. Thine, Ph.D., D-ABFA.
  p. cm.
  Includes biographical references and index.
ISBN 978-0-398-07949-9 (hard)–ISBN 978-0-398-07950-5 (pbk.)
1. Human skeleton–Analysis. 2. Human skeleton–Growth. 3. Human body–
Composition–Age factors. 4. Forensic athropology. 5. Forensic osteology. 6.
Dental anthropology. I. Latham, Krista E. II. Finnegan, J. Michael. III.
Buikstra, Jane E. IV. Rhine, Stanley, V. Title.

GN70.A34 2010
614'17–dc22   2010016116

AGE ESTIMATION
OF THE
HUMAN SKELETON

To the memory of:
Alice M. Brues (1913–2007)
and
Sheilagh T. Brooks (1923–2008)

CONTRIBUTORS

JEREMY J. BEACH, M.S.
Purdue University, Department of Anthropology
700 West State St., Suite 219
West Lafayette, IN 47907
beachj@purdue.edu

CARRIE A. BROWN, M.A.
Joint POW/MIA Accounting Command Central Identification Laboratory
310 Worchester Ave., Bldg. 45
Hickam AFB, HI 96853-5530
carrie.brown@jpac.pacom.mil

AMBER R. CAMPBELL HIBBS, M.A.
Emory University, Department of Anthropology
1557 Dickey Dr.
Atlanta, GA 30322
amber.rae.campbell@gmail.com

CHRISTIAN CROWDER, PH.D., D-ABFA
Deputy Director of Forensic Anthropology Office of Chief Medical Examiner
520 First Ave.
New York, NY 10016
ccrowder@ocme.nyc.gov

JANENE M. CURTIS, M.S.
Forensic Identification Services, RCMP K Division HQ
11140 109 St.
Edmonton, AB, Canada T5G 2T4
jmcurtis11@hotmail.com

MICHAEL FINNEGAN, PH.D., D-ABFA
Osteology Laboratory Professor, Department of Sociology, Anthropology and Social Work
204 Waters Hall, Kansas State University
Manhattan, KS 66506
finnegan@ksu.edu

HEATHER M. GARVIN, M.S.
Johns Hopkins School of Medicine, Center for Functional Anatomy & Evolution
1830 E Monument St.
Baltimore, MD 21205
heamarie@jhmi.edu

JENNIFER L. HARMS-PASCHAL, M.S.
Clinical Data Manager
7551 Metro Center Dr.
Austin, TX 78744
jennpaschal@gmail.com

CAROLYN V. HURST, M.A.
Michigan State University, Department of Anthropology
354 Baker Hall
East Lansing, MI 48824
hurstcar@msu.edu

ANGIE HUXLEY PH.D., D.O.
St. Joseph's Hospital and Medical Center, Department of Internal Medicine
350 W. Thomas Rd.
Phoenix, AZ 85013
akhuxley@pol.net

DUSTIN M. JAMES, B.A.
Department of Anthropology, University of Memphis
316 Manning Hall
Memphis, TN 38152
dmjames1@memphis.edu

KRISTA E. LATHAM, PH.D.
Assistant Professor of Biology & Anthropology, Research Associate, University of Indianapolis
Archeology & Forensics Laboratory
1400 East Hanna Ave.
Indianapolis, IN 46227
lathamke@uindy.edu

STEPHEN P. NAWROCKI, PH.D., D-ABFA
Sease Distinguished Professor of Forensic Studies, Professor of Biology & Anthropology
Director, Graduate Human Biology Program, Co-Director, University of Indianapolis
Archeology & Forensics Laboratory
1400 E. Hanna Ave.
Indianapolis, IN 46227
snawrocki@uindy.edu

NICHOLAS V. PASSALACQUA, M.S.
Michigan State University, Department of Anthropology
354 Baker Hall
East Lansing, MI 48823
passala5@msu.edu

SUSAN PFEIFFER, PH.D.
University of Toronto Professor, Anthropology Department
19 Russell St.
Toronto, ON, M5S Canada 2S2
susan.pfeiffer@utoronto.ca

CHRISTOPHER W. SCHMIDT, PH.D.
Indiana Prehistory Laboratory Associate Professor, Department of Anthropology,
University of Indianapolis
1400 E. Hanna Ave.
Indianapolis, IN 46227
cschmidt@uindy.edu

RACHEL A. SHARKEY, B.S.
University of Indianapolis, Department of Anthropology
1400 East Hanna Ave.
Indianapolis, IN 46227
lockhartra@uindy.edu

EMILIE L. SMITH, M.S., M.P.A.S., P.A.-C.
Board Certified Physician Assistant,
University of Texas Health Science Center at San Antonio
3537 County Rd. 4220
Commerce, TX 75428
els711@gmail.com

MARGARET STREETER, PH.D.
Associate Professor, Department of Anthropology, Boise State University
1910 University Dr.
Boise, ID 83725
margaretstreeter@boisestate.edu

KYRA E. STULL, M.S.
Coordinator, Forensic Anthropology Center, Department of Anthropology
Texas State University - San Marcos
601 University Dr., ELA 232
San Marcos, TX 78666
ks47@txstate.edu

DOUGLAS H. UBELAKER, PH.D., D-ABFA
Department of Anthropology, Smithsonian Institution
NMNH, MRC 112
Washington, DC 20560-0112
ubelaked@si.edu

NATALIE M. UHL, M.S.
Department of Anthropology, University of Illinois at Urbana-Champaign
109 Davenport Hall, 607 S. Mathews Ave.
Urbana, IL 61801
uhl1@illinois.edu

DIANA M. WILBERT, B.S.
Department of Sociology, Anthropology and Social Work
204 Waters Hall, Kansas State University
Manhattan, KS 66506

FOREWORD

In ascertaining that a set of remains are both human and of medicolegal significance, the forensic anthropologist absorbs many impressions. These form an instant conclusion, a skeletal gestalt. However, most practitioners agree that creation of a biological profile should be undertaken in a very compartmentalized fashion, independently assessing sex, age, ancestry and stature. Later, one can more fully evaluate other attributes; ante-, peri- and postmortem trauma, state of health and other idiosyncratic features that might be useful in narrowing down the search for identity, and for attributes that would illuminate time since death, cause of death and other matters of medicolegal interest.

Aging younger individuals has traditionally depended upon an assessment of the maturation of the skeleton; the appearance of centers of ossification, epiphyseal fusion, development and eruption of the teeth, and in the very young, direct measurement of the bony elements. In older individuals the age estimation process has focused on degeneration of the skeleton as reflected in various joints of the body, such as the pubic symphysis, auricular surface and cranial sutures. Each of these continues to be the focus of ever-closer analytical scrutiny.

In the past few decades there has been a growing interest in assessing age by an analysis of the fine structure of bones and teeth. It may seem that this continued finer focus provides an alternate, more exotic, hardware-dependent and time-demanding analysis. Yet, not all of these methods will be used on a single case. Instead, we have an ever-expanding galaxy of potential approaches that can be selectively applied to any case.

Clearly, no single criterion is adequate for estimating age. Any estimate of age (or any other quality) is made more reliable and accurate by employing multiple approaches with multiple bones. While age may be estimated from the state of the pubic symphysis (for example), it is dangerous to place all of one's eggs in that—or any other—single basket. Evaluation of multiple bones through a combination of anthropometric, anthroposcopic and histological means offers convergent conclusions from methodologically independent sources, and thus the most robust results.

This volume effectively illustrates that the study of human osteology in a forensic context continues to become both wider and deeper.

STANLEY RHINE

INTRODUCTION

Age Estimation of the Human Skeleton represents a collection of some of the latest research in age at death estimation indicators of human skeletal remains using dental, gross morphological, histological and multifactorial techniques. The papers represent scientific research that has been conducted and presented at scientific forums within the past several years, and encompasses age estimation methods from all life-stage categories, including: fetal, subadult, and adult. This book will serve as a convenient starting point for practical and research applications.

INSPIRATION FOR THE VOLUME

This volume arose from various symposia at recent Mountain, Desert and Coastal Forensic Anthropologists meetings, focusing on methods of age estimation from the human skeleton. The symposia were organized by the editors, who noticed a great deal of research being conducted on this topic. The editors also recognized a need for an up-to-date book on aging human skeletal remains, as the last text available for this purpose was compiled in 1989, and significant scientific advances have been made since that time. There are several books available that have one or two chapters devoted to skeletal aging techniques. However, the full spectrum of techniques cannot be covered in one or two chapters and an entire volume on this topic is needed.

THE MOUNTAIN, DESERT AND COASTAL
FORENSIC ANTHROPOLOGISTS

The Mountain Desert & Coastal Forensic Anthropologists meeting (MD&C) celebrates its thirtieth anniversary in 2010. From the beginning, MD&C has served as a forum to foster the presentation of new research and a continuing discussion of pertinent topics surrounding skeletal biology and forensic anthropology. This volume celebrates that legacy.

Looking Back

MD&C officially met for the first time in 1981 with nine attendees at the Southern Utah State College's mountain cabin. The first three meetings focused on regional variation of human skeletal remains, and resulted in the first MD&C inspired publication: *Skeletal Attribution of Race* (Gill and Rhine, 1990). These early accommodations were very rustic and remote, a combination that kept attendee numbers small and meetings very informal.

The MD&C meeting location changed to the Lake Mead Lodge in Boulder City, Nevada in 1986. With the change of venue came more attendees and the need for more organization. By 1988 the number of attendees rose to 41 and by 1989 MD&C had its first official schedule of presentations and first annual t-shirt. In 1991, *The Connective Tissue* became the official journal of the Mountain, Desert and Coastal Forensic Anthropologists.

The silver anniversary of MD&C was celebrated in 2005 with 37 attendees. By this time the atmosphere had shifted to a more balanced group of forensic anthropologists and eager students. The number of individuals wanting to present new or refined research grew to the point that a moderator was required to keep track of time. The Lake Mead Lodge closed its doors in 2008, and MD&C had to move to yet another location in Boulder City. Younger attendees try to maintain the original intent of the MD&C founders, while adapting to changing times. As attendee numbers rise and fall from year-to-year, one thing remains the same: MD&C is a favorite meeting for many anthropologists (historical information summarized from various volumes of *The Connective Tissue*).

Looking Ahead

MD&C was created as a way to gather forensic anthropologists and their advanced graduate students from the mountain, desert and coastal western part of the United States together in a friendly informal atmosphere to discuss the field of forensic anthropology. As attendee numbers have grown and demographics have changed, so has the face of the meeting. However, MD&C remains consistent in bringing out the best in its attendees. MD&C is distinct from other meetings with its informal attire and no titles attitude. This creates an environment where old and young, experienced and naive, debate and share ideas. A glance at regular attendees of the past and present reveal a long list of able-bodied forensic anthropologists. The first 30 years of MD&C have inspired numerous researchers and two volumes, and it is expected that there is still much to come.

K.E.L.

REFERENCES

Gill, G. W., & Rhine, S. (Eds.). (1990). Skeletal attribution of race. Albuquerque, New Mexico: Maxwell Museum of Anthropology Anthropological Papers No 4.

Finnegan, M. (Ed.). (2000). *The connective tissue 16*(1). Manhattan, Kansas.

Finnegan, M. (Ed.). (2001). *The connective tissue 17*(4). Manhattan, Kansas.

Finnegan, M. (Ed.). (2002). *The connective tissue 18*(4). Manhattan, Kansas.

Finnegan, M. (Ed.). (2005). *The connective tissue 21*(2). Manhattan, Kansas.

A HISTORY OF METHODOLOGY IN THE ESTIMATION OF AGE AT DEATH FROM THE SKELETON

Douglas H. Ubelaker

The history of the methodology of estimating age at death from the human skeleton is complex and incorporates a large and diverse literature. Given the limited space available for this section, I have chosen to focus only on key thematic developments as presented in landmark synthetic works. Special attention is devoted to the development of approaches based on newly recognized anatomical areas and perspective, which continued to influence research in later times. This approach, by necessity, limits literature coverage and indicates that some key individual studies are not examined exhaustively.

THOMAS DWIGHT'S PIONEER STUDIES

The work of Thomas Dwight (1843–1911) represents a useful entry point into the history of age at death estimation. T. D. Stewart (1901–1997) considered him to be the "father of forensic anthropology in the United States (Stewart, 1979, xii) since he became involved in forensic cases and made significant early contributions to the field. Working in Boston, Dwight conducted research and taught anatomy for decades, holding the Parkman Professorship of Anatomy at Harvard. Although he made significant research contributions to methods of age estimation (Dwight, 1881, 1890a,b) his reputation in forensic anthropology became established through his key prize-winning publication in 1878 *The Identification of the Human Skeleton, A Medico-Legal Study*. Given its historical prominence, this essay presents a useful platform to launch this examination of the history of age estimation.

Although Dwight's essay was general in nature, it addressed key points in age estimation that continue in importance today. Much of the most relevant discussion is presented in Chapter IV (Dwight's volume) entitled "The Age." In his introduction to this chapter, Dwight noted that age can "rarely be given with any great accuracy" (Dwight, 1878:36). He highlighted the importance of sex difference in aging and that different methods apply to different general stages of life. Dwight recognized an immature stage up to age 25 in males and 22 in females, a young adult stage extending to about age 30, a mature stage from 30 to 60 and the "senile" stage "which may begin at a very variable period" (Dwight, 1878:37). For the immature stage, he stressed bone size and epiphyseal union, noting differences between beginning and final fusion and recognizing considerable variation in the timing of development. Dwight was so impressed with the likely variation that he refused to put these data in tabular form noting "The fact is, that the careful observations of some hundreds of skeletons of known ages, needed to settle this point, are yet to be made" (Dwight, 1878:37–38). This attitude contrasts with views presented in various anatomy texts of the time and such a cautious approach likely contributed to the honor Stewart later bestowed upon him.

Dwight also called attention to age changes in his young adult, mature, and senile stages, but was similarly concerned that variation was extensive and solid research needed to be completed. In a cautionary statement regarding cranial suture closure, which was later overlooked by others, he noted "the closure of the sutures which usually begins in the mature stage is another of those signs that are too variable to be depended on" (Dwight, 1878:38). He also cautioned of the variability in third molar eruption "they are like the trains of some railroads, due when they arrive" (Dwight, 1878:39).

In summary, Dwight's essay departed from texts of the time and likely won the award and Stewart's praise not because of the wealth of dogma, but because he called attention to how little was really known about variation in age progression and the need for research.

H. H. WILDER (1890–1971)

A professor at Smith College in Massachusetts, Wilder's name is closely linked with methodology relating to personal identification issues, including facial approximation. Trained as a zoologist in Europe, he became involved in forensic issues late in his career and coauthored a key synthetic work on personal identification (Wilder and Wentworth, 1918). Although much of Wilder's volume focuses on fingerprint analysis and other aspects of soft tissue identification, it contains a robust section entitled "identification of fragmentary, decomposed or dried remains; identification of bones and teeth." This particular section (Chapter VI in Wilder's volume) includes summary information on age estimation that reveals developments in thinking by that time.

Like Dwight, Wilder called attention to variation but was much more willing to offer specifics for age changes in bones and teeth. According to Wilder "the age of a person under twenty-five may be quite definitely calculated from the skeleton, or even, occasionally, from a single bone" (1918:85). The Wilder and Wentworth publication (1918:87) provides a chart listing the fusion of the coracoid process of the scapula with the "main bone" at puberty, fusion of the basilar synchondrosis at the 16th year, fusion of the "three parts of the os innominatum" by the 18th–20th year and fusion of the iliac crest by the 25th–28th year. Dental eruption is discussed but not dental formation. Criteria for estimating age in the adult years focuses on obliteration of the cranial sutures, shifts in the mandibular angle and "the reduction of the angle between the neck, and shaft of the femur" (Wilder and Wentworth, 1918:88). Wilder does not discuss the database that such opinions are based upon and fails to echo Dwight's cautionary appeals for additional research.

HRDLIČKA'S "ANTHROPOMETRY" (1920)

Although Aleš Hrdlička (1869–1943) was known primarily for his contributions to other areas of anthropology (Stewart, 1940), he also made significant and pioneering efforts in forensic applications (Ubelaker, 1999). In an early synthetic work, which became a standard reference work for practicing physical anthropologists, Hrdlička (1920) addressed age estimation from skeletal remains. In this work, Hrdlička summarized basic age changes discussed by others above but stressed factors which in his considerable experience were especially useful. For the early adult years he emphasized the regularity of fusion of the basilar synchondrosis and reported age ranges of one to five years for complete fusion at various bone sites. He called attention to population variation in the timing of tooth eruption and dental wear. Hrdlička noted the age changes in cranial suture closure and suggested that considering suture closure and dental wear together, "we may correctly estimate the age of the adult subject to within, perhaps, ten years" (1920:99).

Hrdlička also noted "the pubic articulation shows important changes with age" (1920:98). Although no detail is provided, he cited a recently published study by T. Wingate Todd (1885–1938) "Age changes in the Pubic Bone" (1920) in the *American Journal of Physical Anthropology*. Since Hrdlička was editor of that journal at the time, he likely had an early exposure and positive impression of the content in that key article. This seminal article by Todd resulted from the then recent assemblage of anatomical collections of known age at death at the Anatomical Laboratory of Western Reserve University in Cleveland, Ohio, and set the stage for later developments in age estimation from the pubic symphysis.

Hrdlička's *Practical Anthropometry* published in 1939 presents a revised version of his 1920 publication and a glimpse at the minimal developments in age estimation methodology in the intervening 19 years. This version differs little from the previous volume, but provides a more specific guide to age changes in dental attrition. The previously mentioned quote in regards to age estimation from cranial sutures and dental observations was modified to suggest an accuracy of "within less than ten years" (1939:47). For detail on recent research developments, Hrdlička refers readers in a footnote to publications by Todd (1930) on the pelvis and Graves (1922) on the scapula. Hrdlička also called attention to the importance of osteophytosis in age evaluation but presented no detail.

KROGMAN'S "GUIDE" (1939)

Historians of forensic anthropology (e.g., Stewart, 1979) have identified Wilton Marion Krogman's 1939 publication as a key development in the field. For the first time, Krogman (1903–1987) assembled important information on human identification from skeletal remains for publication in an outlet oriented toward law enforcement. The publication revealed to that community the value of scientifically-oriented analysis of human skeletal remains in the identification process. Although much of the general information is presented in a manner similar to publications by Hrdlička and others cited above, Krogman presented greater detail. He presented age information on different stages of cranial suture closure (begin, rapid, final) and added information on the dates of appearance of ossification centers.

In contrast to Hrdlička's publications, Krogman presented considerable detail on age changes at the pubic symphysis. He called attention to the gradual loss of billowing on the symphyseal face as well as the formation of "nodules," pitting and erosion. Krogman also noted how the use of x-rays could be valuable, highlighting changes seen in four stages of below 25 years, between 26 and 39, between 40 and 55 and over 56 years. Since the text is not referenced, it is not clear if Krogman's information was derived from the literature and/or from his own research.

STEWART'S EDITION OF HRDLIČKA'S *PRACTICAL ANTHROPOMETRY* (1952)

Following Hrdlička's retirement and death, T. D. Stewart published a revision of the classic reference work *Practical Anthropometry*. Although he kept Hrdlička's name in the title, Stewart put his own mark on the volume by significantly updating much of the information. Changes were minimal in the skeletal aging section with the most significant addition being a footnote calling attention to the then recent publication (1950) of the *Radiographic Atlas of Skeletal Development of the Hand and Wrist by Greulich and Pyle.*

MCKERN AND STEWART'S *SKELETAL AGE CHANGES IN YOUNG AMERICAN MALES* (1957)

In 1954, T.D. Stewart traveled to Kokura, Japan to participate in a military identification effort of United States soldiers killed during the Korean conflict. Data on various skeletal age changes were collected during the identification process on 450 young American males. These data later became the basis for the classic monograph published in 1957. In assembling these data, Stewart recognized the need for information derived from new samples in order to capture information on the vast range of human variation. He also recognized the existing paucity of data on relatively young individuals since most of the available anatomical collections were comprised of older adults. Stewart also suspected that most of the reported age ranges for various skeletal indicators were too restricted and did not take adequate account of the range of variation and the various stages of development and expression of the traits examined. The military sample offered a partial remedy to many of these issues.

Although the study was restricted to males, it represents an historical leap forward in that it examined age changes in greater detail than had been the case previously. For example, observations on cranial suture and epiphyseal closure were broken down into individual sutures and epiphyses and by four stages of closure (in addition to no closure). This approach yielded unique data on age variation in closure as well as information on population variation.

In their treatment of the pubic symphysis, McKern and Stewart decided to abandon the typological approach advanced earlier by Todd (1920, 1921) in favor of a more dynamic formula process. The authors were impressed with the approach taken by William Herbert Sheldon (1898–1977) in his efforts to study human physique. Sheldon's (1940) somatotype formula utilized three components of seven grades to characterize individual body type. Incorporating a simplified version of this concept, McKern and Stewart settled on the three component, five-subdivision system that was eventually published and widely utilized. This system recognized that the various components of the symphyseal face do not always occur in the same pattern and sequence as suggested by the Todd system.

KROGMAN'S *THE HUMAN SKELETON IN FORENSIC MEDICINE* (1962)

This classic text represents the first major synthesis of methodology in age estimation. Although the volume covered many aspects of forensic anthropology, 93 pages were devoted to the estimation of age at death. In contrast to his 1939 publication, the 1962 volume is very well referenced, so much so that it is difficult to separate Krogman's own data and opinions from the compilation from the literature. Reflecting his career interest in growth and development, the section on "the earlier years" is uniquely comprehensive for its time, presenting detailed information on bone formation and a summary of the already complex literature on epiphyseal formation and closure. Absent from this section is information on dental development and eruption, keeping with the emphasis on the "skeleton" implied in the title. Although little totally new information is presented in the text, it presents for the first time an exhaustive survey of the published literature with insightful commentary from a very experienced practitioner.

Krogman dedicated the book to T. Wingate Todd "with whom I studied and from whom I learned." Thus it is not surprising that Todd's work is prominently presented in the volume. He presented both the Todd, and McKern and Stewart systems of assessment of the symphysis pubis, but commented "with the basic work of Todd and the refinements introduced by Brooks and by McKern and Stewart, the pubic symphysis takes it place as the most reliable indicator of age in the human skeleton" (1962:105). Although Krogman provides considerable discussion of variation of age indicators, much of the data presented seem to be overly concise even by standards of the time. He concludes the aging sections with the statement referring to the third and fourth decades "using pubic symphysis plus other skeletal criteria, I'd venture an accuracy of plus or minus two years" (1962:111).

STEWART'S *ESSENTIALS OF FORENSIC ANTHROPOLOGY* (1979)

As with Krogman's 1962 volume, a major segment (62 pages) of Stewart's synthetic volume focused on methodology relating to the estimation of age at death. In contrast to the Krogman volume, Stewart included a carefully selected literature review, which reflected his sense of the most appropriate techniques available. In addition to the approaches to immature age estimation included in the Krogman volume, Stewart added a robust discussion of dental formation and eruption, noting the importance of teeth in age estimation of the young.

For adult estimation, Stewart included the then recent study of Gilbert and McKern (1973), which extended the McKern and Stewart system of evaluating the pubic symphysis to females. He also provided detail from the literature and his own research on arthritic type change in joints, histological dental approaches, studies of change in cancellous tissue, and bone microstructure including Ellis R. Kerley's (1924–1998) studies of age changes in histological features of compact bone (Kerley, 1965, 1969, 1970). The volume is distinctive from previous works in: (1) producing methodology focusing on a broader range of anatomical structures, (2) increasing awareness of variation in most age changes, and (3) the need to be selective in consulting the supportive published literature.

SUMMARY

In this survey of historical developments in methodology to estimate age at death from skeletal remains several trends are apparent. The most obvious development is the gradual recognition through research that different areas of the skeleton convey distinct information on age change. For adults, the early reliance on dental attrition and cranial suture closure gradually shifted as new techniques came on line. While evaluation of the pubic symphysis barely was discussed in Hrdlička's time, it gradually began to dominate adult age estimation with later research efforts by Todd, McKern and Stewart, and Gilbert and McKern. Clearly the discussion of histological methods, which are so prominently featured in Stewart's 1979 volume, were not on the radar screen of earlier synthesizers.

Another clear development is the gradual recognition of the importance of variation in age estimation and its resulting impact on error. In hindsight, modern forensic anthropologists likely would consider the very early attempts at age estimation to be overly precise with insufficient recognition of the actual error involved. This early naïve precision was a product of the available data and lack of research on samples of more diverse origins and of greater age range. Gradually such research has been conducted with the growing perception of human variation in most of the attributes developed.

Another trend apparent in the literature examined here is the increasing awareness of the need for additional research and access to larger and more diverse samples. While Dwight recognized aspects of this need, real progress had to await the acquisition of suitable samples of individuals of known age at death. Such samples were gradually assembled either by the careful curatorial efforts of anatomists such as T. Wingate Todd or the more opportunistic data collection by T. D. Stewart in his human identification efforts.

An additional recognizable pattern involves more complex and sophisticated methodology. Approaches have a growing tendency to recognize that different methods are more appropriate and effective for different age ranges. Increasingly, methodology calls for combining different approaches with the realization that combined approaches are frequently more effective than isolated ones.

Although these developments play prominent roles in the history outlined here, they do not stop with Stewart's 1979 synthesis. These trends continue into more recent periods and play dominant roles in the material presented in this volume. Existing efforts to improve methodology in the estimation of age at death build on the accomplishments and revelations of past initiatives. Many of the developments recognized as being important by our academic ancestors remain key today.

xxiv *Age Estimation of the Human Skeleton*

REFERENCES

Dwight, T. (1878). *The identification of the human skeleton. A medico-legal study.* Boston: David Clapp & Son, Printers.

Dwight, T. (1881). The sternum as an index of sex and age. *Journal of Anatomy and Psysiology* 15:327–330.

Dwight, T. (1890a). The sternum as an index of sex, height and age. *Journal of Anatomy and Psysiology 24*:527– 535.

Dwight, T. (1890b). The closure of the cranial sutures as a sign of age. *Boston Medical and Surgical Journal 122*(17):389–392.

Gilbert, B. M., & McKern, T. W. 1973). A method for aging the female os pubis. *American Journal of Physical Anthropology 38*(1):31–38.

Graves, W. W. (1922). Observations on age changes in the scapula. A preliminary note. *American Journal of Physical Anthropology 5*(1):21–33.

Greulich, W.W., & Pyle, S.I. (1950). *Radiographic atlas of skeletal development of the hand and wrist.* Stanford, CT: Stanford University Press.

Hrdlička, A. (1920). *Anthropometry.* Philadelphia: The Wistar Institute of Anatomy and Biology.

Hrdlička, A. (1939). *Practical anthropometry.* Philadelphia: The Wistar Institute of Anatomy and Biology.

Kerley, E. R. (1965). The microscopic determination of age in human bone. *American Journal of Physical Anthropology 23*(2):149–163.

Kerley E. R. (1969). Age determination of bone fragments. *Journal of Forensic Sciences 14*(1):59–67.

Kerley, E. R. (1970). Estimation of skeletal age after about age 30. In: T. D. Stewart (Ed.), Personal identification in mass disasters. pp. 57–70. Washington (D.C.): National Museum of Natural History.

Krogman, W. M. (1939). A guide to the identification of human skeletal material. *FBI Law Enforcement Bulletin 8*(8):3–31.

Krogman, W. M. (1962). *The human skeleton in forensic medicine.* Springfield, IL: Charles C Thomas Publisher.

McKern, T. W., & Stewart, T. D. (1957). Skeletal Age Changes in Young American Males. Natick (MA): Headquarters Quartermaster Research & Development Command, Quartermaster Research & Development Center, Environmental Protection Research Division. Technical Report EP-45.

Sheldon, W. H. (1940). *The varieties of human physique: An introduction to constitutional psychology.* New York: Harper & Brothers Publishers.

Stewart, T. D. (1940). The life and writings of Dr. Aleš Hrdlička, 1869–1939. *American Journal of Physical Anthropology 26*:3–40.

Stewart, T. D. (1952). *Hrdlička's practical anthropometry.* Philadelphia: The Wistar Institute of Anatomy and Biology.

Stewart, T. D. (1979). Essentials of forensic anthropology: especially as developed in the United States. Springfield, IL: Charles C Thomas.

Todd, T. W. (1920). Age changes in the pubic bone. I. The Male White Pubis. *American Journal of Physical Anthropology 3*(3):285–334.

Todd, T. W. (1921). Age changes in the pubic bone. II. Pubis of Male Negro-White hybrid. *American Journal of Physical Anthropology 4*(1):1–70.

Todd, T. W. (1930). Age changes in the pubic bone: VIII Roentgenographic differentiation. *American Journal of Physical Anthropology 14*(2):255–271.

Wilder, H. H., & Wentworth, B. (1918). *Personal identification: Methods for the identification of individuals, living or dead.* Boston: Richard G. Badger, The Gorham Press.

Ubelaker, D. H. (1999). *Human skeletal remains, excavation, analysis, interpretation* (3rd ed.). Washington (D.C.): Taraxacum.

ACKNOWLEDGMENTS

The editors would like to acknowledge all those who have participated in the Mountain Desert and Coastal Forensic Anthropologists (MD&C) meetings over the past thirty years. MD&C provides a forum for the presentation and discussion of scholarly work in the field of forensic anthropology, and it was at MD&C that the majority of these papers were originally presented and at which the inspiration for this volume was realized.

We would like to extend our gratitude to Drs. Bruce Anderson, Jerry Melbye and P. Willey for reviewing the material and providing feedback regarding the papers in this volume, and to Amandine Eriksen for designing the cover illustration. Our thanks to those individuals who assisted with the preparation of the volume, especially Elizabeth DeVisser, Elena Madaj, Megan Madonna and Imran Musaji. We also wish to acknowledge the patience and support of our friends and family during the preparation of this volume.

Finally, the editors would like to thank the contributors to this volume for their hard work and efforts. It has been a pleasure working with you all over the past two years. Our gratitude to Mr. Michael Thomas of Charles C Thomas Publisher, Ltd. for his patience and assistance throughout this process.

CONTENTS

SECTION 2: OSTEOLOGICAL AGING TECHNIQUES

SECTION 3: HISTOLOGICAL AND MULTIFACTORIAL AGING TECHNIQUES

AGE ESTIMATION
OF THE
HUMAN SKELETON

Section 1

DENTAL AGING TECHNIQUES

Chapter 1

DENTAL AGING TECHNIQUES: A REVIEW

JEREMY J. BEACH, CHRISTOPHER W. SCHMIDT, AND RACHEL A. SHARKEY

INTRODUCTION

Determining the age at death for skeletal remains has always been a primary concern of the biological anthropologist and dental remains, in particular, can play a central role in assessing the age of an individual. Teeth are usually available to the anthropologist for the construction of a biological profile because they are durable and preserve very well, even when other aspects of the skeleton have long since decomposed. Their ubiquity in archeological and forensic contexts has led to a plethora of literature regarding dental aging techniques. This chapter provides a summary of some of those techniques in an effort to assist biological anthropologists in distilling the vast literature that currently exists, but, by no means constitutes an exhaustive reporting of all techniques, regardless of their efficacy. Instead, we have chosen to highlight some of the more useful approaches to aging teeth, both past and present as the intended audience includes biological anthropologists, professional and student, as well as those in forensic odontology and forensic dental anthropology (e.g., Schmidt, 2008).

Usually, the first stage of any skeletal study is the determination of the biological profile, which minimally consists of the individual's age, sex, and ancestry. The indicators used to create the biological profile, of course, depend on those anatomical landmarks that are present at the time of the study. The fact that tooth enamel is nearly 100 percent mineral makes it an extremely durable substance. The density of enamel also makes it quite impervious to many taphonomic effects. As a result, tooth crowns are usually present for anthropological examinations. In addition, the root structures of teeth are housed in the alveolar bone of the mandible and maxillae, which protect them from degradation. Thus, entire dentitions are often available for age determination.

Dental aging techniques can be broken down into two major categories. The first of these categories is centered on the developmental changes that occur to the human dentition while the teeth are growing and emerging into the oral cavity, and the second involves the degenerative changes that occur once the teeth have erupted and begin to wear down.

DEVELOPMENTAL AGING TECHNIQUES

Hard Tissue Formation

Tooth formation begins very early in the life of an individual. By six weeks *in utero* tooth primordia are lining up along the margin of what will soon be the embryonic mouth. These buds are derived from the same embryonic tissues that make the skin, thus teeth are a function of both the skin and the skeleton. Over time the cells in the buds make the shape of the tooth and eventually enamel and dentin are placed down to form the crown and root, respectively. Thus, a fetus that is no more than a few months old has dental hard tissues present in both its upper and lower jaws. By the time a baby is born, all of its deciduous crowns have either formed or are in the process of forming, and even one adult tooth crown, that of the first molar, is in the initial stages of development.

Documenting the sequence of dental formation is an avenue of research that has been greatly studied in the past, and of these earlier studies Moorrees et al. (1963a, b) is probably the best known. This radiographic study looked at the formation of both the coronal and radical portions of the permanent dentition as well as the eventual apical closure. From these observations, Moorrees and colleagues (1963a, b) came up with a standard rate and sequence of formation that could be used to estimate age more precisely than using eruption alone. The method involves scoring each tooth for its developmental stage, then comparing those scores to values representing a particular age. For example, a deciduous first incisor crown that is fully formed and is recovered adjacent to a deciduous second incisor crown that is only three-fourths complete is consistent with a single individual aging to less than 6 months old. But, if a complete deciduous second molar is found in association with these two teeth, then suspicion might be raised that more than one individual is present because deciduous molars usually do not complete their formation until after the age of two. Thus, the analyst determines an MNI or minimum number of individuals represented in any assemblage simply by inventorying the teeth. Should a particular tooth be present more than once, or should teeth of disparate developmental age be found commingled, the dental inventory will show that more than one person is present.

The chronological development of dental hard tissues is not a uniform process that is identical in all populations. Differences have been noted between groups of different ethnic backgrounds (Harris and McKee, 1990; Harris, 2007; Blankenship et al., 2007). In particular, Harris and McKee (1990) noted that tooth mineralization of populations of African ancestry from the American south matured at a significantly faster rate than comparable populations of European ancestry by about as much as 5 percent. This is why it is so vitally important that the biological anthropologist be well experienced and versed in how human variation is manifest in the human skeleton and dentition. Improper application of dental aging techniques can lead to inappropriate assessment of a biological profile.

The Demirjian (1973, 1976, 1980) technique of scoring dental maturity has been frequently applied for aging individuals of unknown age within the realm of forensic science (TeMoananui et al., 2008; Tunc and Koyuturk, 2008; Rózylo-Kalinowska et al., 2008; Martin-de las Heras et al., 2008). The technique was intended as a measure of maturity of the dentition of younger individuals. Each tooth in the dentition is scored on an ordinal scale and from these values a composite score is computed that represents the overall developmental state of the individual. While this approach has been valuable in those instances where the dentition is complete, as Hillson (1996) points out, this methodology is not applicable when some teeth are missing, as is the case in certain archeological populations where tooth loss due to cavities or extreme wear is common. Moreover, when the Demirjian technique was applied to populations other than those with which Demirjian developed his standard, it was found that the methodology tended to overestimate age (Moananui et al., 2008; Tunc and Koyuturk, 2008; Rózylo-Kalinowska et al., 2008).

Dental Eruption

Schour and Massler's well-known 1941 and 1944 studies detail the eruption sequences of the human dentition by establishing 22 eruption stages and their associated ages. In order to assess the age of an unknown individual, the biological anthropologist compares postmortem radiographs of the individual to the eruption standards produced by Schour and Massler. Attempts have been made to take the Schour and Massler standard and to modify it for particular populations. Ubelaker (1989) modified the eruption sequence of Schour and Massler's standard by adding one stage and removing another to better fit eruption timing in prehistoric Native Americans. Despite its population-specific nature this study is still widely utilized for subadult aging (Buikstra and Ubelaker, 1994). Work on improving dental eruption standards for various populations continues and newer studies have been conducted that incorporate a wide variety of samples from modern contexts (Smith, this volume).

Third Molar Development

The appearance of the third molar has long been utilized as a biological sectioning point that demarcates between two stages of life, subadulthood and adulthood (Mincer et al., 1993). Traditionally, third molar age determination is accomplished by determining the stage of development by comparison to a standard (e.g., Schour and Massler, 1941). Mincer et al. (1993) found that the third molar is a reasonably reliable indicator of age even in modern populations, and Solari and Abramovitch (2002) report an age estimation accuracy that is within 3 years for the Hispanic populations utilized during their study.

In general, third molar emergence tends to be around 17–19 years of age for European Americans, with the third molars of males tending to emerge before the third molars of their female counterparts. This is a divergence from what is seen in the rest of the dentition where girls' teeth erupt somewhat earlier (Ten Cate, 1994). For both males and females, third molar roots complete their formation by the early 20s. However, third molars are highly variable teeth, in terms of their overall morphology as well as their formation and eruption timing. In fact, it is not at all uncommon for third molars to be reduced in size or not formed at all (agenesis). Several studies point out population specific third molar developmental idiosyncrasies that may have archeological and forensic significance. For example, Sarnet et al. (2003) and Orhan et al. (2007) found that agenesis was not unheard of in Israeli and Turkish children, respectively. During their research they determined that if no radiographic evidence of third molar translucency was present by the age of 14 they could conclude agenesis of the tooth within that individual. Studies of third molar development have been extended out to other populations as well (e.g., Arany et al., 2004; Bolaños et al., 2003; Solari and Abramovitch, 2002; Mincer et al., 1993).

It is imperative that radiographs be taken of jaws to aid with age determination. A jaw may not show an erupted third molar, but that tooth may be developing it its crypt out of view. Another possibility is that a tooth has become impacted and is unable to erupt, even though it has completed development. In dry bones, unerupted third molars can be viewed via a window in the bone through which the tooth will eventually erupt, although this view does not usually allow the observer to see the root. Thus, only via radiography can the observer accurately document the developmental stages of unerupted teeth.

Dental Measurements

An alternative to making qualitative assessment of a tooth's growth stage is to measure the length of the tooth (e.g., Liversidge et al. 1993, 1999; Cardoso 2007a, b). Measuring tooth lengths entails determining the distance from the incisal edge of the tooth to the apical termination of growth on either the crown or root. The research of Liversidge (1993), conducted on the known age at death, Christ Church, Spitalfields collection, looked at the development of both the mandibular and maxillary deciduous and permanent dentitions in individuals aged between birth and 5.4 years old. The permanent dentition was limited to the incisors, canines, and first molars. Regression equations for each tooth were produced. Liversidge and Molleson (1999) later expanded the sample from the Christ Church collection to include individuals up to the age of 19. In this particular study, data from the maxillary and mandibular teeth were combined. Cardoso (2007a) found that consistent estimates could be attained with this technique when applied to both mandibular and maxillary permanent teeth. However, he noted that aging using the maxillary teeth alone tended to overage people. Two additional insights were also produced from Liversidge and Molleson's study. First, they found that the growth pattern follows an s-shaped curve with an initial rapid growth, followed by a decrease, and finally followed by a spurt that occurs around the time that the mid root is formed. Second, it also found that reliable measurements could be taken from radiographs. However, the radiographs must be unmagnified and undistorted. The methodologies of Liversidge are different from the other dental developmental studies noted so far because of its quantitative approach. Rather than qualitatively comparing eruption sequences to charts, either direct measurements of teeth or indirect measurements of radiographs are made. Cardoso (2007b) claimed that when testing the Liversidge and Molleson method on a Portuguese sample, and using a 95 percent confidence interval, an age estimate of ± 0.1 years could be achieved when several teeth were used.

DEGENERATIVE AGING TECHNIQUES

Hard Tissue Obliteration

Almost as soon as a tooth enters the mouth it begins to wear down. During mastication the upper and lower teeth are forced tightly together as they attempt to break down food. The food, contaminants such as sand, and even the teeth themselves create small scratches and pits on the occlusal surfaces that eventually wear the teeth away at the macroscopic level. Cusps go from being pointed to rounded to being worn completely flat if the diet is abrasive enough. Eventually, all of the occlusal enamel may be worn away and the underlying dentin is exposed. Wear is usually scored by ranking the tooth's degree of obliteration (e.g., Smith, 1984; Scott, 1979; Molnar, 1971). The Smith (1984) system is generally used for the incisors, canines, and premolars. It ranks wear in eight categories starting with rounded cusps and ending with all of the enamel missing. Stage one is little or no wear while two through five simply rank the relative size of the exposed dentin, from a pinpoint spot to a facet that dominates the occlusal aspect of the tooth. Stages six through eight range from a thin rim of enamel to its complete loss. The Scott (1979) system is used on molars and scores each molar quadrant separately on a scale from one to ten. Like the Smith system, the scale goes from rounded cusps to a complete absence of enamel. Since each quadrant is scored independently, a composite score is computed that ranges from four to 40.

There is an intuitive connection between tooth wear and age as those with more wear tend to be older. However, research has shown that wear rates are highly relative and the wear in one skeletal series may not at all reflect the rate of wear in another (Johannson et al., 1992, 1993). For example, living populations tend to have much lower rates of wear than people who lived hundreds or thousands of years ago. Essentially, most modern diets are pre-masticated in that cereal grains and other hard foods are mechanically processed prior to consumption. By contrast, ancient populations consumed foods that were inherently abrasive and ground those foods with stone tools adding more abrasives to the diet. Pre-agriculture populations who lived in prehistoric North America between 6,000 and 3,000 years ago had very rapid rates of wear. Molars were often worn completely flat and dentin exposure dominated tooth surfaces by the time people were in their 20s or 30s. It was common for teeth to be worn down to the pulp cavity at the center of the tooth, exposing blood vessels and nerves and leading to tooth infections and abscesses. By contrast, agriculturists from about 1,000 years had molars with much less wear and one had to be well into late adulthood before they had wear comparable to young adult pre-agriculturists (Schmidt, 1998). This means that each of these populations must have their own age standard, and applying a wear standard derived from agricultural people to those who lived before agriculture would lead to a gross overestimation of age where even young people would be considered old.

Overall, many factors can affect wear rates, including tooth size, bruxism, diet, culturally mitigated uses of teeth (such as using the teeth as a tool), health, medication, and even the environment (e.g., Walker et al., 1991; Hillson, 1996; Ball, 2002). Traditional populations of the Arctic often used their teeth to soften frozen seal skins. This process leads to excessive wear and even chipped teeth (Hylander, 1977). Sandy locales, for example, tend to create greater rates of wear, regardless of the diet consumed (Johansson et al., 1991; Fareed et al., 1990). Likewise, Johansson et al. (1992, 1993) were able to demonstrate higher rates of wear amongst extant Saudi populations when compared to populations from Sweden. Most likely this difference is attributable to cross-cultural differences in food preparation, as well as environmental differences.

Dental wear varies within populations, and the factors that separate populations cross-culturally are the same that lead to variations within groups, such as certain individuals within a group may consume different foods than the rest, leading to different wear patterns. People today who drink large quantities of carbonated beverages often suffer from rapid wear because the acids in those drinks compromise the integrity of the enamel (Ten Cate, 1994). Individuals with particular diseases can suffer from rapid dental wear because certain conditions lead to poor quality teeth including Amelogenesis Imperfecta and Down Syndrome (Pindborg, 1970). Certain occupations can increase tooth wear, especially if it exposes people to high levels of airborne grit or requires extramasticatory use of the teeth. In fact, although unrelated to age, some wear patterns can be diagnostic of particular tooth usages including smoking a pipe for prolonged periods of time or even tasks associated with an individuals occupation (Prpić-Mehicić, 1998).

Therefore, the biological anthropologist must be well aware of the types of samples studied via dental wear and the limits of the assessment, taking into account the nature of inter- and intrasite wear variation. The resulting age estimates should likewise be conservative and should place people into broad age categories (as recommended by Buikstra and Ubelaker, 1994) and not into more specific age ranges until eventual studies produce confidence intervals allowing for such precision. Based upon his stody of a Medieval Danish village, Boldsen (2005) asserts that aging based upon attrition scores are impossible. However, population specific wear standards have been constructed. Lovejoy (1985) developed one that is appropriate for late prehistoric agriculturists from eastern North America. His study correlated tooth wear with skeletal age determined from the skull and *os coxae*. Brothwell (1981, 1989) developed a similar system from archaeological burials from England. His study looks at cusp removal and dentin exposure and places individuals into broad overlapping age groups (17–25, 25–35, 35–45, and "about 45").

The Miles aging system (Miles, 1962) is yet another methodology that the biological anthropologists can utilize that is based upon the attrition of dental hard tissues on molars. This system is based upon samples gathered from Anglo-Saxon archaeological samples in England. It differs from the other methods in that it looks at relative wear. Molars erupt at predicable intervals, usually M1 around age 6, M2 around age 12, and M3 around age 18. The Miles system looks at how quickly each molar wears by the time the following molar erupts. For example, one population may have first molars that are worn flat by the time the second molar erupts. In other populations, the first molar may only have been lightly rounded. Like the other systems, a score is given and placed on an ordinal scale that is correlated with skeletal age. Researchers have applied Brothwell's and Miles' aging systems to various skeletal samples from different cultural backgrounds and temporal horizons. Santini and colleagues (1990) tested the accuracy of Brothwell's chart and found that is was inconsistent when applied to Chinese skeletal samples of known age.

Other systems include Kim (2000) and Yun (2007) for modern Korean populations. Wear-related aging techniques certainly have value, but some populations may be more suitable than others. Some industrial diets are so soft, that wear changes are generally too modest for effective age estimation (Hillson, 2005). Moreover, some populations have such carious diets that a sizable percentage of the population is missing most of its teeth, or the remaining teeth are relatively unworn because chewing is too painful.

Dentin Sclerosis and Associated Techniques

Dentin sclerosis is an age-related phenomenon where tubules within dentin become filled with transparent crystals over time. It is similar in concept to the way costal cartilage ossification is associated with age-related changes. As an individual grows older the dentin of a tooth undergoes mineralization. As this mineralization process takes place the once opaque tissue becomes transparent allowing light to pass through. The progression of this transparency begins at the apex of the roots and continues towards the crown. Gustafson (1950) and Maples (1978) used root transparency as part of their multiple regression formulae for age determination. Gustafson originally published a technique (1947) that utilized four dental age indicators. This technique was later expanded and modified (Gustafson, 1950) to incorporate a total of seven dental anatomical features that included: dentin sclerosis, root resorption, apposition of cementum, secondary dentin apposition, periodontosis, and dental attrition. Several researchers continued to test and make improvements based upon the research of Gustafson (Burns and Maples, 1976; Maples and Rice, 1979). Although a promising approach, especially in its multivariate setup, it should be noted that this particular approach involves the preparation and analysis of histological thin ground sections (0.25 mm as described by Metzger et al., 1980). There are both advantages and caveats that must be heeded whenever utilizing histological techniques, all of which will be discussed in further detail in later chapters in this volume. In general, without the proper amount of training and experience it is easy to improperly section a tooth and therefore be analyzing the wrong portion of the tooth resulting in incorrect conclusions. Metzger et al. (1980) address the problem of improper sectioning by proposing a thick ground section technique (1.0 mm section), which minimizes overgrinding, a problem that can occur even among experienced histologists. Also, without proper care it is easy to produce a tooth slide that is not suitable for study because it is heavily fractured, too thick, too thin, uneven in thickness, or improperly mounted. Dental histology is a valuable analytical tool that should be utilized by the biological anthropologist if they are properly versed in histological procedures. However, it is important for analysts to understand that histology is a destructive process. Teeth should be fully studied for morphology, photographed, radiographed, and molded before being sectioned.

Observing root sclerosis does not necessarily require dental histology and several techniques have been proposed that use a light source behind the tooth to display root transparency. The Lamendin technique is a two-step process. First, the researcher must identify and measure the amount of periodontosis (Lamendin et al., 1992). This usually leaves a small marking on the tooth as the periodontal ligament and alveolar bone recede with time, thus exposing the root of the tooth during life. Second, the amount of dentin transparency must be identified and measured. Since the sclerosis advances from the root apex toward the cervix, calipers are placed at the root tip and at the point where the sclerosis gives way to non-transparent dentin. The light source behind the tooth does not need to be powerful and a standard light table with a 60-watt or equivalent bulb suffices.

Sclerosis measurements are put into Lamendin's regression formula to produce an estimated age. When compared to other methodologies (such as the Gustafson methodology) it is an accurate approach (Lamendin et al., 1992). Lamendin produced a single regression formula that did not control for sex and ancestry and he found that his approach is most accurate in older individuals. However, there are several advantages to utilizing a technique such as this. Overall, the method is fast and efficient; compared to the Gustafson technique, no intricate equipment is needed (other than a pair of sliding calipers) and the remains are not compromised as they are with histological aging techniques. Finally, several studies have compared the accuracy of the Lamendin technique to other popular skeletal aging techniques (such as Lovejoy's auricular surface aging, Suchey-Brooks' pubic symphysis aging, and Îscan's sternal rib aging technique). According to Martrille et al. (2007) the Lamendin technique is the most accurate technique for middle-age adults (ages 41–60), when compared to six other aging methods. This age range is on par with the age Lamendin stated in his research. In addition, Baccino et al. (1999) found that the Lamandin technique, when compared to three other skeletal aging techniques (sternal 4th rib end, pubic symphysis, and femoral cortical remodeling), was the most effective method in remains that were 25 years and older.

Prince and Ubelaker (2002) utilized the same criteria that Lamendin proposed and found that the technique yielded comparable results when applied to a non-French sample. In addition, Prince and Ubelaker added the variable of sex and ancestry, thus producing separate equations for each (black male, black female, white male, white female). These additional variables decreased the mean error for each group, thus yielding more precise age estimates. In comparisons of the Lamendin and Prince-Ubelaker techniques, researchers (González-Colmenares et al., 2007) have found that the Prince-Ubelaker method tends to produce age estimates that are more accurate than results produced by the original Lamendin method.

CONCLUSION

Proper application of dental aging techniques is imperative. For this to happen biological anthropologists must know the context of the dental remains they are studying to insure that proper aging techniques are applied and that the results are interpreted appropriately. There are many useful aging techniques available that include every aspect of dental formation and degeneration. Each has its value, but it is possible that not all techniques will be available because some approaches are population-specific and tooth preservation can vary. Thus, a competent analyst is aware of and capable of employing a wide range of dental aging techniques either in isolation or in conjunction with others. In doing so, the analyst is better equipped to produce an accurate age estimate that can contribute to biological profiles in both archeological and forensic contexts.

REFERENCES

Arany, S., Iino, & M., Yoshioka, N. (2004). Radiographic survey of third molar development in relation to chronological age among Japanese juveniles. *Journal of Forensic Sciences 49:*534–538.

Baccino, E., Ubelaker, D., Hayek, L. A., & Zerilli, A. (1999). Evaluation of Seven methods of estimating age at death from mature human skeletal remains. *Journal of Forensic Sciences 44.*931–936.

Ball, J. 2002. A critique of age estimation using attrition as the sole indicator. *Journal of Forensic Odonto-Stomatology 20:*38–42.

Blankenship, J. A., Mincer, H. H., Anderson, K. M., Woods, M. H., & Burton, E. L. (2007). Third molar development in the estimation of chronologic age in American blacks as compared with whites. *Journal of Forensic Sciences 55*(2):428–433.

Bolaños, M. V., Moussa, H., Manrique, M. C., & Bolaños, M. J. (2003). Radiographic evaluation of third molar development in Spanish children and young people. *Forensic Science International 133:*212–219.

Boldsen, J. L. (2005). Analysis of dental attrition and mortality in the medieval village of Tirup, Denmark. *American Journal of Physical Anthropology 126:*168–176.

Brothwell, D. R. (1981). *Digging up bones.* Ithaca: Cornell University Press.

Brothwell, D. R. (1989). The relationship of tooth wear to aging. In: M. Y. Îscan (Ed.), *Age markers in the human skeleton,* pp. 303–316. Springfield, IL: Charles C Thomas.

Buikstra, J. E., &Ubelaker, D. H. (1994). Standards for data collection from human skeletal remains (Archeological Survey Research Series No. 44). Fayetteville: Arkansas Archeological Survey.

Burns, K. R., & Maples, W. R. (1976). Estimation of age from individual adult teeth. *Journal of Forensic Sciences 21:*343–356.

Cardoso, H. F. (2007). Accuracy of developing tooth length as an estimate of age in human skeletal remains: the deciduous dentition. *Forensic Science International 172*:17–22.

Cardoso, H. F. (2007b). A test of the differential accuracy of the maxillary versus the mandibular dentition in age estimations of immature skeletal remains based on developing tooth length. *Journal of Forensic Sciences 52*:434–437.

Demirjian, A., & Goldstein, H. (1976). New systems for dental maturity based on seven and four teeth. *Annals of Human Biology 3*:411–421.

Demirjian, A., Goldstein, H., & Tanner, J. M. (1973). A new system of dental age assessment. *Human Biology 45*:211–227.

Demirjian, A., & Levesque, G-Y. (1980). Sexual differences in dental development and prediction of emergence. *Journal of Dental Research 59*:1110–1122.

Fareed, K., Johansson, A., & Omar, R. (1990). Prevalence and severity of occlusal tooth wear in a young Saudi population. *Acta Odontologica Scandinavica 48*:279–285.

Gonzalez-Colmenares, G., Botella-Lopez, M. C., Moreno-Rueda, G., & Fernandez-Cardenete, J. R. (2007). Age estimation by a dental method: A comparison of Lamendin's and Prince and Ubelaker's technique. *Journal of Forensic Sciences 52*:1156–1160.

Gustafson, G. (1950). Age determination of teeth. *Journal of the American Dental Association 51*:45–54.

Gustafson, G. (1947). Microscopic examination of teeth as a means of identification in forensic medicine. *Journal of the American Dental Association 35*:720–724.

Harris, E. F. (2007). Mineralization of the mandibular third molar: A study of American blacks and whites. *American Journal of Physical Anthropology 132*:98–109.

Harris, E. F., & McKee, J. H. (1990). Tooth mineralization standards for blacks and whites from the middle southern United States. *Journal of Forensic Sciences 35*:259–272.

Hillson, S. (2005). *Teeth* (2nd ed.). Cambridge: Cambridge University Press.

Hillson, S. (1996). *Dental anthropology*. Cambridge: Cambridge University Press.

Hillson, S., FitzGerald, C., & Flinn, H. (2005). Alternative dental measurements: Proposals and relationships with other measurements. *American Journal of Physical Anthropology 126*:413–426.

Hylander, W. L. (1977). The adaptive significance of Eskimo craniofacial morphology. In A. A. Dahlberg & T. M. Graber (Eds.), *Orofacial growth and development,* pp. 129–169. The Hague: Mouton Publishers.

Johansson, A. (1992). A cross-cultural study of occlusal tooth wear. *Swedish Dental Journal Supplement 86*:1–59.

Johansson, A., Fareed, K., & Omar, R. (1991). Analysis of possible factors influencing the occurrence of occlusal tooth wear in a young Saudi population. *Acta Odontologica Scandinavica 49*:139–145.

Johansson, A., Omar, R., Fareed, K., Haraldson, T., Kiliaridis, S., & Carlsson, G. E. (1993). Comparison of the prevalence, severity and possible causes of occlusal tooth wear in two young adult populations. *Journal of Oral Rehabilitation 20*:463–471.

Kim, Y. K., Kho, H. S., & Lee, K. H. (2000). Age estimation by occlusal tooth wear. *Journal of Forensic Sciences 45*:303–09.

Lamendin, H., Baccino, E., Humbert, J. F., Tavernier, J. C., Nossintchouck, R. M., & Zerilli, A. (1992). A simple technique for age estimation in adult corpses: the two criteria dental method. *Journal of Forensic Sciences 37*:1373–1379.

Liversidge, H. M., Dean, M. C., & Molleson, T. I. (1993). Increasing human tooth length birth and 5.4 years. *American Journal of Physical Anthropology 90*:307–313.

Liversidge, H. M., & Molleson, T. I. (1999). Developing permanent tooth length as an estimate of age. *Journal of Forensic Sciences 44*:917–920.

Lovejoy, C. O. (1985). Dental wear in the Libben population: Its functional pattern and role in the determination of adult skeletal age at death. *American Journal of Physical Anthropology 68*:47–56.

Maples, W. R. (1978). An improved technique using dental histology for estimation of adult age. *Journal of Forensic Sciences 23*:764–770.

Maples, W. R, & Rice, P. M. (1979). Some difficulties in the Gustafson dental age estimations. *Journal of Forensic Sciences 24*:118–172.

Martrille, L., Ubelaker, D., Cattaneo, C., Sequret, F., Tremblay, M., & Baccino, E. (2007). Comparison of four skeletal methods for the estimation of age at death of white and black adults. *Journal of Forensic Sciences 52*:302–07.

Martin-de las Heras, S., García-Fortea, P., Ortega, A., Zodocovich, S., & Valenzuela, A. (2008). Third molar development according to chronological age in populations from Spanish and Magrebian origin. *Forensic Science International 174*:47–53.

Metzger, Z., Buchner, A., & Gorsky, M. (1980). Gustafson's method for age determination from teeth–A modification for the use of dentists in identification teams. *Journal of Forensic Sciences 25*:742–749.

Miles, A. E. W. (1962). Assessment of the ages of a population of Anglo-Saxons from their dentitions. *Proceedings of the Royal Society of Medicine 55*:881–886.

Mincer, H. H., Harris, E. F., & Berryman, H. E. (1993). The A.B.F.O. study of third molar development and its use as an estimator of chronological age. *Journal of Forensic Sciences 38*:379–390.

Moananui, R. T., Kieser, J. A., Herbison, P., & Liversidge, H. M. (2008). Advanced dental maturation in New Zealand, Maori, and Pacific Island children. *American Journal of Human Biology 20*:43–50.

Molnar, S. (1971). Human tooth wear, tooth function and cultural variability. *American Journal of Physical Anthropology 34*:175–190.

Moorrees, C. F. A., Fanning, E. A., & Hunt, E. E. (1963). Age variation of formation stages for ten permanent teeth. *Journal of Dental Research 42*:1490–1502.

Moorrees, C. F. A., Fanning, E. A., & Hunt, E. E. (1963). Formation and resorption of three deciduous teeth in children. *American Journal of Physical Anthropology 21*:205–213.

Orhan, K., Ozer, L., Orhan, A. I., Dogan, S., & Paksoy, C. S. (2007). Radiographic evaluation of third molar development in relation to chronological age among Turkish children and youth. *Forensic Science International 165*:46–51.

Pindborg, J. J. (1970). *Pathology of the dental hard tissues.* Philadelphia: W.B. Ssaunders.

Princ, D. A., & Ubelaker, D. (2002). Application of Lamendin's adult dental aging technique to a diverse skeletal sample. *Journal of Forensic Sciences 47*:107–116.

Prpić-Mehicić, G., Buntak-Kobler, D., Jukić, S., & Katunarić, M. (1998). Occupational toothwear in clothing industry workers. *Collegium Antropologicum Supplement*:241–249.

Rózy_o-Kalinowska, I., Kiworkowa-Raczkowska, E., & Kalinowski, P. (2008). Dental age in Central Poland. *Forensic Science International 174*:207–216.

Santini, A., Land, M., & Raab, G. M. (1990). The accuracy of simple ordinal scoring of tooth attrition in age assessment. *Forensic Science International 48*:175–184.

Sarnat, H., Kaffe, I., & Amir, E. (2003). Developmental stages of the third molar in Israeli children. *Pediatric Dentistry 25*:373–377.

Schmidt, C. W. (1998). Dietary reconstruction among prehistoric humans from Indiana: An analysis of dental macrowear, dental pathology, and dental microwear. Doctoral Dissertation. Purdue University, West Lafayette, IN.

Schmidt, C. W. (2008). Forensic dental anthropology: Issues and guidelines. In J. D. Irish & G. C. Nelson (Eds.), *Techniques and application in dental anthropology*, pp. 266–292. Cambridge: Cambridge University Press.

Schour, I., & Massler, M. (1944). *Development of human dentition chart* (2nd ed.). Chicago: American Dental Association.

Schour, I., & Massler, M. (1941). The development of the human dentition. *Journal of the American Dental Association 28*:1153–1160.

Scott, E. C. (1979). Dental wear scoring technique. *American Journal of Physical Anthropology 51*:213–218.

Smith, B. H. (1984). Patterns of molar wear in hunter-gatherers and agriculturalists. *American Journal of Physical Anthropology 63*:39–56.

Solari, A. C., & Abramovitch, K. (2002). The accuracy and precision of third molar development as an indicator of chronological age in Hispanics. *Journal of Forensic Sciences 47*:531–535.

TeMoananui, R., Kieser, J. A., Herbison, G. P., & Liversidge, H. M. (2008). Estimating age in Maori, Pacific Island, and European children from New Zealand. *Journal of Forensic Sciences 53*:401–404.

Ten Cate, A. R. (1994). *Oral histology, development, structure and function* (4th ed.). St. Louis: Mosby.

Tunc, E. S., &Koyuturk, A. E. (2008). Dental age assessment using Demirjian's method on northern Turkish children. *Forensic Science International 175*:23–26.

Ubelaker, D. H. (1989). *Human skeletal remains, excavation, analysis, interpretation* (2nd ed.). Washington D.C.: Taraxacum.

Walker, P. L., Gean, G., & Shapiro, P. (1991). Estimating age from tooth wear in archaeological populations. In M. A. Kelley & C. S. Larsen (Eds.), *Advances in dental anthropology*, pp. 143–169. New York: Wiley-Liss.

Yun, J. I., Lee, J. Y., Chung, J. W., Kho, H. S., & Kim, Y. K. (2007). Age estimation of Korean adults by occlusal tooth wear. *Journal of Forensic Sciences 52*:678–683.

Chapter 2

THE ESTIMATION OF AGE AT DEATH THROUGH THE EXAMINATION OF ROOT TRANSPARENCY

Jennifer L. Harms-Paschal and Christopher W. Schmidt

INTRODUCTION

The determination of age at death is a crucial component of the biological profile one creates in forensic and bioarchaeological casework. Age, sex, stature, and ancestry are all distinct characteristics determined individually, but used collectively to create a profile that describes the individual's characteristics during life. Analyses of forensic skeletal and dental human remains are performed with the understanding that the determination of the biological profile will facilitate identification and each attribute contributes significantly to the identification process. Age estimation is vital and the need for accurate aging techniques is imperative. The reliability of any aging technique must fulfill the needs of police and anthropologists alike, and several demands must be met for any technique to be considered dependable enough to be used in a systematic manner.

PURPOSE AND HYPOTHESIS

Dental hard tissue is often extremely well-preserved in archaeological and forensic contexts due to its high mineral content, and is occasionally the only tissue remaining in analyzable condition. These lasting characteristics make teeth of particular value in the determination of age in skeletal analyses. Thus, dental aging is relied upon for identification when osseous elements are missing and additionally when DNA comparison is not possible.

The purpose of this study is to independently evaluate the efficacy of root transparency as a predictor of age at death. The methods and statistical equations of Bang and Ramm (1970) are applied to a modern sample while controlling for sex and ancestry. While Bang and Ramm (1970) did not control for ancestry, the current study will only examine teeth from individuals of Euro-American descent, eliminating any ancestral differences that may influence root transparency. In addition, new regression equations are constructed from the sample studied in this investigation to further explore the usefulness of root transparency and to generate new regression formulae that may be used in future analyses.

THE STUDY SAMPLE

The study sample consists of teeth extracted from human cadavers housed at Indiana University Medical Center (Indianapolis, IN), the University of Indianapolis (Indianapolis, IN), Michigan State University (East Lansing, MI), the University of Chicago (Chicago, IL), and The Ohio State University (Columbus, OH). Cadaver teeth were chosen for this investigation because the majority of these individuals have a recorded sex and age at death. The complete sample includes a total of 280 teeth from 82 individuals. Of these individuals, 32 are male and 50 are female. One hundred five teeth were from male cadavers and the remaining 175 teeth were from females. The total age range extends from 29 to 100 years, with males ranging from 54 to 93 and females ranging from 29 to 100. The mean age of the entire sample was 77.4 years, the most frequent age was 92 years, and the median age was 80 years.

A total of four teeth were taken from each individual. One of which came from each of the following areas: upper canines/incisors, lower canines/incisors, upper premolars and lower premolars. The dental abbreviations used herein are, incisors (I), canines (C), third premolars (PM3), and fourth premolars (PM4). Unfortunately, due to edentulous jaws and complex dental restorations, fewer than four teeth were removed from several individuals. Teeth were primarily removed from the right side of the dental quadrant, although left teeth were extracted when the right was unavailable. Of the 280 teeth collected, 176 were anterior teeth and 104 were posterior. The anterior teeth included 134 canines and 42 incisors. The posterior teeth included 83 third premolars and 21 fourth premolars.

Each measurement was recorded without the knowledge of the age or sex of the individual to which each tooth belonged. All measurements were taken with digital sliding calipers and recorded to the nearest 0.1 mm. The type and location of all restorations and decay was noted. Root length was recorded as the distance from the midpoint of the buccal dento-enamel junction to the root apex. If the buccal dento-enamel junction was destroyed by decay or restorations, the measurement was recorded from the lingual surface. Transparency was recorded from the mesial or distal aspect of the tooth.

RESULTS

Intra-observer Error

To determine whether the method used in the study sample was reliable and repeatable, 30 teeth were randomly selected and re-measured approximately 100 days after the original measurements were taken. Only relative values of root transparency were used in the analysis. The measurements from the retest were compared to the original measurements. A Pearson correlation coefficient of $r = 0.514$ at a level of significance of $p = 0.004$ was obtained.

Pearson's Correlation

A correlation matrix was constructed to determine the strength and direction of the relationships of the 29 variables to age (Table 2.1). The variables include each tooth used separately, a combination of all anterior teeth, all posterior teeth, and all teeth combined. Additional variables tested were those that combined tooth types. All incisors, canines, third premolars, and fourth premolars were examined as separate groups. Tests revealed a strong relationship among canines and, more specifically, among right canines. Therefore, the correlation matrix also includes a variable for all right canines. After examining the correlation coefficients for the third premolars, an additional variable, right third premolars, was created and correlated with age. Upper right third premolars and lower right third premolars examined alone did not exhibit very strong correlations with age, but improvements were obtained when the teeth were combined. The grouping of these teeth omitted the influence of the poorly-correlated left third premolars and resulted in a higher correlation. Of the 29 variables, 13 are significantly correlated with age.

Of the 13 variables that are significantly correlated with age, three (URP4,

TABLE 2.1
CORRELATION MATRIX RESULTS FOR ALL 29 VARIABLES OF
RELATIVE LENGTH OF TRANSPARENCY WITH AGE. BOLD RESULTS
ARE FOR THE 10 VARIABLES USED IN SUBSEQUENT ANALYSES

Tooth	Sample Size (n)	Correlation Coefficient (r)	p-value
Upper Right First Incisor	6	-0.429	0.397
Upper Right Second Incisor	6	-0.188	0.721
Upper Right Canine	**35**	**0.592**	**0.000**
Upper Right Third Premolar	22	0.401	0.064
Upper Right Fourth Premolar	7	0.954	0.001
Upper Left First Incisor	1	na	na
Upper Left Second Incisor	5	0.526	0.363
Upper Left Canine	8	0.387	0.344
Upper Left Third Premolar	3	0.999	0.022
Upper Left Fourth Premolar	1	na	na
Lower Right First Incisor	2	-1.000	na
Lower Right Second Incisor	11	-0.395	0.229
Lower Right Canine	**58**	**0.405**	**0.002**
Lower Right Third Premolar	46	0.207	0.167
Lower Right Fourth Premolar	9	0.906	0.001
Lower Left First Incisor	1	na	na
Lower Lefty Second Incisor	8	0.407	0.317
Lower Left Canine	31	0.129	0.489
Lower Left Third Premolar	11	0.521	0.100
Lower Left Fourth Premolar	1	na	na
All Incisors	32	0.190	0.299
Right Canines	**65**	**0.423**	**0.000**
All Canines	**76**	**0.330**	**0.004**
Right Third Premolars	**54**	**0.275**	**0.044**
All Third Premolars	**60**	**0.290**	**0.024**
All Fourth Premolars	**17**	**0.766**	**0.000**
All Anterior Teeth	**78**	**0.418**	**0.000**
All Posterior Teeth	**65**	**0.391**	**0.001**
All Teeth	**81**	**0.443**	**0.000**

TABLE 2.2
CORRELATION COMPARISON BETWEEN RELATIVE OR ABSOLUTE
MEASUREMENTS OF ROOT TRANSPARENCY LENGTH AND AGE

Tooth	Sample Size (n)	Relative Root Transparency Length	Absolute Root Transparency Length
Upper Right Canine	35	0.592	0.492
Lower Right Canine	58	0.405	0.350
Right Canines	65	0.423	0.352
All Canines	76	0.330	0.308
Right Third Premolars	54	0.275	0.216
All Third Premolars	60	0.290	0.271
All Fourth Premolars	17	0.766	0.583
All Anterior Teeth	78	0.418	0.354
All Posterior Teeth	65	0.391	0.345
All Teeth	81	0.443	0.389

ULP3, and LRP4) were excluded from further consideration because the sample sizes were less than 10. For the remaining 10 variables, correlations of absolute root transparency length versus age were calculated and compared to the values obtained using relative length. As seen in Table 2.2, relative length outperformed absolute length in all comparisons, with the exception of one tooth (LRP3). The improvement in relative values is undoubtedly due to the fact that a relative measure standardizes for variation in overall tooth size. Therefore, only relative lengths of transparency for these 10 variables are used in generating age-predictive equations.

Descriptive Statistics

Descriptive statistics of the 10 variables and combinations of teeth used throughout the remainder of this study are presented in Table 2.3. A one-sample Kolmogorov-Smirnov test was performed to test the distribution of relative length of root transparency for each variable. Each variable proved to be normally distributed allowing for the subsequent use of normal, parametric statistical analyses (Table 2.3).

Absolute root transparency values range from 2.40 mm to 17.70 mm with a mean of 9.7 mm, whereas root transparency values relative to root length

TABLE 2.3
DESCRIPTIVE STATISTICS AND NORMALITY FOR RELATIVE ROOT LENGTH OF TRANSPARENCY FOR THE 10 VARIABLES USED IN SUBSEQUENT ANALYSES

Tooth	*n*	*Standard Deviation*	*Variance*	*Normal Distribution*
Upper Right Canine	35	14.279	203.686	Y
Lower Right Canine	58	20.546	422.139	Y
Right Canines	65	17.591	309.450	Y
All Canines	76	17.191	295.547	Y
Right Third Premolars	54	15.090	227.734	Y
All Third Premolars	60	14.809	219.327	Y
All Fourth Premolars	17	19.553	382.306	Y
Anterior Teeth	78	15.418	237.714	Y
Posterior Teeth	65	14.886	221.584	Y
All Teeth	81	14.077	198.174	Y

range from 21.72 percent to 100 percent with a mean of 61.8 percent. Absolute values are the actual measurements in millimeters that represent the length of the transparent zone. Relative measurements are obtained by dividing the absolute measurement by the total root length. Relative measurements take into consideration the effects that varying root lengths may have on root transparency analyses.

ANCOVA

Analysis of covariance (ANCOVA) was used to determine if there are significant relationships between root transparency, age, and sex. Type I sums of squares was used because the covariate, age, is continuous. Overall results indicate that there is no significant influence of sex on root transparency measurements for individual teeth across all teeth and tooth combinations. Therefore, males and females can be examined together in the subsequent statistical analyses. Age does covary with root transparency (Table 2.4). Age was significant in all 10 ANCOVAs.

TABLE 2.4
ANCOVA RESULTS WITH RELATIVE LENGTH OF
TRANSPARENCY AS THE DEPENDENT VARIABLE

Tooth	*n*	*Sex p-value*	*Age p-value*
Upper Right Canine	35	0.272	0.000
Lower Right Canine	58	0.185	0.002
Right Canines	65	0.484	0.000
All Canines	76	0.177	0.003
Right Third Premolars	54	0.404	0.045
All Third Premolars	17	0.266	0.024
All Fourth Premolars	60	0.650	0.001
All Anterior Teeth	78	0.225	0.000
All Posterior Teeth	65	0.285	0.001
All Teeth	81	0.706	0.000

Linear Regression

The data points of each of the 10 selected variables were entered into a scatterplot to determine visually if the relationship was linear. Each data set exhibited a linear relationship and therefore only linear regression formulae were created from the sample study. A total of 10 linear regression equations were created (Table 2.5). Regression statistics for each equation are presented in Table 2.6. R-squared is the percent of variance in age that is explained by the variance in the relative length of root transparency within the sample study. Adjusted r-squared predicts the explained variance in the parent population as a whole, and is therefore a more realistic measure of the equations' predictive abilities in the real world. The standard error of the estimate should be doubled to produce an approximate (but slightly underestimated) 95 percent error interval for a predicted age. Of the 10 linear regression equations, the variables upper right canine, fourth premolars, and all teeth have the lowest standard error of the estimates.

As can be seen in Table 2.7, inaccuracy for each equation hovers around 10 years, meaning that, on average, each individual's estimated age was off by 10 years. Note that inaccuracy is a smaller measure of error than the standard error of the estimate (Table 2.5) and should not be used to construct prediction intervals for individual cases. Bias for each equation is zero as a forced

TABLE 2.5
REGRESSION EQUATIONS CREATED FROM THE CURRENT
STUDY SAMPLE USING RELATIVE LENGTH OF
TRANSPARENCY AS THE INDEPENDENT VARIABLE (X)

Tooth	Regression Formulae with standard error of the estimate (in ± years)
Upper Right Canines	Age = 36.7569 + 0.6599(x) ± 13.016
Lower Right Canines	Age = 58.8041 + 0.2868(x) ± 13.437
Right Canines	Age = 54.7066 + 0.3489(x) ± 13.242
All Canines	Age = 59.4081 + 0.2814(x) ± 13.909
Right Third Premolars	Age = 59.4025 + 0.2734(x) ± 14.542
All Third Premolars	Age = 58.5075 + 02850(x) ± 14.024
All Fourth Premolars	Age = 30.3796 + 0.6787(x) ± 11.519
All Anterior Teeth	Age = 52.6773 + 0.3940(x) ± 13.289
All Posterior Teeth	Age = 53.2359 + 0.3754(x) ± 13.256
All Teeth	Age = 49.3551 + 0.4540(x) ± 13.008

TABLE 2.6
REGRESSION STATISTICS FOR EQUATIONS PRESENTED IN TABLE 2.5

Tooth	Sample Size (n)	Correlation Coefficient (r)	Adjusted r-Squared	p-value
Upper Right Canine	35	0.592	0.331	0.000
Lower Right Canine	58	0.405	0.149	0.002
Right Canines	65	0.423	0.166	0.000
All Canines	76	0.330	0.097	0.004
Right Third Premolar	54	0.275	0.058	0.044
All Third Premolars	60	0.290	0.069	0.024
All Fourth Premolars	17	0.766	0.558	0.000
All Anterior Teeth	78	0.418	0.164	0.000
All Posterior Teeth	65	0.391	0.139	0.001
All Teeth	81	0.443	0.186	0.000

TABLE 2.7
INACCURACY AND BIAS RESULTS OF THE EQUATIONS DEVELOPED IN
THE STUDY SAMPLE. RESULTS ARE ALSO PRESENTED FROM ENTERING THE STUDY
SAMPLE INTO THE EQUATIONS OF BANG AND RAMM.

Equation	Inaccuracy	Bias	Sample Size
Current Study			
Age = 36.7569 + 0.6599(x) ± 13.016	9.963	0.000	35
Age = 58.8041 + 0.2868(x) ± 13.437	10.209	0.000	59
Age = 54.7066 + 0.3489(x) ± 13.242	10.231	0.000	66
Age = 59.4081 + 0.2814(x) ± 13.909	10.700	0.000	77
Age = 59.4025 + 0.2734(x) ± 14.542	10.921	0.000	54
Age = 58.5075 + 02850(x) ± 14.024	10.600	0.000	60
Age = 30.3796 + 0.6787(x) ± 11.519	9.074	0.000	17
Age = 52.6773 + 0.3940(x) ± 13.289	10.546	0.000	79
Age = 53.2359 + 0.3754(x) ± 13.256	10.068	0.000	65
Age = 49.3551 + 0.4540(x) ± 13.008	10.012	0.000	82
Bang & Ramm	**10.233**	**0.000**	
Method with recommended polynomial	14.509	7.275	274
Method with unrecommended polynomial	15.295	9.869	274

result of the least-squares regression method (Table 2.7). In other words, when each sample is resubstituted back into the equation from which it was constructed, the degree of overestimations and underestimations is perfectly balanced. However, bias will not usually be zero if the equations are used on new, different samples.

Comparison to Bang and Ramm (1970)

Inaccuracy and bias statistics were calculated to determine the predictive ability of the Bang and Ramm (1970) equations using the current sample (Table 2.7). Absolute transparency measurements for all teeth in the study sample were entered into each Bang and Ramm formula. Their formulae are specific for each individual tooth type and they suggest using the first degree polynomial if the transparency measurement is greater than 9.0 mm and the second degree polynomial if the measurement is equal to or less than 9.0 mm.

The method tended to underestimate age by 7.275 years on average (Table 2.7), and the average error was 14.509 years. Absolute measurements of root transparency also were entered into the unrecommended formulae. For example, Bang and Ramm (1970) suggest using the second degree polynomial if the extent of transparency is less than or equal to 9.0 mm. In this case, if the measurement was less than 9.0 mm, the unrecommended formula would be the first degree polynomial. The resulting errors were greater than those for the recommended formulae (Table 2.7).

DISCUSSION AND CONCLUSIONS

In this study, age affects the variation of root transparency, including both absolute values and relative values standardized by total root length. This study supports previous investigations that have found a relationship between age and root transparency. Although the techniques and statistical analyses developed by Bang and Ramm (1970) prove to be somewhat difficult to repeat, the method shows promise and can be applied to independent samples in order to determine age at death.

Intra-observer Error

Close attention was paid to the explanations of measuring root transparency by Bang and Ramm in hopes that the current study would duplicate the technique and achieve similar statistical results. An intra-observer test of error was used to determine whether the method of measurement was consistent with the investigator throughout the study. With a correlation coefficient of 0.514 at a level of significance $p = 0.004$, the method proves to be difficult to repeat.

The sample study contained many teeth that exhibited indistinct limits of transparency. In numerous situations the limits of transparency within the same tooth varied drastically from the buccal to the lingual side of either the mesial or distal aspect of the tooth. Both measurements were taken, although drastically different, and their averages may not have truly reflected the length of transparency. The technique also became difficult to master due to the way the extent of transparency fluctuated as the tooth changed direction while being held in front of the light source. The problems encountered in distinguishing actual limits of transparency within the current sample accounts for the greater part of intra-observer error.

When the limit of transparency was not an even line across the root, a minimum and maximum length of transparency was needed. The average of these two measurements was used to represent the extent of root transparency for the particular tooth. Two measurements were necessary 62.8 percent of the time in the current study. Bang and Ramm (1970) noted that a minimum and maximum extension was only necessary in 7.8 percent of their intact root cases. In many cases, roots looked transparent along the sides and opaque down the middle of the root. In these situations, the decision of where to "draw the line" became vague. Bang and Ramm possibly measured the bottom extension of the opaque region more often, ignoring the transparency along the sides of the roots. This would explain the marked difference between the two studies regarding minimum and maximum transparency limits.

These aspects of measurement could also account for the low r-value found in the intra-observer error test. A correlation coefficient of $r = 0.514$ is a significant value, but the value may have been higher if the limits of transparency had not been so vague. In the current study, the technique almost certainly improved over time and was reflected in more accurate, but differing second measurements of root transparency. The sparse publications of other investigators' intra-observer errors make comparisons quite difficult. However, higher correlation coefficients produced by other studies do suggest that measuring performances have been less of a problem than encountered here.

Pearson's Correlation

Correlation coefficients were calculated for each individual tooth and several combinations of teeth. Upon analysis of the correlation matrix, several individual teeth exhibited poor correlations with age, while others performed quite well. Some teeth were combined with similar teeth in an attempt to increase the sample sizes in a number of categories. No combination of incisors gave acceptable results except when they were combined as a whole with all of the canines to represent an "anterior tooth" variable, or combined with all other teeth in the "all teeth" variable.

Correlation coefficients obtained by Bang and Ramm are considerably higher than those obtained in this study. Their coefficients consistently fluctuate between 0.600 and 0.900+. The highest significant r-value in the present analysis is 0.766 for all fourth premolars, although the average of all coefficients is only $r = 0.433$. The Bang and Ramm method appears to be easily duplicated by some investigators, while difficult to repeat by others. Statistics from previous studies must be considered when deciding what aging technique to apply to unique casework. The composition of a sample may drastically affect the outcome of age predictions when using the Bang and Ramm method of measuring and analyzing root transparency.

ANCOVA

Exploration of the relationship of sex and root transparency development indicated that sex is not a variable that contributes significantly to variation in root transparency. The analysis of covariance indicates a generalized, systematic development of root transparency in adult human beings. Therefore, the sample is pooled with regard to sex for all statistical analyses.

Linear Regression

Linear regression equations were created for the 10 variables that showed the strongest correlations with age. Regression analysis takes two variables that correlate with each other and uses the correlation as the basis for the prediction of the value of one variable from the value of the other (Salkind, 2000). Here, age is predicted from the extent of root transparency relative to root length.

These 10 variables differ from Bang and Ramm because combinations of teeth are included as well as individual teeth, whereas the previous investigators only examined the correlations of individual teeth. Bang and Ramm's ability to devise formulae for each individual tooth was due to their large study sample. The construction of a separate formula for each tooth removes the concern of including multiple data points from one individual, which would ultimately create regressions and correlations that are artificially inflated since multiple data points from one individual will tend to cluster around each other (Nawrocki, personal communication, 2004). The current study presents several variables that require the combination of several teeth. For example, the variable "all teeth" could potentially include every tooth within the dentition (excluding molars). The transparency measurements of each tooth are averaged, producing a single number that represents one individual, avoiding the problem of artificial inflation.

Standard errors produced from equations in the study sample range from ± 11.519 to ± 14.542 years, with a mean of ± 13.324 years. Few comparisons can be made to previous investigations due to the lack of published error results, or because the published error results are difficult to interpret. Standard error of the estimate calculations most comparable to the current study are those of Drusini (1991) in his analysis of the influence of sex in root transparency. His combination of all anterior teeth from both sexes resulted in an error of ± 11.15 years, whereas the current study produced ± 13.289 years. Although all other methods mentioned thus far have lower error estimations than the present study sample, the observations of Solheim and Sundess (1980) may lead one to be cautions when applying the methods of Bang and Ramm. Within their study, the Bang and Ramm method produced a comparatively wide range of errors and they suggest that these results may indicate potential and occasional failures of the Bang and Ramm method. Additional comparisons of the current study to the Bang and Ramm method follow.

Comparison to Bang and Ramm

The techniques of measuring root transparency as developed by Bang and Ramm were followed in the current study. Although Bang and Ramm outlined a method of standardizing root transparency by dividing the extent of transparency by total root length, they only used absolute values in the creation of their regression formulae. They note that the differences in results when using either relative or absolute values is minor, and therefore conclude that root transparency does not advance at differing rates within roots of varying size. If root transparency is systematic as Bang and Ramm state, then why do their results become less accurate when teeth from older individuals are examined? Their sample consists of a small amount of older age individuals, possibly accounting for the unexpected predictions. They state that the predictive ability of the method is improved when the first degree polynome is used when transparency measurements are high. When they used the second degree polynomial with higher values, the results suggested that root transparency decreases at around the age of seventy. Due to the fact that this is biologically difficult to assess, they used the first degree polynomial for these values and improved the predictions for older individuals (Bang and Ramm, 1970).

While the ability to choose from several polynomials is acceptable, the consideration of root length may allow for one equation to be applied to individuals of all ages. The ages of older individuals possessing small roots may be underestimated if root length is not taken into account. If the entire root is transparent, the root length becomes the absolute measurement. If the root is small and the individual is old, the prediction will always be underestimated.

If the amount of transparency is standardized against root length, the percentage will be 100 and a more accurate prediction will be attained. Both relative and absolute values from the present sample were correlated to age. Relative values consistently produced higher correlation coefficients, and therefore only these measurements were used in subsequent statistical analysis. The equations produced from the present study may be relevant to investigators analyzing a population consisting of older individuals, given that the value entered into the equation is a percentage versus an actual measurement. The consideration of root transparency in relation to root length may possibly improve predictions in such situations.

The inaccuracy of the Bang and Ramm method applied to the study sample is 14.509 years. This indicates that on average, the predicted age is incorrect by about 14 years. These results are comparable with other skeletal aging methods whose inaccuracies are approximately ± 10 years of the actual age. The poor intra-observer error obtained in the study sample may suggest that the inclusion of several aging techniques for various regions of the dentition and osseous elements may improve age predictions.

Limitations of the Study

The low correlation coefficients produced in the current investigation may have been affected by the low reliability that is evident in the intra-observer error results. The lower the reliability a sample possesses, the more unsystematic error, and thus the lower the Pearson correlation coefficients. With this in mind, several variables may have been inappropriately omitted due to an artificially deflated correlation coefficient. There is certainly a possibility that several tooth variables that may have been significantly correlated with age were not given further consideration in the current investigation. These negative affects also would have masked the complete truth regarding regression errors and values. The low reliability also would be reflected in higher standard errors of the regression equations, inaccurate regression slopes, and deflated r-squared values. This information must be considered when the conclusions of the current study are being examined since these affects would make the method look a lot less useful than it might have been otherwise. Assuming that the reliability did not affect the magnitude and range of the coefficients, the results of the current study may be applied and compared to subsequent investigations.

Significance of the Study

Root transparency is systematically affected by the age of an individual. As age increases root transparency increases, supporting the findings that higher percentages of root transparency tend to exist within the roots of older individuals (Bang and Ramm, 1970; Burns and Maples, 1976; Dalitz, 1962; Drusini et al., 1989; Gustafson, 1950; Johansen, 1971; Johnson, 1968; Kayshap and Koteswara, 1990; Lamendin et al., 1992; Lopez-Nicolas et al., 1996; Lucy et al., 1995; Maples and Rice, 1979; Prince and Ubelaker, 2002; Sengupta et al., 1999; Whittaker and Bakri, 1996). Previous studies have determined which teeth and combinations of teeth correlate more strongly with age. The strongest correlations tend to vary from one study to the next and nearly every tooth or combination of teeth at one time or another has been favored by correlation analysis. The current investigation found significant relationships between age, several individual teeth, and several combinations of teeth (Table 2.1). Regression equations, presented in Table 2.5, have been designed for each variable and are available for future root transparency analyses.

The use of Bang and Ramm's technique and statistical analysis is cautioned when predicting the unknown age of an individual. The method of measurement outlined by Bang and Ramm is not as easily interpreted as previously thought, although it can be easily improved for future application. The identification of the exact limits of transparency can be difficult to distinguish. This is not a reflection of the method, simply an artifact of the way root transparency develops. Improvements in the method would include a more detailed explanation of how to determine the limits of transparency when the junction between opaque and transparent dentin becomes unclear. The Bang and Ramm regression equations may possibly be more confidently applied to a broader range of individuals than the equations developed from the current sample. The predictive ability of the regression formulae created by Bang and Ramm is assessed and the results indicate that the use of their technique can be beneficial when aging unidentified individuals, but predictions will most likely improve with the inclusion and comparison of multiple dental and osseous age techniques. In situations where dental material is the only tissue complete enough to analyze, prediction improvements also may be obtained by including multiple age-related dental changes in regression analysis.

GENERAL CONCLUSIONS

The methods of Bang and Ramm (1970) are worthy of consideration when determining the age of an unknown individual. The method is an additional tool that can be used in conjunction with other aging techniques in the creation of a biological profile. This investigation supports previous findings that root transparency correlates with age. Future analyses can only improve the existing literature, methods, and techniques and will be of benefit to the field of dental and forensic anthropology.

ACKNOWLEDGMENTS

This project was funded in part by The Connective Tissue Research Fund. I would like to thank those who graciously allowed me to study their cadaver collections: Dr. David Burr, IU-Medicine and Dentistry; Dr. John Langdon, University of Indianapolis; Betty Kastaros, University of Chicago; Kristin Liles, Michigan State University; Mark Whitmer and Connie Young; The Ohio State University. I would also like to extend my gratitude to Dr. Matthew Hill, and Dr. Stephen Nawrocki who lent their time, equipment and expertise.

REFERENCES

Bang, G., & Ramm, E. (1970). Determination of age in humans from root dentin transparency. *Acta Odontologica Scandinavica 28*:3-35.

Burns, K. R., & Maples, W. R. (1976). Estimation of age from individual adult teeth. *Journal of Forensic Sciences 21*:343-356.

Dalitz, G. D. (1962). Age determination of adult human remains by teeth examination. *Forensic Science Society 3*:11-21.

Drusini, A. (1991). Age-related changes in root transparency of teeth in males and females. *American Journal of Human Biology 3*:629-637.

Drusini, A., Businaro, F., & Volpe, A. (1989). Age determination from root dentin transparency of intact human teeth. *Cahiers d'Anthropologie et Biometrie Humaine 7*(1-2):109-127.

Gustafson, G. (1950). Age determination on teeth. *The Journal of the American Dental Association 41*:45-54.

Johansen G. (1971). Age determinations from human teeth. *Odontologisk Revy 22, Supplement 22*:5-126.

Johnson, C. C. (1968). Transparent dentine in age estimation. *Journal of Oral Surgery 25*:834-838.

Kayshap, V. K., & Koteswara, R. (1990). A modified Gustafson method of age estimation from teeth. *Forensic Science International 47:*237-247.

Lamendin, H., Baccino, E., Humbert, J. F., Tavernier, J. C., Nossintchouk, R. M., & Zerilli A. (1992). A simple technique for age estimation in adult corpses: The two criteria dental method. *Journal of Forensic Sciences 37*(5):1373-1379.

Lopez-Nicolas, M., Morales, A., & Luna, A. (1996). Application of dimorphism in teeth to age calculation. *The Journal of Forensic Odonto Stomatology 14*(1):10-13.

Lucy, D., Pollard, A. M., & Roberts, C. A. (1995). Comparison of three dental techniques for estimating age at death in humans. *Journal of Archaeological Science. 22:*417-428.

Maples, W. R., & Rice, P. M. (1979). Some difficulties in the Gustafson dental age estimations. *Journal of Forensic Sciences 24:*168-172.

Prince, D. A., & Ubelaker, D. H. (2002). Application of Lamendin's adult dental aging technique to a diverse skeletal population. *Journal of Forensic Science 47(1):*107-116.

Salkind, N. J. (2000). *Statistics for people who think they hate statistics.* Thousand Oaks, London, New Dehli: Sage Publications, Inc.

Sengupta, A., Whittaker, D. K., & Shellis, R. P. (1999). Difficulties in estimating age using root dentine translucency in human teeth of varying antiquity. *Archives of Oral Biology 44*(11):889-899.

Solheim, T., & Sundess, P. K. (1980). Dental age estimation of Norwegian adults. A comparison of different methods. *Forensic Science International 16:*7-17.

Whittaker, D. K., & Bakri, M. M. (1996). Racial variation in the extent of tooth root translucency in ageing individuals. *Archives of Oral Biology 41*(1):15-19.

Chapter 3

AGE ESTIMATION BY ROOT DENTIN TRANSPARENCY OF SINGLE ROOTED TEETH

Amber R. Campbell Hibbs and Michael Finnegan

INTRODUCTION

The approximation of an individual's age at death is a primary concern of physical anthropologists, skeletal biologists and bioarchaeologists attempting to create accurate demographic reconstructions of archaeological collections, as well as forensic anthropologists working to identify individuals' remains. Because teeth tend to survive longer in the taphonomic environment and thus remain when many other parts of the body have been destroyed, a reliable estimation of age based on dental material is of obvious utility. A variety of dental aging methods have been formulated, and these traditional methods will be critically reviewed by Beach and colleagues (this volume). Many of these techniques for age estimation are complex and require instrumentation and equipment not readily available to the majority of individuals working within the forensic sciences to identify unknown individuals (Pretty, 2003). This chapter provides a relatively straightforward method for the estimation of age from sectioned teeth based upon root dentin transparency. This technique eliminates the need for costly equipment, as it requires only a light microscope and sliding calipers to observe and measure the amount of dentin transparency per individual tooth.

Age estimation for juveniles and young adults is generally accurate given the consistent nature of developmental changes in the human skeleton; however, methods for aging older adults are generally based on degenerative changes which are more variable between individuals and populations due to the huge environmental component of degenerative change (Cox, 2001). Research into the estimation of age from root dentin transparency has been ongoing since Gustafson (1950) first employed this technique. He incorporated dentin transparency as one of six tooth characteristics deemed of value in age estimation. Since Gustafson's initial report, several researchers have developed, tested, and compared different methods of transparency measurement as a possible means of age estimation (Bang and Ramm, 1970; Finnegan, 1981; Harms, 2004; Lamendin et al., 1992; Prince and Ubelaker, 2002).

DENTIN TRANSPARENCY

The dentin becomes transparent over time as the dentin tubules narrow, causing a hardening of its tubular structure. This process can begin as early as 20 years of age and is not generally affected by the health of the tooth pulp or the sex of the individual (Ermenc, 1997; Lorensen and Solheim, 1989; Maples, 1978; Nalbandian et al., 1960; Pilz et al., 1974; Condon and Charles, 1983). The transparency first becomes evident at the root apex and moves towards the crown of the tooth (Ermenc, 1997). Thus, root transparency as a means of age estimation is applicable throughout adult life in the period in which dental eruption cannot provide reliable age estimates and can be especially useful when the sex of the individual has not yet been or cannot be determined.

MATERIALS AND METHODS

The study sample consists of permanent teeth from two collections housed at the Human Osteology Laboratory in the Anthropology Department of Kansas State University. The first set of teeth comes from a collection extracted by dental professionals at the Fort Riley Dental Clinic (FRDC), Fort Riley, KS. FRDC serves military personnel and their families, and the samples were collected during 1979 and 1980 (N = 176). The sex, race, and age of each individual were recorded at the time of extraction. The second set of teeth were extracted from human cadavers at the George Washington University Medical School (GWUMS) Department of Anatomy, Washington, D.C. during 1980 and 1981 (N = 28). The sex, race and age at death of each individual are also known. The study sample utilized in this investigation originates from

103 (94 FRDC, 9 GWMS; 77 male, 26 female) individuals. Most of these teeth were removed as single extractions; however, the sample includes as many as ten teeth from a single individual. The sample set ranges in age from 13 to 89 years with a mean age of 38.8 years, and a standard deviation of 16.7 years. Only single rooted teeth (incisors, canines, and first premolars) were analyzed. For information on aging multiple rooted teeth see (Wilbert and Finnegan, this volume).

All teeth were prepared similarly regardless of the collection from which they came. Each tooth was fully immersed in isopropyl alcohol for dehydration, and was considered dehydrated once the volume of alcohol had totally evaporated. The tooth was then numbered and imbedded in Liquid Bio-Plastic™ (Ward's Natural Science, Rochester, NY). The imbedded tooth was set in a vacuum chamber so that internal structures, such as microfractures would be impregnated with the plastic. After the plastic cured, the tooth was sectioned on a Buehler (Lake Bluff, IL) slow speed Isomet saw (Model No. 11-1180) with a diamond blade of approximately 300 microns (μm) in thickness. A buccal-lingual bisection of the tooth was cut and polished on 400, 600, and 1000 aluminum oxide grit. These sections were interpreted using a Bosch and Lomb (Madison, NJ) stereoscopic dissecting microscope (Finnegan, 1981).

While many researchers have utilized backlighting of thin sections in order to visualize root dentin transparency, this technique requires consistency in the thickness of the tooth sections for consistency between samples. It also destroys most of the tooth in the process of preparing a thin section. This study provides information on the use of thick sections as they minimize the destruction of the dental material and reduce the labor intensiveness of section preparation. There are, however, a number of inherent drawbacks to the use of thick sections. First, the visible transparency is directly dependent on the thickness of the sample, and the relative anatomical position of the observed section within the tooth. As the dentin closest to the apex becomes transparent first, creating and observing a section which represents as accurately as possible the equal bisection of the tooth including the anatomical apex is necessary to achieve the best possible results with this method.

Imprecise sectioning of the tooth can create the appearance of the root apex at the tip of the section regardless of the actual origin of the section (i.e., a section which does not include the tip because the cut made was not in line with the anatomical apex still appears to include the tip because of the conical nature of the root). During the investigation, it became apparent that many of the samples utilized in this study were not sectioned directly through the center of the root apex. Thus, depending on the cutting plane, the apparent total root length in the section and the observable length of dentin transparency in the section could vary substantially. The longer of the two sections of each tooth was deemed both most complete and most likely to provide the best approximation of the bisection desired. It was therefore used for measurement.

Measurements of the root and root dentin transparency length were taken using a digital sliding caliper to the nearest 0.1 mm by a single investigator (A.R.C.). The root length (RL) was measured as the distance between the root apex and the midpoint of the line connecting the dento-enamel junction on either side of the tooth (Figure 3.1). A single measurement of transparency length (TL) was taken for those teeth possessing a roughly horizontal distinction between transparency and opaqueness. In situations where there was an uneven delineation due to differential transparency on either side of the sectioned tooth, two measurements (TL1 and TL2) were taken and the mean transparency length (MTL) was utilized in the regression formulae (Figure 3.1). Since transparency tends to extend farther up the tooth at the periphery, the shortest observable measurement of transparency on either side of the tooth was recorded and used in the construction of the age regression equations. Prominent pathology and decay were noted in most all teeth, as expected based on the origin of the sample, but the MTL was not adjusted as tooth pathology has not been associated with atypical dentin transparency in previous studies (Ermenc, 1997).

An intraobserver error test was used to determine whether the measurements taken by the investigator were consistent throughout the study. Fifty teeth from the original sample of 204 were randomly selected for reexamination three weeks after the initial study was completed. The mean of the differences between initial and later measurements was not statistically significantly different from zero (student's t-test, p = 0.53). Statistical analysis resulted in correlation coefficients of greater than r = 0.92 when comparing initial and later measurements of both absolute and relative transparency length with an average difference in the estimated age of less than a year. Harms (2004) had more trouble replicating her results due to 'indistinct limits of transparency." The determination of limits of transparency corresponds directly with the usefulness of this technique (Figure 3.1). Adherence to similar standards for the limits of transparency is essential to the reproducibility of age estimations and the accuracy of estimations produced using the equations provided.

FIGURE 3.1
TRANSPARENCY MEASUREMENTS

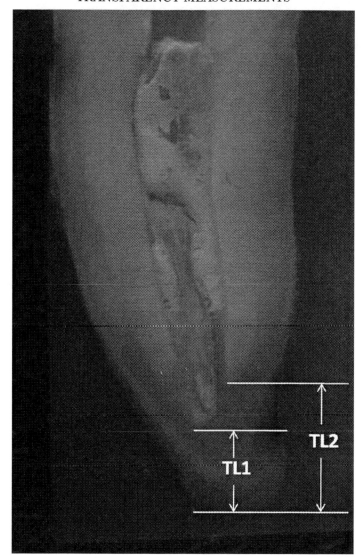

RESULTS

Transparency lengths ranged from 0 to 7.4 millimeters (mm). Transparency appeared as early as age 13, but two individuals, age 22 and 35, had no observable transparency. Correlation coefficients and p-values were obtained for the relationship between root dentin transparency length and age for each

TABLE 3.1
CORRELATION MATRIX FROM INDIVIDUAL TEETH AND TEETH GROUPS

Tooth	Sample Size	Absolute Length Correlation Coefficient	Absolute Length p-value	Relative Length Correlation Coefficient	Relative Length p-value
All First Incisors	70	.383	.001	.394	.001
All Second Incisors	60	.519	.000	.488	.000
All Canines	34	.538	.001	.550	.001
All First Premolars	40	.534	.000	.475	.002
All Teeth	204	.470	.000	.463	.000

tooth (first incisors, second incisors, canines, and first premolars) as well as all of these teeth grouped together. Correlation coefficients and p-values were also obtained for the relationship between relative transparency length (TL/RL) and age. These correlation coefficients and p-values are provided in Table 3.1.

Regression formulae were developed for both absolute and relative length of root dentin transparency as neither consistently outperformed the other in this study. The only real performance advantage at this point appears to be the reduction in the number of errors possible by limiting the total number of measurements involved. Examination of the scatter plots revealed the relationships to be roughly linear; therefore, linear regression formulae were the only regressions produced (Tables 3.2 and 3.3). The formulae were generated using the least squares method, and produced equations with standard errors that hover around 14 years.

TABLE 3.2
REGRESSION FORMULAE CREATED FOR ABSOLUTE TRANSPARENCY LENGTH

Tooth	Regression Formulae
First Incisors	Age $= 29.7 + 4.9$ (MTL) ± 14.2
Second Incisors	Age $= 20.6 + 7.7$ (MTL) ± 12.2
Canines	Age $= 21.5 + 6.4$ (MTL) ± 16.1
First Premolars	Age $= 17.2 + 5.3$ (MTL) ± 14.0
All Single Rooted Teeth	Age $= 23.5 + 6.0$ (MTL) ± 14.4

TABLE 3.3
RELATIVE TRANSPARENCY LENGTH REGRESSION FORMULAE

Tooth	*Regression Formulae*
First Incisors	Age = 30.3 + 57.1 (MTL/RL) ± 14.1
Second Incisors	Age = 22.3 + 91.9 (MTL/RL) ± 12.8
Canines	Age = 22.4 + 94.2 (MTL/RL) ± 15.9
First Premolars	Age = 17.8 + 68.8 (MTL/RL) ± 14.5
All Single Rooted Teeth	Age = 24.1 + 75.9 (MTL/RL) ± 14.6

APPLICATION

To estimate the age of an individual from a transparency measurement, simply substitute the measurement into the appropriate regression formula. For example, if the absolute mean transparency length (MTL) of an individual canine is 1.9 mm this measurement would be substituted into the equation as

$$Age = B0 + B1(MTL) \pm SE$$
$$Age = 21.5 + 6.4(1.9) \pm 16.1 = 33.7 \pm 16.1 \text{ years}$$

Thus, the estimated age of the individual is roughly 34 years with a range from 17.6 to 49.8 years. To estimate the age using the relative transparency length regression formula one would also need the total root length (RL). In this case the RL was 15.3mm. Substituted into the equation this gives

$$Age = B0 + B1(MTL/RL) \pm SE$$
$$Age = 22.4 + 94.2 \ (1.9/15.3) \pm 15.9$$
$$Age = 22.4 + 94.2 \ (.12) \pm 15.9 = 34.1 \pm 15.9 \text{ years}$$

We would again estimate the individual's age at around 34 years with a range between 18.2 and 50.0 years. The actual age of the individual was 38 years.

Again, the equations provided here are dependent upon the use of the transparency observation and measurement method described above and should not be employed when transparency is measured using the back lighting technique.

DISCUSSION

There are two main sources of error in age estimates: (1) variability in the aging process between individuals/populations, and (2) methodological bias (Schmitt et al., 2002).

Variability in Aging

Variability in the aging processes of individuals ensures that skeletal age as measured by indicators of biological maturation is not directly correlated with chronological age, which corresponds with the length of exposure to risk of death and disease (Lovejoy et al., 1997). As a result, ages derived from skeletal remains are "well-founded estimates" (Kemkes-Grottenthaler 2002: 48).

Error can also result from differences in the rate of skeletal maturation in the reference population from that in the unknown individual. One of the most fundamental assumptions made by paleodemographers and forensic anthropologists is that the pattern and rate of aging of one temporal or geographic population are not significantly different from those seen in the reference populations from which the aging estimation methods are derived (i.e., that chronological age and skeletal age are correlated in the same manner) (Hoppa, 2000; Howell, 1976; Paine, 1997). Critics of uniformitarian theory question the ability of modern populations to provide valid analogs to past populations (Paine, 1997). Research with known-age populations has shown that the mean age of individuals possessing skeletal elements having the same indicator state may vary significantly from the mean of the reference population (Hoppa, 2000; Pal and Tamankar, 1983; Schmitt et al., 2002; Sinha and Gupta, 1995). Empirical evidence supporting the basic assumptions of uniform aging processes across populations and time to identify age indicators which are valid across cultural settings is needed (Usher, 2002). This information as well as data on the variation between populations will improve the comparability of age estimations.

Methodological Bias

The use of multiple teeth from a single individual suggests possible issues resulting from covariance between these teeth, which others have attempted to resolve by using measurement averages of all teeth taken from a single individual (Harms, 2004). As the current sample has a very small number of contralateral teeth (a maximum of ten in the "All Teeth" group of 204), it was not considered to be a significant factor.

Whereas forensic researchers are most concerned with the accuracy of the age estimates made for a specific individual, the validity of paleodemographic reconstruction is based upon the ability to achieve an unbiased estimate of the distribution of age in the skeletal series (Hoppa, 2002; Lovejoy et al., 1985). As such, errors in age estimation which, although sizeable, are not biased in any systematic way are preferable to more precise, but biased estimates (Lovejoy et al., 1985). Lovejoy and colleagues (1985) also suggest the value of an age indicator in paleodemography should be based on minimizing possible bias rather than the accuracy of the method in individual cases. This method does not show any systematic bias in age estimates for the reference sample, which is a forced result of least-squares method of linear regression. A test of regression equations through estimation of age for another known age sample would provide a measure of the bias in these equations.

While the current technique can provide useful information on the age of an individual, its destructive nature and large standard error estimate (especially relative to less destructive techniques for age estimation from the pubic symphysis, etc.) makes this technique more appropriate for estimation of age in forensic cases in which the materials available for age estimation are extremely limited, than mass aging of archaeological skeletal series of relatively complete skeletons. This is due to both a large standard error of the method and an attempt to preserve finite dental remains.

The regression equations resulting from this study differ from those obtained by previous researchers on transparency (Harms, 2004; Bang and Ramm, 1970; Ermenc, 1997). The constants or y-intercepts of regression lines for individual teeth calculated in this study are generally smaller by ten to twenty years than Bang and Ramm propose. The constant for all teeth is nearly half (10 versus 20) of that suggested by Harms. This difference is probably due to the age bias in each of the samples used and is not surprising considering that the average age of the sample used in this study is roughly half that in Harms' study (38 years versus 76 years). With a large number of younger individuals the y-intercept values would be expected to drop using the least squares method of regression.

Another possible cause for the difference is the amount of pathological material in the current sample. All but 28 of the teeth used in this study were extracted from living individuals as deemed necessary by dental health professionals. Roughly half of Bang and Ramm's sample was extracted for similar reasons while the other half was extracted from cadavers with varying levels of pathology. In Harms' study, all the teeth were removed from cadavers. If significant pathology increases the rate at which root dentin becomes transparent, it could account for the reduction in the y-intercept. However, Gustafson (1950) suggests that root transparency is not greatly affected by pathology or treatment.

CONCLUSION

Measurement of root dentin transparency is a straightforward method for the estimation of age. This readily observable characteristic allows age estimation from sectioned teeth with only the use of a light microscope and sliding calipers, in addition to the sectioning supplies. This technique can thus be undertaken in most any reasonably equipped laboratory without the use of complex or excessively costly equipment. The ability to utilize root dentin transparency with confidence when the sex of the individual is unknown or cannot be determined, as well as the broad range of ages utilized in the derivation of these age regression formulae, improves the ability of this technique to provide an age estimate in most forensic cases. However, due to the complexity of the aging process and variability with reference to innumerable intrinsic and extrinsic factors "all markers employed in skeletal age assessment are inherently flawed" (Kemkes-Grottenthaler, 2002). Age estimates based on root dentin transparency are no exception. A single root dentin transparency measure can provide only a rough estimate of the age of an unknown individual. Given the large standard error estimates, this method of age estimation should not be used alone when the remains allow for additional means of age estimation. More complex dental and post-cranial aging techniques can provide more precise estimations of individual age, and age estimations based on root dentin transparency should be utilized as part of a mosaic of age estimation techniques when the skeletal material necessary is available.

The equations developed in this research should be an immediate substantial aid in situations in which only a single tooth or teeth are available for the purposes of age estimation. Equations provided here are dependent upon the use of the transparency observation and measurement method described above and should not be employed when transparency is measured using the back lighting technique.

ACKNOWLEDGMENTS

This material is based upon work supported under a National Science Foundation Graduate Research Fellowship. Any opinions, findings, conclusions or recommendations expressed in this publication are those of the author(s) and do not necessarily reflect the views of the National Science Foundation.

REFERENCES

Bang, K. R., & Ramm, E. (1970). Determination of age in humans from tooth dentin transparency. *Acta Odontologica Scandinavica 28*:3–35.

Condon, K. W., & Charles, D. K. (1983). An evaluation of the cemental annulation aging technique. *American Journal of Physical Anthropology 60*:183.

Cox, M. (2001). Assessment of age at death and sex. In D. Brothwell & A. Pollard (Eds.), *Handbook of archaeological sciences,* pp. 237–247. Chinchester: Wiley.

Ermenc, B. (1997). Metamorphosis of root dentine and age. *International Journal of Osteoarchaeology 7*:230–234.

Finnegan, M. (1981). An analysis of age determination by a modified Gustafson method. 33rd annual meeting of the American Academy of Forensic Sciences. Los Angeles, California.

Gustafson, G. (1950). Age determination on teeth. *The Journal of the American Dental Association 41*:45–54.

Harms, J. (2004). The determination of age at death through the examination of root dentin transparency. Master's Thesis: University of Indianapolis.

Hoppa, R. D. (2000). Population variation in osteological aging criteria: an example from the pubic symphysis. *American Journal of Physical Anthropology 111*:185–191.

Hoppa, R. D. (2002). Paleodemography: looking back and thinking ahead. In R. D. Hoppa & J. W. Vaupel (Eds.), *Paleodemography: Age distributions from skeletal samples,* pp. 9–28. Cambridge: Cambridge University Press.

Howell, N. (1976). Toward a uniformitarian theory of human paleodemography. *Journal of Human Evolution 5*:25–40.

Kemkes-Grottenthaler, A. (2002). Aging through the ages: historical perspectives on age indicator methods. In R. D. Hoppa & J. W. Vaupel (Eds.), *Paleodemography: Age distributions from skeletal samples,* pp. 48–72. Cambridge: Cambridge University Press.

Lamendin, H., Baccino, E., Humbert, J. F., Tavernier, J. C., Nossintchouk, R. M., & Zerilli, A. (1992). A simple technique for age estimation in adult corpses: The two criteria dental method. *Journal of Forensic Sciences 37*:1371–1379.

Lorensen, M., & Solheim, T. (1989). Age assessment based on translucent dentine. *Journal of Forensic Odontal-Stomatol 7*:3–9.

Lovejoy, C. O., Meindl, R. S., Mensforth, R. P., & Barton, T. J. (1985). Multifactorial determination of skeletal age at death: A method and blind tests of its accuracy. *American Journal* of *Physical Anthropology 68*:1–14.

Lovejoy, C. O., Meindl, R. S., Tague, R. G., & Latimer, B. (1997). The comparative senescent biology of the Hominoid pelvis and its implications for the use of age-at-death indicators in the human skeleton. In R. R. Paine (Ed.), *Integrating archaeological demography,* pp. 43–63. Carbondale, IL: Southern Illinois University.

Maples, W. (1978). An improved technique using dental histology for estimation of adult age. *Journal of Forensic Sciences 23*:764–770.

Nalbandian, J., Gonzales, F., & Sognnaes, R. F. (1960). Sclerotic age changes in root dentine of human teeth as observed by optical, electron, and X-ray microscopy. *Journal of Dental Research 39*:598–607.

Paine, R. R. (1997). Uniformitarian models in osteological paleodemography. In R. R. Paine (Ed.), *Integrating archaeological demography,* pp. 191–204. Carbondale, IL: Southern Illinois University.

Pal, G., & Tamankar, B. (1983). Determination of age from the pubic symphysis. *Indian Journal of Medical Research 99*:694–701.

Pilz, W., Reiman, W., & Krause, D. G. (1974). Medizin fur Stomatologen. Leipzig: J. A. Barth.

Pretty, I. (2003). The use of dental aging techniques in forensic odontological practice. *Journal of Forensic Sciences 48*:1127–1132.

Prince, D. A., & Ubelaker, D. H. (2002). Application of Lamendin's adult dental aging technique to a diverse skeletal sample. *Journal of Forensic Sciences 47*:107–116.

Schmitt, A., Murail, P., Cunha, E., & Rouge, D. (2002). Variability of the pattern of aging on the human skeleton: evidence from bone indicators and implications on age at death estimation. *Journal of Forensic Sciences 47*: 1203–1209.

Sinha, A., & Gupta, V. (1995). A study on estimation of age from pubic symphysis. *Forensic Science International 75*:73–78.

Usher, B. M. (2002). Reference Samples: The first step in linking biology and age in the human skeleton. In R. D. Hoppa & J. W. Vaupel (Eds.), *Paleodemography: Age distributions from skeletal samples,* pp. 2–47. Cambridge: Cambridge University Press.

Chapter 4

AGE ESTIMATION BY ROOT DENTIN TRANSPARENCY OF DOUBLE ROOTED MANDIBULAR MOLARS

Diana M. Wilbert and Michael Finnegan

INTRODUCTION

For over fifty years researchers have been developing, testing, and analyzing different methods to use in the age estimation of individuals based on dental elements (Bang and Ramm, 1970; Burns and Maples, 1976; Gustafson, 1950; Harms, 2004; Lamendin et al., 1992; Maples and Rice, 1979; Prince and Ubelaker, 2002). Dental material is often well preserved in archaeological and forensic contexts due to its high mineral content, making human dentition extremely valuable for use in the estimation of age at death in forensic and bioarchaeological cases. Due to its high preservation rate, researchers continue to formulate new equations and methods for determining age by use of dental material.

In the past, researchers have avoided the use of multi-rooted (molar) teeth (Bang and Ramm, 1970), suggesting the determination of transparency to be too difficult in such circumstances. However, it is likely that molar teeth will be represented more often than the anterior teeth in forensic and bioarchaeological contexts due to protection from the cheek muscles and reduced post-mortem loss afforded by the clutching roots of multi-rooted teeth as compared to the conical shaped roots of most anterior single-rooted teeth, and these statements need to be systematically evaluated. Molar teeth are not only the largest teeth found in the human mouth, but they are also the strongest and most likely to withstand stresses that destroy the smaller teeth.

Gustafson (1950) pioneered dental aging techniques, and his work has served as a foundation for the development of subsequent dental aging methods (Bang and Ramm, 1970; Burns and Maples, 1976; Finnegan, 1981; Harms, 2004; Campbell and Finnegan 2006; Lamendin et al., 1992; Maples and Rice, 1979; Prince and Ubelaker, 2002). The purpose of this study is to investigate the feasibility of utilizing root dentin transparency in multi-rooted teeth by investigating first, second, and third mandibular molar teeth. Mandibular molar teeth were chosen due to their symmetrical structure in having either two or four roots. Maxillary molar teeth are more likely to have an odd number of roots, with the most common number being three.

MATERIALS AND METHODS

The first, second, and third molars utilized in this study were extracted by dental professionals at the Fort Riley Dental Clinic during 1979 and 1980. The age, race, and sex of most individuals were noted at the time of extraction (Table 4.1). Table 4.1 includes two unknowns for sex. These are included as we are not separating the sample by sex.

Of the 328 teeth used for this investigation 105 were first molars, 105 were second molars, and 118 were third molars.

Each tooth was placed in a sufficient amount of isopropyl alcohol to completely cover the specimen. The isopropyl alcohol served as a dehydrating agent, and was allowed to completely evaporate. Then each tooth was assigned a number, imbedded in Ward's bioplastic (Ward's Natural Science, Rochester, NY), and placed in a vacuum chamber to allow for internal structures and breaks to be impregnated with the plastic.

Once the plastic was fully cured, each tooth was sectioned into buccal and lingual halves by a Buehler (Lake Bluff, IL) low speed isomet saw (Model No.

TABLE 4.1
SAMPLE COMPOSITION

	N	*Age Range*	*Mean Age*
Males	269	17–65	23.8
Females	57	15–44	22.7
Unknown	2	19–21	20
Total	328	15–65	23.6

11-1180) with a diamond blade 300 microns in thickness. Each tooth section was polished using a 400, 600, and 1,000 aluminum oxide grit. It should be noted that these sections are thicker than those utilized by Bang and Ramm. Bang and Ramm's study involved the use of both intact and longitudinal sections of only 400 micron thickness, while this study uses sections varying from two to six millimeters in thickness.

A Stereo Eighty (Swift Instruments International S.A., San Jose, CA) dissecting microscope with available magnification of 2X and 4X was used for observations and an electronic digital sliding caliper was used for taking measurements. This device has an accuracy of ± 0.02 millimeters and measures up to one hundred millimeters. All measurements in this study were below twenty millimeters.

Measurements were taken of root length (RL), transparency length one (TL1) and transparency length two (TL2). Figure 4.1 illustrates where these measurements are taken on any given root. RL is measured from the root apex to the upper peak on the dentin central to the present section of the tooth. TL1 is the primary transparency and is most commonly found beginning at the apex and continuing superiorly for measurement. TL1 should be easily recognizable while TL2, on the other hand, may appear to be a transi-

FIGURE 4.1
MOLAR TOOTH MEASUREMENTS

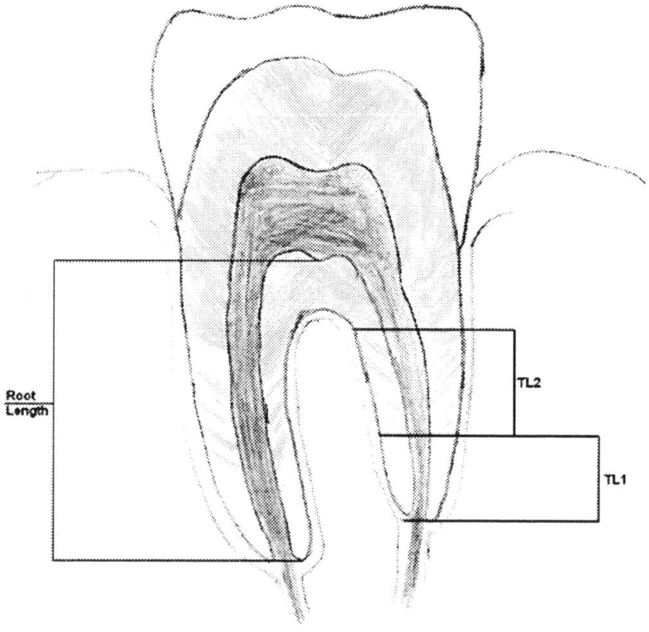

tional area between transparency and opaqueness. It is important to note that all specimens do not have both TL1 and TL2. Some only have one or the other. As such, both measurements were used to determine final formulae. These measurements were taken on both the mesial and distal roots. In most cases differences were noted between roots of the same tooth, leading to the more complex formulae discussed later.

Definitive decay and pathologies were noted, but not unexpected given the origin of the sample in which a large portion includes extractions for dental health reasons. However, Gustafson (1950) noted that dental pathologies had little, if any affect on dentin transparency.

RESULTS

P-values and correlation coefficients were obtained for the relationship between age and transparency for each root type, along with all teeth. The teeth were further subdivided by mesial or distal root to provide more accurate data. Data were also obtained for the relationship between age and relative transparency length (TL/RL). These data are presented in Tables 4.2 and 4.3. Table 4.2 utilizes TL1 values, while Table 4.3 uses TL2 values for comparison.

Most of the statistically significant values, both for correlation coefficients and p-values, are found in relation to TL1 measurements. These also tend to fall in the absolute length categories, although a few do exist in the relative form. Since there are only a few significant values present in both categories, regression analysis was performed using both absolute and relative data.

Data analysis and related scatter plots showed the relationships to be fairly linear, therefore, linear regression analysis was utilized and formulae were produced. Formulae for both absolute and relative transparency lengths are presented in Tables 4.4 and 4.5 respectively.

APPLICATION

Determination of left and right sides of the tooth were used to facilitate identification of buccal and lingual sections. This sample was not subdivided based on sex or race, and equations are therefore applied to all individuals despite sex, race, or side of origin (left or right). For example, if the absolute values of an individual M1 are LMTL1 = 0.31 mm, LDTL2 = 0 mm, LDTL1

TABLE 4.2
CORRELATION MATRIX BASED ON T1 VALUES FROM INDIVIDUAL TEETH
AND ALL TEETH. (VALUES IN BOLD REPRESENT STATISTICAL
SIGNIFICANCE; * INDICATES P = 0.05; ** INDICATES P = 0.01)

Tooth	Section	Root	Sample Size	Absolute Length Correlation Coefficient	Absolute Length p-value	Relative Length Correlation Coefficient	Relative Length p-vale
1st Molar	Buccal	Mesial	105	**0.316**	0.099	0.239	0.506
1st Molar	Buccal	Distal	105	0.159	0.706	0.103	0.771
2nd Molar	Buccal	Mesial	105	0.228	0.516	0.164	0.929
2nd Molar	Buccal	Distal	105	**0.421**	0.071	0.287	0.270
3rd Molar	Buccal	Mesial	118	0.064	0.620	0.036	0.753
3rd Molar	Buccal	Distal	118	**0.333**	0.082	0.234	0.322
All Molars	Buccal	Mesial	328	0.138	0.859	0.088	0.594
All Molars	Buccal	Distal	328	0.297	**0.014***	0.196	0.097
1st Molar	Lingual	Mesial	105	**0.321**	0.056	0.266	**0.033***
1st Molar	Lingual	Distal	105	**0.401**	**0.007****	**0.363**	**0.000****
2nd Molar	Lingual	Mesial	105	0.211	0.351	0.172	0.813
2nd Molar	Lingual	Distal	105	0.316	0.918	0.220	0.715
3rd Molar	Lingual	Mesial	118	0.039	0.125	-0.021	0.167
3rd Molar	Lingual	Distal	118	**0.314**	**0.014***	0.237	**0.050***
All Molars	Lingual	Mesial	328	0.205	0.853	0.140	0.545
All Molars	Lingual	Distal	328	**0.352**	**0.000****	0.278	**0.000****

= 1.91 mm, and BMTL1 = 1.50 mm the measurements would be substituted into the equation:

Age = 19.4 + 1.21(LMTL1) + 0.743(LDTL2) + 1.79(LDTL1) + 0.967(BMTL1) ± SE
Age = 19.4 + 1.21(0.31 mm) + 0.743(0 mm) + 1.79(1.91 mm) + 0.967(1.50 mm) ± 6.98 years = 24.64 ± 6.98 years or between 17.66 and 31.62 years of age.

To estimate the same individual's age using relative transparency length a different equation would be used. RLDTL1 is calculated from the lingual dis-

TABLE 4.3
CORRELATION MATRIX BASED ON T2 VALUES FROM INDIVIDUAL TEETH
AND ALL TEETH. (VALUES IN BOLD REPRESENT STATISTICAL
SIGNIFICANCE; * INDICATES P = 0.05; ** INDICATES P = 0.01)

Tooth	*Section*	*Root*	*Sample Size*	*Absolute Length Correlation Coefficient*	*Absolute Length p-value*	*Relative Length Correlation Coefficient*	*Relative Length p-vale*
1st Molar	Buccal	Mesial	105	0.119	0.837	0.089	0.761
1st Molar	Buccal	Distal	105	0.180	0.318	0.169	0.523
2nd Molar	Buccal	Mesial	105	0.274	0.087	0.215	0.191
2nd Molar	Buccal	Distal	105	0.064	0.836	0.031	0.899
3rd Molar	Buccal	Mesial	118	0.298	0.067	0.247	**0.030***
3rd Molar	Buccal	Distal	118	0.243	0.338	0.225	0.145
All Molars	Buccal	Mesial	328	0.212	0.143*	0.167	.0193
All Molars	Buccal	Distal	328	0.152	0.741	0.130	0.870
1st Molar	Lingual	Mesial	105	0.061	0.055	0.083	0.375
1st Molar	Lingual	Distal	105	0.183	**0.043***	0.152	0.063
2nd Molar	Lingual	Mesial	105	**0.392**	0.454	**0.417**	**0.016***
2nd Molar	Lingual	Distal	105	**0.309**	0.749	0.223	0.834
3rd Molar	Lingual	Mesial	118	0.257	0.429	0.164	0.846
3rd Molar	Lingual	Distal	118	0.172	0.405	0.153	0.290
All Molars	Lingual	Mesial	328	0.250	0.383	0.250	**0.031***
All Molars	Lingual	Distal	328	0.245	0.064	0.192	0.082

tal TL1 being divided by the lingual distal root length (0.26 mm). Similarly RLMTL1 is calculated from the lingual mesial TL1 being divided by the lingual mesial root length (0.03 mm). This calculation is shown below.

Age = 20.7 + 6.92(RLDTL1) + 16.5(RLMTL1) ± SE
Age = 20.7 + 6.92(0.26) + 16.5(0.03) ± 6.97 years = 22.99 ± 6.97 years or between 16.02 and 29.96 years of age. The actual age of this individual was 19 years.

While a standard error of almost seven years remains to be very significant,

TABLE 4.4
ABSOLUTE TRANSPARENCY LENGTH REGRESSION FORMULAE FOR TEETH
BASED ON STATISTICALLY SIGNIFICANT CORRELATIONS AND/OR P-VALUES

Tooth	*Regression Formula*	*Standard Error (SE)*	*Average Known Age*	*Adjusted R2*
1st Molars	Age = 19.4 + 1.21(LMTL1) + 0.743(LDTL2) + 1.79(LDTL1) + 0.967(BMTL1)	6.98 years	23.19 years	0.196
2nd Molars	Age = 21.6 + 2.95(BDTL1) + 1.04(BMTL2)	7.61 years	24.73 years	0.197
3rd Molars	Age = 20.3 + 1.53(BMTL2) + 0.823(BDTL1) + 1.33(LDTL1)	4.62 years	22.91 years	0.209
All Molars	Age = 20.5 + 1.76(LDTL1) + 0.947(LDTL2) + 0.991(BDTL1)	6.63 years	23.6 years	0.18

TL1 = Transparency Length 1 (Primary)   L = Lingual
TL2 = Transparency Length 2 (Secondary)   B = Buccal
R____ = Relative Length   D = Distal
    M = Mesial

TABLE 4.5
RELATIVE TRANSPARENCY LENGTH REGRESSION FORMULAE FOR TEETH
BASED ON STATISTICALLY SIGNIFICANT CORRELATIONS AND/OR P-VALUES

Tooth	*Regression Formula*	*Standard Error (SE)*	*Average Known Age*	*Adjusted R2*
1st Molars	Age = 20.7 + 6.92(RLDTL1) + 16.5(RLMTL1)	6.97 years	23.19 years	0.175
2nd Molars	Age = 22.8 + 17.1(RLMTL2)	7.84 years	24.73 years	0.165
3rd Molars	Age = 21.1 + 9.47(RBMTL2) + 8.95(RLMTL1)	4.91 years	22.91 years	0.107
All Molars	Age = 22.0 + 6.90(RLDTL1) + 8.21(RLMTL2)	6.79 years	23.6 years	0.114

TL1 = Transparency Length 1 (Primary)   L = Lingual
TL2 = Transparency Length 2 (Secondary)   B = Buccal
R____ = Relative Length   D = Distal
    M = Mesial

this is an improvement from past formulae. This method could be used to help confirm an age or narrow down an age range. In older individuals a spread of twelve to fourteen years is considered fairly acceptable. The standard errors found in this study all fall well below those involving suture closure, which at this point makes the analysis of molar teeth a good choice in age determination of mandibles.

DISCUSSION

This study looks at age estimation by use of root dentin transparency in mandibular molar teeth. Correlations are significantly lower than those obtained by Bang and Ramm (1970), which place them closer to those obtained in the recent study by Harms (2004). This is likely due to the differences in sample size and age variations between studies. The Harms (2004) sample had a mean age of 77.4 years, while this study has a mean age of 23.6. The Harms (2004) sample leans more toward older, elderly individuals and the present study includes more young adults. Both lack an even distribution in age range.

The standard error is reduced in this study as compared to those in the past. For example, the current study has a standard error falling around five to seven years. The Harms (2004) study has an average standard error around thirteen years, and the Bang and Ramm (1970) study had standard errors ranging around nine to ten years. Additional research is required to investigate whether this is due to the increased technology available and/or the better data available through use of molar teeth.

Sixty sections (buccal or lingual halves) were randomly selected from the original sample of 328 in order to conduct an intraobserver error test. This was used to determine whether the measurements taken by the investigator were significantly different and was conducted after half of the study was completed. Data gathered from the intraobserver test were set aside for later comparison. Two weeks after completion of the entire sample thirty sections were randomly selected for a second intraobserver test. The data from the mid-study test and the post-test were combined and compared to the final data. Statistical analysis resulted in correlation coefficients greater than 0.96.

According to Bang and Ramm (1970) most researchers who utilize multi-rooted teeth have been confronted with difficulties when determining root dentin transparency. This could be due to the limited resources available at the time their research was conducted. This study has found the task of measuring multi-rooted teeth no more difficult than that of single-rooted teeth. Difficulties lie more in the extra statistical analysis necessary to ultimately determine simple, but useful equations. Researchers should grasp the opportunity to study multi-rooted teeth, especially mandibular molars.

REFERENCES

Bang, K. R., & Ramm, E. (1970). Determination of age in humans from tooth dentin transparency. *Acta Odontologica Scandinavica 28*:3–35.

Burns, K. R., & Maples, W. R. (1976). Estimation of age from individual adult teeth. *Journal of Forensic Sciences 21*:343.

Campbell, A., & Finnegan, M. (2006). Age estimation by root dentin transparency of single-rooted teeth. Paper presented at the 26th Annual Meeting of the Mountain, Desert and Coastal Forensic Anthropologists, 24–26 May 2006, at Lake Mead, Boulder City, Nevada.

Finnegan, M. (1981). An analysis of age determination by a modified Gustafson method: 33rd Annual Meeting of the American Academy of Forensic Sciences. Los Angeles, California.

Gustafson, G. (1950). Age determination on teeth. *The Journal of the American Dental Association 41*:45.

Harms, J. (2004). The determination of age at death through the examination of root transparency. University of Indianapolis Master's Thesis.

Lamendin, H., Baccino, E., Humbert, J. F., Tavernier, J. C., Nossintchouk, R. M., & Zerilli, A. (1992). A simple technique for age estimation in adult corpses: the two criteria dental method. *Journal of Forensic Sciences 37*:1371.

Maples, W. R, & Rice, M. P. (1979). Some difficulties in the Gustafson dental age estimations. *Journal of Forensic Sciences 24*:168.

Prince, D. A, & Ubelaker, D. H. (2002). Application of Lamendin's adult dental aging technique to a diverse skeletal sample. *Journal of Forensic Sciences 47*:107.

Chapter 5

AGE ESTIMATION OF SUBADULT REMAINS FROM THE DENTITION

EMILIE L. SMITH

INTRODUCTION

Norms of dental development provide a means for aging subadult human skeletal remains by giving anthropologists a method of estimating the unknown chronological age from known morphology. Age can be estimated by comparing information obtained from the skeleton, in this case the teeth, and then translating this morphology into an approximate chronological age.

In forensic anthropology and odontology, age at death is estimated by comparing the decedent's teeth with a series of standardized images of dentitions at different known ages presented on comprehensive charts. A target estimate is then assigned to the unknown individual. The two main charts utilized by anthropologists were prepared by Schour and Massler (1944) and Ubelaker (1978; 1989). These charts are similar and provide line drawings of the teeth in 21 different developmental stages from just prior to birth to early adulthood. However, there are some differences between them in their depiction of the development and eruption of specific teeth, and in their designated error intervals. The charts are not sex-specific even though many authors have noted a distinct sexual dimorphism in the formation and eruption of the teeth (Schour and Massler, 1941; Steggerda and Hill, 1942; Gleiser and Hunt, 1955; Lewis and Garn, 1960; Glister et al., 1964; Ubelaker, 1978; Smith, 1991).

Schour and Massler's and Ubelaker's dental aging charts were tested to determine if their use is appropriate for age estimation in modern American children. Since these charts are both used regularly by anthropologists to estimate age at death from subadult remains, it seemed appropriate to subject them to testing with a known-age sample.

DEVELOPMENT OF THE DENTAL AGING CHARTS

The first chronologies of dental formation can be attributed to Legros and Magitot (1880, 1881; quoted from Smith, 1991:145). These authors developed tables that displayed the appearance of dental tissues and structures for both the deciduous and permanent teeth, with emphasis on prenatal formation. In 1933, Logan and Kronfeld examined children with various dental abnormalities, including cleft palate and linear enamel hypoplasias, and discussed the errors found in Legros and Magitot's chart of calcification. The authors found that within the table, all permanent teeth, from central incisor to second premolar in both upper and lower jaws, are shown as beginning calcification at one month after birth, but in reality they noted differences of almost two years between formation of the dentin of the central incisor and second bicuspid. Logan and Kronfeld also noted that while the chart contains many inaccuracies, it has been accepted and used without modification for four decades. Smith (1991) cites the errors found in Legros and Magitot's chart as a result of their data being poorly translated into English and their table of development being partially misprinted. Later developmental charts appeared in American dental journals in 1883 (Black) and 1884 (Peirce) without any description of the methods or sample subjects, and in 1924, Brady printed a chart that pictographically shows stages of dental development, eruption, and resorption that he developed from more than 25 years of study. His chart displays both the upper and lower dentition beginning at the 17th week and extending through 15 years of age.

In 1940b, Schour and Massler researched the incremental growth of teeth and produced a table modifying data from Logan and Kronfeld (1933) and Kronfeld (1935a, b) on the initiation of calcification of the permanent teeth. They also included a "diagrammatic representation of the chronology and mode of development of human upper teeth" (1940b), which appears to combine some of the Logan and Kronfeld data as well as their own (Schour and Hoffman, 1939a, b; Schour and Kronfeld, 1938; Schour and Massler, 1940a, b). However, critiques were raised against the reuse of Logan and Kronfeld's data because of the small sample and the fact that many of these individuals had died from illnesses, which could have potentially had an effect on their dental development (Garn et al., 1959; Miles, 1963; Lunt and Law, 1974; Ubelaker, 1987). Additionally, they seem to ignore previous findings that the Logan and Kronfeld ranges were too narrow and that many children fell outside of the published ranges (Garn et al., 1959; Lewis and Garn, 1960).

Despite using the same manner of presentation, Schour and Massler do not reference Brady's (1924) earlier diagram, and a comparison of the two uncovers many noticeable discrepancies. Most conspicuously, Brady indicates that the permanent teeth begin formation at 14 months of age, with the calcification of the central permanent incisor crown. Schour and Massler, however, show in their chart that the permanent teeth begin formation at 6 months of age with calcification of the crowns of both the medial incisor and canine. Schour and Massler's developmental chart more closely depicts published data for these rates of formation, and shows 21 developmental stages of the upper dentition from 5 to 8 months in utero, birth, 6 months, 9 months, and then chronologically from 1 to 14 years of age.

Schour and Massler later modified their pictorial chart in 1941, with 22 developmental stages for the first 35 years of life. They eliminated the 13 and 14-year age stages and included new stages at ages 15, 21, and 35. Differences between the 1940b and the 1941 charts are minor, with dissimilarities beginning at the 2-year stage. Their older chart (1940b) shows the second permanent premolar beginning cusp formation at age 2; however, this is not seen in the new chart until age 3. Additionally, the third molar at age 15 in the 1941 chart shows the same stage of root development as the eliminated age 13 in the older version. Schour and Massler describe their chart as having six overall phases of development, including prenatal, birth/neonatal, infancy, childhood, grade school, and adulthood, and additional subdivisions of these phases.

The Schour and Massler chart appears in a slightly modified version in 1944 as a wall-sized chart entitled "Development of the Human Dentition" distributed by the American Dental Association. This chart notes that it is a second edition; however, it is uncertain which version of the previous two charts is considered to be the "first." The library at the American Dental Association in Chicago was unable to locate an earlier edition of the wall-sized chart and the only other versions of the Schour and Massler chart were published by the *Journal of the American Dental Association* in 1940 and 1941. The newer 1944 chart is similar to the 1941 version; however, one noticeable difference is the addition of error ranges. It is not certain how the error ranges were derived as there are no data accompanying this new chart in the form of published research. Other differences include the elimination of postnatal ages of 6 and 8 months and the addition of an 18-month age stage (1.5 years). The newly added 18-month age group most closely resembles the 1941 stage at 2 years. Beginning with 6 months of age, there are apparent differences in the formation of the dentition, with root development in the later Schour and Massler chart being more advanced at almost every stage. Despite this progression, the ages for loss and eruption are still the same for both charts. The phases mentioned by Schour and Massler in 1941 are now partially visualized in their 1944 chart. This chart is grouped by deciduous dentition, mixed dentition, and permanent dentition categories. The deciduous dentition includes two subgroups, infancy (5 months to 18 months) and early childhood/preschool age (2 to 6 years). The mixed dentition includes late childhood/school age children aged 7 to 10 years, and the permanent dentition grouping includes "adolescence and adulthood" individuals aged 11 to 35 years.

Yet another chart was developed by Schour and Massler and was printed in their "Atlas of the Mouth and Adjacent Parts in Health and Disease" (Massler and Schour, 1958) published by the American Dental Association. This chart displays many similarities to and a few noted differences from their 1944 chart. However, the 1944 chart is the one most often utilized by anthropologists; hence the newer version of the chart will not be discussed in depth here.

Over the years, these various dental charts have been reevaluated and tested against other samples and populations. Miles (1958) tested Schour and Massler's 1941 chart and found that on individuals up to the age of 12, most were close to their actual estimates, few exceeding their true age by more than one year. After 12 years, Miles found an increasing tendency for the individuals to be scored 2 or more years above or below the actual age. The age estimates found with Schour and Massler's 1941 chart for individuals over 16 years of age were consistently too low, and the author suggests modifying the chart to correct the development of the third molar.

Miles (1963) again critiques Schour and Massler's 1941 chart, citing that it is limited to individuals below 15 years because no stages of growth for the third molar are recorded for the critical formation ages between 15 and 21 years. Miles claims that "where material of unknown sex is concerned, estimates of age based on the dentition are more likely to be correct than those based on osseous development" because sex differences in the skeleton are about three times greater than those for tooth development (258). Scheuer and Black (2000) recommend that Schour and Massler's 1941 chart is best used when examining infancy and early childhood subjects.

In 1978, and again in 1989, Ubelaker expanded and changed many of the error ranges originally given by Schour and Massler in 1944. This change seems to be primarily due to the fact that Ubelaker's chart was developed for analysis of Indigenous Americans and other non-white dentitions after determining that Schour and Massler's chart consistently overestimates their ages at death and underestimates their actual growth rate (Merchant and Ubelaker, 1977). Despite these modifications, Ubelaker's chart has now become a recognized world standard for all ancestral groups. Ubelaker also made minor adjustments to the original pictorial depictions of the rates of formation and eruption of the teeth, with the most distinct visual difference being in the development of the canine from the age of 18 months to 2 years. The changes made by Ubelaker are associated with various author's findings of earlier formation and development of the dentition of indigenous American individuals.

There seems to be spontaneously generated or tacitly modified differences among all of the dental aging charts with no mention as to where these differences were generated. For example, Ubelaker's 1989 chart was reproduced in a text by Ubelaker and Buikstra (1994:51), and while Ubelaker's 1989 text gave a target age with error range as 12 years $\pm$ 30 months, the 1994 text gave an error range for the same age of $\pm$ 36 months with no mention as to why this change was made. Additionally, Ubelaker's newer 1999 edition of his 1989 book replicates the chart again with the error age at 12 years $\pm$ 30 months, and he notes that his ranges express variability within the literature and the error intervals may be inexact by as much as 5 years, especially among the older ages.

There do not appear to be any tests of Ubelaker's chart. There was a modification made by WEA (1980) that can be viewed in Scheuer and Black (2000), which was based on Ubelaker's 1978 chart. The only major difference in this newer chart is that the error interval at 15 years has been narrowed from 15 $\pm$ 36 months, as was previously found in Ubelaker's chart, to 15 $\pm$ 30 months. Additionally, in the WEA chart, at 6 months of age the permanent cusps are beginning in the mandible, which is not present in Ubelaker.

The history of the development of dental aging charts is long and complex. It appears that there are gaps in their construction and many lack vigorous testing. The few tests that have been performed do not recommend any major changes; however, there is a need to determine if their use is appropriate for age estimation in modern American children.

MATERIALS AND METHODS

Clinical Sample

The data for this longitudinal study consists of 419 randomly selected American children of European ancestry from 5 to 15 years of age, and includes approximately equal numbers of males and females for each year of age. Panoramic dental radiographs were collected until approximately twenty males and twenty females were obtained for each age or until the existing supply of records for that age was exhausted. Panoramic radiographs were chosen because they provide comprehensive coverage of all teeth, and the film includes the "maxillary region extending to the superior third of the orbit, and the entire mandible including the temporomandibular joint region" (Miles and Parks, 2004:72).

Individuals not of European-American ancestry were excluded from this study in order to concentrate on variation within one ancestral group and to maximize homogenous sample sizes. Other groups eliminated included all patients with orthodontia (such as braces) or more than one absent tooth. Siblings were also excluded.

Scoring Systems

Specific dental stage numbers were assigned to Ubelaker's (1978) and Schour and Massler's (1944) dental charts, beginning with 1 for the "birth" stage and ending with 18 at the age 21 stage. Since the ages in the study range from 5 to 15, stages 9 through 17 were generally assigned for those ages. The left side of each panoramic radiograph (including both the mandible and the maxilla) was compared to Ubelaker's (1978) dental aging charts and given a dental stage number according to which Ubelaker stage the radiograph most closely matched. Then all pictures were reexamined using Schour and Massler's (1944) chart. The target age for each dental stage was the predicted age given by each chart, which was then compared with the actual chronological age.

RESULTS

Qualitative Results

Slight nuances were detected when assigning individuals to the 9–17 stages using the Ubelaker (1989) and the Schour and Massler (1944) charts. For example, in stage 9, the first molars have begun root formation in Ubelaker's chart; however, in Schour and Massler's chart, they have only just completed crown formation. This difference caused some individuals to be classified as one stage later when using Schour and Massler's chart. Stages 10 and 11 were very similar between the two charts and no problems were noted in these stages.

Beginning with stage 12, additional differences can be observed between the charts. At this stage in Ubelaker's chart, the first and second permanent incisors are at stage 13 in Schour and Massler's. This led to some differences when scoring the study sample. In addition, in Schour and Massler's stage 12, the canine is underdeveloped relative to Ubelaker's chart (the root should be developed at approximately $1/2$ its full length but it is shown at $1/4$). This difference led to some individuals being placed into Schour and Massler's stage 13 when the root was further developed.

At stage 13, the second molar in Ubelaker's chart is shown with roots developing, however, in Schour and Massler, root formation has not yet begun. It was observed that Ubelaker's chart more accurately depicted the state of tooth development in the study sample in this respect. In Ubelaker's chart the development of the roots of the first and second incisors at stage 13 were at stage 14 in Schour and Massler's chart. However, while these differences were noticeable, they did not affect the stage placement because the overall eruption pattern had not advanced to Schour and Massler's stage 14.

It should be noted that in evaluations of Schour and Massler's stage 13, in most cases the mandibular teeth were more advanced than they should be (especially the roots of the 1st and 2nd permanent premolars) while the maxillary teeth tended to match the depictions in the chart very well. Another general irregularity in both charts involves the formation of the permanent second premolar, shown as being developmentally the same as the first premolar. However, the P2 was found to be less developed than the P1 in most cases. This difference was especially noted in stages 13 and 14.

Another scoring difficulty for both Schour and Massler's and Ubelaker's charts was distinguishing between stages 14 and 15. The major difference between these stages is the transition from mixed dentition to permanent dentition. Thus, for both charts, even if most of the teeth were in stage 15, if any deciduous teeth were present, they were placed into stage 14. The unintended effect of this strategy was to dramatically reduce the number of individuals in stage 15. For both charts, the difference between stages 16 and 17 is slight. If root formation for the M2 and the P2 was incomplete, the specimen was classified as stage 16, and if all of the apices were closed, the specimen was placed into stage 17. Differences in the development of the third molar between stages 16 and 17 were observed, but these differences were highly variable and did not appear to be stage-specific.

Overall, it seemed that the Ubelaker chart performed better than the Schour and Massler chart in both placing individuals correctly in the stage that they should have belonged in and in the correct phase of development for each tooth in the diagrams.

Quantitative Results

Method 1: Range of Ages Per Stage

A comparison of the distribution of individuals by age per observed stage was evaluated and shows a fairly linear progression from stages 9–13 for Ubelaker's chart with some disparity for ages 10, 11, 13, and 14. The trend for Schour and Massler's chart is also fairly linear. While both tables lack a strong grouping of individuals for stages 12 and 15, overall, both charts seem to track the age of individuals fairly well. A total of 37 percent of the children up to and including stage 16 scored with Ubelaker's chart fell in the predicted stage, while a total of 36 percent of the children scored with Schour and Massler's chart fall in their predicted stage.

Method 2: Comparing the Means

The mean ages for each chart are summarized in Table 5.1, and it can be seen that the study sample tracks the predicted ages on the charts fairly well, but are mostly overestimated. Much of this overestimation, however, is due to the authors of these charts rounding down their age designations in each category to obtain whole numbers. In both charts, it was observed that stages 14 and 15 appear to have similar mean ages, and t-tests indicate that the mean ages for these stages are not statistically different (Ubelaker: $t = 1.34$, $p = 0.18$, $df = 64$; Schour and Massler: $t = 1.32$, $p = 0.19$, $df = 63$). Therefore, in order for these charts to be used in a rigorous fashion, stages 14 and 15 may need to be combined into a single stage. However, the similarity may simply be a result of the small sample size for stage 15. The mean age for stage 16 for the study sample shows the greatest difference from the chart means, probably because at this age, juvenile dental formation and eruption has slowed and both Ubelaker and Schour and Massler combined 12, 13, and 14 year age

TABLE 5.1
OBTAINED MEAN AGES FOR UBELAKER AND
SCHOUR AND MASSLER STAGES. (SEXES COMBINED)

Ubelaker				*Schour & Massler*			
Actual Stage	*Obtained Mean Age*	*(n)*	*Ubelaker Predicted Age*	*Actual Stage*	*Obtained Mean Age*	*(n)*	*S & M Predicted Age*
9	5.75	19	5	9	5.69	15	5
10	6.57	43	6	10	6.51	49	6
11	7.80	58	7	11	7.81	52	7
12	8.43	45	8	12	8.22	38	8
13	9.59	52	9	13	9.42	61	9
14	11.14	59	10	14	11.07	62	10
15	11.64	16	11	15	11.64	16	11
16	13.34	83	12	16	13.33	84	12
17	14.53	43	15	17	14.58	42	15

groups, so the use of age 12 as the predicted age for stage 16 is misleading. Stage 17 is underestimated when comparing the obtained mean age with the charts' predicted ages probably because the study sample was restricted to individuals under the age of 16, resulting in artificial truncation.

Method 3: Assessing Mean Error

The mean error for each chart was determined by calculating bias and inaccuracy statistics for the study sample for each stage, using Ubelaker's and Schour and Massler's predicted ages. The bias for both charts was negative across all stages indicating a systematic underestimation of the true ages by about seven-tenths of a year. This underestimation is largely a result of the target ages for each stage on the original charts being rounded to the nearest whole year. Therefore, any juvenile age estimate based on these charts will always underestimate the actual age of the subject unless the radiograph was taken on their birth date. For example, for a random sample of 5-year-old children, it would be expected that the mean age would be approximately 5.5 years of age. Consequently, for each dental stage given in whole years, the expected baseline bias should be -0.5 year. When the rounding error on both charts is taken into account, the obtained bias values are reasonable and not much more than the predicted 0.5 year, indicating that overall, the chart diagrams perform well. The only exceptions that are readily observed are stages 14 and 16 in both charts, which seem to underestimate the ages of the study sample more than would be predicted by the rounding errors (Stage 14 Bias - Ubelaker: -1.04, Schour and Massler: -1.05; Stage 16 Bias - Ubelaker: -1.34, Shour and Massler: -1.34).

Inaccuracy values are predictably higher than the bias values, ranging from about 0.7 to 1.5 years. Again, 0.5 year of this error is due to the rounding of the chart ages to the nearest year. As before, stages 14 and 16 performed less well than the others. Overall, Schour and Massler's chart performs slightly better than Ubelaker's with both lower inaccuracy and bias values for nearly every stage.

Method 4: Assessment of Predicted Error Ranges

The number of individuals correctly falling in the predicted error ranges as given for each stage was evaluated to examine the performance of the charts (Table 5.2). For Ubelaker's chart, the actual age correctly falls within the predicted age ranges 91 percent of the time for the entire sample, and no stage performs below about 79 percent. Schour and Massler's chart, however, did not perform as well, with only 44 percent of the individuals falling within the predicted ranges for the entire sample. The difference in success between the two charts is partly due to Ubelaker's predicted age ranges including two standard deviations around each mean age, while Schour and Massler's ranges are considerably narrower, using only one standard deviation. However, even when Schour and Massler's error ranges are doubled, only 69.7 percent of the individuals fall within the range limits. Stage 16 of the Schour and Massler chart performs very poorly with only 18 percent success when using the non-doubled error range. Note that between stages 16 and 17, there is a gap between ages 12.5 and 14.5 years in which no individual can be placed. Therefore, it is technically impossible to age an individual at, say, 13 years with their chart. Their most accurate stage was stage 12, with 65.8 percent of the individuals correctly falling within the (narrow) error range.

These results suggest that Ubelaker's (1989) dental aging chart is superior to Schour and Massler's (1944) with respect to the robusticity of its error ranges. However, Schour and Massler's chart has lower inaccuracy and bias values. Both charts produce similar mean ages for each stage and demonstrate equivalent regularity across the age range.

TABLE 5.2
COMPARISON OF CORRECT AGE ASSESSMENT USING UBELAKER
AND SCHOUR AND MASSLER'S CHARTS. (SEXES COMBINED)

Observed Ubelaker Stage	Predicted Ubelaker Range (in years)	# Individuals Within Range	%	Observed S & M Stage	Predicted S & M Range (in years)	# Individuals Within Range	%
9	3.70–6.30	15/19	78.9	9	4.25–5.75	9/15	60.0
10	4.00–8.00	40/43	93.0	10	5.25–6.75	28/49	57.1
11	5.00–9.00	52/58	89.7	11	6.25–7.75	28/52	53.8
12	6.00–10.00	41/45	91.1	12	7.25–8.75	25/38	65.8
13	7.00–11.00	49/52	94.2	13	8.25–9.75	28/61	45.9
14	7.50–12.50	52/59	88.1	14	9.25–10.75	25/62	40.3
15	8.5–13.50	16/16	100.0	15	10.25–11.75	8/16	50.0
16	9.00–15.00	71/83	85.5	16	11.50–12.50	15/84	17.9
17	12.00–18.00	43/43	100.0	17	14.50–15.50	19/42	45.2
TOTAL (all stages)		379/418	90.7	TOTAL (all stages)		158/419	44.0

Sex Differences

When analyzing the distribution of individuals by age per observed stage, separated by sex, Ubelaker's chart shows females exhibit a more regular progression of stage per age, while the male's pattern displays more irregularity. Ages 11 and 13 seem problematic for both sexes. Similarly, Schour and Massler's chart is fairly linear among females but more irregular among males. A total of 43.7 percent of the females younger than 14 scored using Ubelaker's chart fall in the predicted stage, while only 32.6 percent of the males are correctly predicted. A total of 41.4 percent of the females younger than 14 scored using Schour and Massler's chart fall in the predicted stage, while only 33.5 percent of the males are correctly predicted. Overall, the two charts seem to perform equivalently.

An analysis of covariance to assess the effects of sex was performed for both Ubelaker's and Schour and Massler's observed stages. The independent variables (sex and age) were found to be highly significant for both Ubelaker's and Schour and Massler's charts, indicating that both variables significantly affect the expressed dental stage.

T-tests were utilized to compare mean age by sex for each stage (see Table

TABLE 5.3
SEX DIFFERENCES IN AGE FOR EACH UBELAKER AND SCHOUR AND MASSLER
STAGE. (BOLD VALUES INDICATE WHICH SEX IS OLDER FOR EACH STAGE)

	Ubelaker				*Schour & Massler*		
Stage	*Obtained Female Mean*	*Obtained Male Mean*	*t-Test Significance (p)*	*Stage*	*Obtained Female Mean*	*Obtained Male Mean*	*t-test Significance (p)*
9	5.54	**5.87**	ns	9	5.45	**5.81**	ns
10	6.45	**6.64**	ns	10	6.37	**6.60**	ns
11	7.72	**7.85**	ns	11	7.75	**7.85**	ns
12	8.15	**8.65**	0.077 df = 43	12	7.75	**8.53**	**0.014 df = 36**
13	9.33	**9.90**	**0.048 df = 50**	13	9.10	**9.79**	**0.007 df = 59**
14	10.80	**11.40**	**0.046 df = 57**	14	10.72	**11.39**	**0.027 df = 60**
15	11.44	**11.91**	ns	15	11.44	**11.91**	ns
16	13.37	13.31	ns	16	**13.35**	13.31	ns
17	14.30	**14.68**	ns	17	14.30	**14.68**	ns

5.3). The differences between sexes in most of the stages are not significant. However, in Ubelaker's chart females and males are at significantly different ages at stages 13 and 14 (ages 9-10) and are approaching significance at stage 12. For Schour and Massler's chart, stages 12, 13, and 14 are significantly different between the sexes. These findings are consistent with published data that females' teeth tend to develop faster than males. As a result, females are reaching these stages earlier than males, as seen with a lower mean age. The mean age by stage is always absolutely higher in males in both charts, except for stage 16. This stage includes individuals aged 12-14, which are the ages in which puberty usually begins. Males may begin to developmentally catch up with girls in this age range due to a later growth spurt. For those stages that are significantly different, there may be a need to differentiate them by sex.

Prediction Intervals

The 95 percent prediction intervals were calculated for all stages and the data can be seen in Table 5.4. This table displays new target ages based on the observed data for this study and the limits of the prediction interval. In addition, the percentage of individuals that correctly fell within these parameters was calculated.

Based on the significant differences found between the sexes for Ubelaker's stages 13 and 14 and Schour and Massler's stages 12, 13, and 14, the 95 percent prediction intervals were also calculated for males and females separately at these stages (Table 5.5).

TABLE 5.4
TARGET AGES AND PREDICTION INTERVALS FOR EACH STAGE BASED ON
UBELAKER AND SCHOUR AND MASSLER'S CHARTS (SEXES COMBINED).
INTERVALS NOT PROVIDED FOR STAGES 9 OR 17 BECAUSE THEY
WERE ARTIFICIALLY TRUNCATED BY THE SAMPLING STRATEGY,
AND TARGET AGES FOR THOSE STAGES ARE SUSPECT

Stage	*Chart*	*(n)*	*Target Age*	*s*	*Observed Range (in years)*	*95% Prediction Interval*	*% within Prediction Interval*
9	Ubelaker	19	(5.75)	0.52	5.0–6.6		
	S & M	15	(5.69)	0.52	5.1–6.6		
10	Ubelaker	43	6.57	0.94	5.0–9.3	4.97–8.17	95.4
	S & M	49	6.51	0.95	5.0–9.3	4.90–8.12	95.9
11	Ubelaker	58	7.80	0.91	6.3–10.4	6.27–9.34	94.8
	S & M	52	7.81	0.95	6.3–10.4	6.20–9.42	96.2
12	Ubelaker	45	8.43	0.94	7.0–10.5	6.83–10.03	91.1
	S & M	38	8.22	0.97	7.0–10.5	6.56–9.88	89.5
13	Ubelaker	52	9.59	1.05	7.2–12.0	7.81–11.37	90.4
	S & M	61	9.42	1.01	7.2–12.0	7.72–11.12	93.4
14	Ubelaker	59	11.14	1.16	8.8–13.9	9.18–13.10	89.8
	S & M	62	11.07	1.20	8.1–13.9	9.06–13.08	88.7
15	Ubelaker	16	11.64	0.84	10.1–13.0	10.12–13.16	100.0
	S & M	16	11.64	0.84	10.1–13.0	10.12–13.16	100.0
16	Ubelaker	16	11.64	0.84	10.1–13.0	10.12–13.16	100.0
	S & M	84	13.33	1.31	10.5–15.8	11.14–15.52	89.3
17	Ubelaker	43	(14.52)	1.05	12.1–16.0		
	S & M	42	(14.58)	1.00	12.1–16.0		

TABLE 5.5
PREDICTION INTERVALS SEPARATED BY SEX FOR UBELAKER'S CHART
(STAGES 13 & 14) AND SCHOUR AND MASSLER'S CHART (STAGE 12, 13, & 14)

Stage	*Sex*	*Chart*	*(n)*	*Target Age*	*s*	*Observed Range (in years)*	*95% Prediction Interval*	*% w/in PI*
12	F	S & M	15	7.75	0.66	7.0–9.3	6.56–8.94	93.3
	M	S & M	23	8.53	1.00	7.2–10.5	6.77–10.29	91.3
13	F	Ubelaker	28	9.33	1.08	7.2–11.3	7.46–11.20	85.7
		S & M	33	9.1	0.93	7.2–9.1	7.49–10.71	90.9
	M	Ubelaker	24	9.90	0.88	8.5–12.0	8.36–11.44	91.7
		S & M	28	9.79	0.96	7.7–12.0	8.13–11.45	89.3
14	F	Ubelaker	26	10.80	1.18	8.8–13.9	8.75–12.85	96.2
		S & M	29	10.72	1.23	8.1–13.9	8.60–12.84	93.1
	M	Ubelaker	33	11.40	1.04	9.6–13.5	9.61–13.19	87.9
		S & M	33	11.39	1.05	9.6–13.5	9.58–13.20	87.9

For the 95 percent prediction intervals separated by sex for stage 12 based on Schour and Massler's chart, both males and females scored higher than when sexes were combined. The 95 percent interval for stage 13 individuals evaluated with Ubelaker's chart was slightly lower for females than for sexes combined, while the male's percentage was slightly higher. For Schour and Massler's 95 percent prediction intervals for stage 13, both males and females scored lower than with sexes combined. At stage 14, for Ubelaker's chart, the prediction intervals for both the males and females performed better than the sex-combined interval. However, when the 95 percent prediction intervals were based on Schour and Massler's chart for stage 14, the females' percentage was higher than the combined sex percentage and the males' score was lower than the sex-combined interval.

A comparison of the 95 percent prediction interval ranges with Ubelaker's ranges and Schour and Massler's predicted ranges are presented in Table 5.6. The prediction intervals calculated here when compared to Ubelaker's intervals have a higher percentage of individuals falling within the determined parameters for all stages except stage 13, with an overall accuracy of 92.4 percent for stages 10 to 16. This figure is slightly better than Ubelaker's overall accuracy of 90.7 percent (or 90.2 percent accuracy for stages 10 to 16). Like-

TABLE 5.6
COMPARISON OF PREDICTION INTERVAL RANGES WITH UBELAKER AND
SCHOUR AND MASSLER'S PREDICTED RANGES AND PERCENTS
OF INDIVIDUALS WITHIN THESE RANGES

Stage	*Chart*	*Predicted Ubelaker Range (in years)*	*% of Individuals Within Range*	*95% PI Range (in years)*	*% of Individuals Within Range*
9	Ubelaker	3.7–6.3	78.9	4.83–6.68	
	S & M	4.25–5.75	60.0	4.74–6.64	
10	Ubelaker	4.0–8.0	93.0	4.97–8.17	95.4
	S & M	5.25–6.75	57.1	4.90–8.12	95.9
11	Ubelaker	5.0–9.0	89.7	6.27–9.34	94.8
	S & M	6.25–7.75	53.8	6.20–9.42	96.2
12	Ubelaker	6.0–10.0	91.1	6.83–10.03	91.1
	S & M	7.25–8.75	65.8	6.56–9.88	89.5
13	Ubelaker	7.0–11.0	94.2	7.81–11.37	90.4
	S & M	8.25–9.75	45.9	7.72–11.12	93.4
14	Ubelaker	7.5–12.5	88.1	9.18–13.10	89.8
	S & M	9.25–10.75	40.3	9.06–13.08	88.7
15	Ubelaker	8.5–13.5	100.0	10.12–13.16	100.00
	S & M	10.25–11.75	50.0	10.12–13.16	100.0
16	Ubelaker	9.0–15.0	85.5	11.13–15.55	91.6
	S & M	11.50–12.50	17.9	11.14–15.52	89.3
17	Ubelaker	12.0–18.0	100.0	12.73–16.31	
	S & M	14.50–15.50	45.2	12.88–16.28	
	Ubelaker	**TOTAL**	**90.7**	**TOTAL**	**92.4**
	S & M	**(all stages)**	**44.0**	**(stages 10–16)**	**92.3**

wise, Schour and Massler's newly determined prediction intervals gave an excellent performance with 92.3 percent of individuals falling within the found range. This highly outperforms the overall accuracy of the original chart of 44 percent. When these prediction intervals were recalculated with the division of sexes for Ubelaker's stages 13 and 14 and the new ranges determined the overall accuracy increased to 93 percent. Schour and Massler's division of sexes for stages 12 to 14 did not increase the overall accuracy, remaining constant at 92.3 percent. It is, therefore, important to note that while the knowledge of sex at stages 13 and 14 when using the Ubelaker chart can increase age prediction accuracy, it is not entirely necessary to identify the sex in order to get a good age estimate.

While the differences are not absolutely great, a general evaluation of the new prediction intervals compared to Ubelaker's ranges show that the new parameters have smaller ranges, allowing for tighter estimates of age. The lower limits of the new intervals are always higher than Ubelaker's lower limits, while the upper limits are more comparable. A noteworthy example can be seen in stage 14, where Ubelaker's age range is 7.5–12.5 years. This study, however, produces a prediction interval beginning 1.7 years later and ending 0.6 year later, at 9.18–13.10 years for the same stage. This range is with the sexes combined, even though they were shown to be significantly different at this stage. It is of importance to note however, that this difference could be due to the scoring strategies at this stage. At stages 14 and 15 the transition begins from mixed dentition to permanent dentition. Thus, for both charts, even if most of the teeth were in stage 15, if any deciduous teeth were present, the individual was placed into stage 14. This could have skewed the data.

CONCLUSION

This study reevaluated and tested known standards of skeletal aging using Schour and Massler (1944) and Ubelaker's (1989) dental aging charts to determine their accuracy when applied to modern subadults, addressed whether their target age and associated error ranges are still applicable, and whether or not these charts need to be differentiated by sex. It is hoped that these results will assist in improving the accuracy of estimating age for unknown subjects from their teeth and that this approach will assist in their identification.

To date, both charts are widely duplicated and both are utilized by anthropologists and odontologists. Therefore, it is the suggestion of this author that the line drawings remain the same, but modifications must be made on the target ages and their associated error intervals. When this study's 95 percent prediction intervals were calculated, both charts performed equally well, thus it is suggested that the prior error intervals be modified for stages 10–16 (ages 6 to 14) to include the newly determined mean age and intervals (see Table 5.7).

TABLE 5.7
COMPARISON OF SCHOUR AND MASSLER AND UBELAKER'S MEAN AGES
AND 95 PERCENT ERROR INTERVALS DERIVED FROM THIS STUDY

	Schour & Massler			*Ubelaker*		
Stage 10	6.51 ± 0.95			6.57 ± 1.60		
Stage 11	7.81 ± 1.61			7.80 ± 1.54		
Stage 12	8.22 ± 1.66	Female	7.75 ± 1.19	8.43 ± 1.59		
		Male	8.53 ± 1.76			
Stage 13	9.42 ± 1.70	Female	9.10 ± 1.61	9.59 ± 1.78	Female	9.33 ± 1.91
		Male	9.79 ± 1.66		Male	9.90 ± 1.58
Stage 14	11.07 ± 2.01	Female	10.72 ± 2.12	11.14 ± 1.96	Female	10.80 ± 2.10
		Male	11.39 ± 1.81		Male	11.40 ± 1.82
Stage 15	11.64 ± 1.52			11.64 ± 1.52		
Stage 16	13.33 ± 2.19			13.34 ± 2.21		

Accordingly, the question remains as to which of the two charts is better. With the newly determined prediction intervals, they are now equally useful in their age determinations. Thus, the slight differences in formation and eruption between these charts are accommodated by the new means and error intervals.

An analysis of covariance for both Ubelaker's and Schour and Massler's charts, found that sex and age are highly significant indicating that both variables affect the expressed dental stage. Additionally, t-tests were used to compare the mean age by sex for each stage with differences between sexes in most stages not being significant. However, in Ubelaker's chart, males and females are significantly different at stages 13 and 14, and in Schour and Massler's chart stages 12, 13, and 14 are significantly different between the sexes. Therefore, in order to obtain the most accurate age estimate, when sex is known, there is a need for both charts to have these ages separated by sex for these stages. It is recommended that these new prediction intervals be used when the sex of an unidentified individual is known.

Since these newly derived intervals have not been widely used, potential limitations have not been delineated. Thus, replication on a larger scale with known-age samples is required to examine the robusticity of this study's results. It is also important to note that these intervals were derived solely from modern individuals of European ancestry, and thus application to individuals from different time periods or of different ancestries must be made with caution.

ACKNOWLEDGMENTS

I would like to thank the faculty members of the Department of Biology at the University of Indianapolis, especially Dr. Stephen Nawrocki. I would also like to thank the Riley Hospital for Children Pediatric Dental Clinic for allowing access to their dental charts.

REFERENCES

Black, G. V. (1883). Lines of contemporaneous calcification of the teeth. *Ill State Dent Soc Trans 1883:* Frontispiece.

Brady, W. J. (1924). *A chart of the average time of development, eruption and absorption of the teeth.* Kansas City: William J. Brady.

Garn, S. M., Lewis, A. B., & Polacheck, D. L. (1959). Variability in tooth formation. *Journal of Dental Research 38:*135–148.

Gleiser, I., Hunt, E. E. (1955). The permanent mandibular first molar: its calcification, eruption, and decay. *American Journal of Physical Anthropology 13:*253–283.

Glister, J. E., Smith, F. H., & Wallace, G. K. (1964). Calcification of mandibular second primary molars in relation to age. *Journal of Dentistry for Children 31:*284–288.

Kronfeld, R. (1935a). First permanent molar: Its condition at birth and its postnatal development. *Journal of the American Dental Association 22:*1131–1155.

Kronfeld, R. (1935b). Postnatal development and calcification of the anterior permanent teeth. *Journal of the American Dental Association 22:*1521–1536.

Legros, C., & Magitot, E. (1880). *The origin and formation of the dental follicle.* Translated from the French by Dean, MS. Chicago: Hansen, McClurg and Co.

Legros, C., & Magitot, E. (1881). *Recherches sur l'evolution du follicle dentaire ches les mammiferes.* Paris: Librairie Germer Ballière.

Lewis, A. B, & Garn, S. M. (1960). The relationship between tooth formation and other maturational factors. *The Angle Orthodontist 30*(2):70–77.

Logan, W. H. G., & Kronfeld, R. (1933). Development of the human jaws and surrounding structures from birth to the age of fifteen years. *Journal of the American Dental Association 20:*379–427.

Lunt, R. C, & Law, D. B. (1974). A review of the chronology of calcification of deciduous teeth. *Journal of the American Dental Association 89:*599–606.

Massler, M., & Schour, I. (1958). *Atlas of the mouth and adjacent parts in health and disease.* Chicago: American Dental Association.

Merchant, V. L., & Ubelaker, D. H. (1977). Skeletal growth of the protohistoric Arikara. *American Journal of Physical Anthropology 46:*61–72.

Miles, A. E. W. (1958). The assessment of age from the dentition. *Proceedings of the Royal Society of Medicine 51:*1057–1060.

Miles, A. E. W. (1963). Dentition in the estimation of age. *Journal of Dental Research Suppl 42:*255–263.

Miles, D. A., & Parks, E. T. (2004). Radiographic techniques. In R. E. McDonald, D. R. Avery, & J. A. Dean (Eds.), *Dentistry for the child and adolescent,* (8th ed.), pp. 59–78. St. Louis: Mosby.

Peirce, C. N. (1884). Calcification and decalcification of the teeth. *Dental Cosmos 26:*449–455.

Scheuer, L., & Black, S. (2000). *Developmental juvenile osteology.* San Diego: Academic Press.

Schour, I., & Hoffman, M. M. (1939a). Studies in tooth development: I. the 16 microns calcification rhythm in the enamel and dentin from fish to man. *Journal of Dental Research 18:*91–102.

Schour, I., & Hoffman, M. M. (1939b). Studies in tooth development: II. the rate of apposition of enamel and dentin in man and other mammals. *Journal of Dental Research 1818:*161–175.

Schour, I., & Kronfeld, R. (1938). Tooth ring analysis. IV. neonatal dental hypoplasia: analysis of the teeth of an infant with injury of the brain at birth. *Archeology Pathology 26:*471–490.

Schour, I., & Massler, M. (1940a). Studies in tooth development: the growth pattern of human teeth. *Journal of the American Dental Association 27:*1778–1793.

Schour, I., & Massler, M. (1940b). Studies in tooth development: The growth pattern of human teeth. Part II. *Journal of the American Dental Association 27:*1918–1931.

Schour, I., & Massler, M. (1941). The development of the human dentition. *Journal of the American Dental Association 28:*1153–1160.

Schour, I., & Massler, M. (1944). *Development of human dentition chart* (2nd ed.). Chicago: American Dental Association.

Smith, B. H. (1991). Standards of human tooth formation and dental age assessment. In M. A. Kelley & C. S. Larsen (Eds.), *Advances in dental anthropology,* pp. 143–168. New York: Wiley-Liss, Inc.

Steggerda, M., & Hill, T. J. (1942). Eruption time of teeth among whites, negroes, and indians. *American Journal of Orthodontics and Oral Surgery 28:*361–370.

Ubelaker, D. H. (1987). Estimating age at death from immature human skeletons: An overview. *Journal of Forensic Sciences 32*(5):1254–1263.

Ubelaker, D. H. (1978). Human skeletal remains, excavation, analysis, Interpretation (1st ed.). Washington D.C.: Taraxacum.

Ubelaker, D. H. (1989). *Human skeletal remains, excavation, analysis, interpretation* (2nd ed.). Washington D.C.: Taraxacum.

Ubelaker, D. H.. (1999). *Human skeletal remains, excavation, analysis, Interpretation* (3rd ed.). Washington D.C.: Taraxacum.

Ubelaker, D. H, & Buikstra, J. E. (1994). Standards for data collection from human skeletal remains. Arkansas Archeological Survey Research. Series No. 44.

Workshop of European Anthropologists (WEA). (1980). Recommendations for age and sex diagnoses of skeletons. *Journal of Human Evolution 9:*517–549.

Section 2

OSTEOLOGICAL AGING TECHNIQUES

Chapter 6

THE NATURE AND SOURCES OF ERROR IN THE ESTIMATION OF AGE AT DEATH FROM THE SKELETON

STEPHEN P. NAWROCKI

The anthropologist can save himself a lot of time by not trying to make more precise estimates of age than are warranted by the nature of the material.
S. L. WASHBURN (1958)

INTRODUCTION

All osteologists know that it is not normally possible to predict an individual's exact age at death from their skeleton. Some degree of error is unavoidable—but why? To understand the sources of error in age estimation, one must first examine the basic process of obtaining an age estimate from the skeleton. (The term "estimation" is used here because age at death is a continuous variable, potentially taking any value between zero and, say, 110 years; for predicting a discontinuous or discrete variable, such as sex, one should use "determination" or some other term that reflects the categorical nature of the variable.)

To estimate age at death, osteologists start by *describing* the morphological appearance or status of the remains. These descriptors take the form of discrete, typological observations, continuous measurements, or something in-between (semi-continuous observations). The first method has been used more frequently. A specific area of the skeleton is observed in a group of individuals of known age and a sequence of discrete morphological variants is generated for the series. These morphological variants are generally called "phases" or "stages" and typically number from 3 to 8, depending on the area scored and the portion of the lifespan that the method covers. Examples of methods developed for subadults include epiphyseal development and fusion (McKern and Stewart, 1957) and dental development and eruption (Smith, 2005). In adults, most methods have focused on degenerative changes to the various joint surfaces, such as the pubic symphysis (Brooks and Suchey, 1990), the auricular surface of the ilium (Lovejoy et al., 1985b), and the cranial sutures (Nawrocki, 1998). Methods using continuous measurements as morphological descriptors include long bone diaphyseal lengths and cranial bone measurements (Fazekas and Kosa, 1978) in subadults, and cortical osteon measurements (Kerley, 1965) and tooth root transparency (Lamendin et al., 1992) for adults.

Morphological indicators of age, both discrete and continuous, reflect the skeleton's continuing adaptation to biomechanical stress and participation in mineral metabolism, growth, remodeling, and disease. Therefore, these indicators will vary across an individual's lifespan and also between individuals of the same calendar age. Together the various morphological indicators constitute a *description* of the actual physical (phenotypic) appearance of the bones at death. This description has been called, by various authors, the "biological age," "skeletal age," "dental age," "physiological age," "developmental age," or "morphological age" of the decedent. A more appropriate substitute for "age" might be "status" (as in "developmental status" for subadults or "degenerative status" for adults), because the use of "age" implies a calendar estimate when in reality the description is not an estimate of actual age–it is simply a statement about the physical *appearance* of the skeleton in question relative to the skeletons used to create the original phase scoring systems.

"Chronological age," in contrast, is the actual calendar age of the decedent as measured in days or years since conception or birth. In the skeletons of vertebrates, biological age covaries with the chronological age of the individual. As time passes, biomechanical and physiological changes accumulate, but this accumulation is not necessarily linear or regular. Therefore, a morphological skeletal indicator will reflect chronological age only indirectly and incompletely. This relationship can be modeled as follows:

Skeletal Indicators ⟷ **Biological Age** ⟷ **Chronological Age**

The individual skeletal indicators (diaphyseal length, joint appearance, etc.) are observed and combined in some fashion into a summary biological age that describes the state of development or degeneration of the skeleton, which in turn can be used to derive an estimated chronological age of the decedent via comparison with skeletal samples with known ages at death.

Estimating chronological age from a skeletal indicator is a *transformative process*–one must transform or translate the descriptive skeletal indicator (a phase or measurement) into another variable (calendar age). To the extent that the indicator and chronological age are imperfectly correlated and indirectly causal, *some error is always involved in the transformation.* A simple analogy clarifies this loose relationship between variation in the skeletal indicator and chronological age. Imagine what happens to an automobile over time. The longer one owns the vehicle, the more the tread wears down on the tires. One might be tempted to say that time somehow "causes" the tire's tread to wear down, because the two variables are indeed correlated. The problem with this line of reasoning becomes apparent if one stores the vehicle in a garage for a year without driving it–the tread doesn't change even though time passes. In this case, time is practically irrelevant compared to the *real* causal factor, which is road friction that the tire experiences during driving. Unfortunately, road friction is much harder for the owner to measure than the chronological age of the car, and so age becomes a proxy or simplified substitute for the more complex, truly causal phenomena that occur and whose effects tend to accumulate only secondarily with the passage of time. A stronger relationship would be found between tire wear and the odometer reading, because rotations of the wheels are measured by the odometer, and the odometer does not change like the calendar does if the vehicle is stored.

The situation is similar to age at death estimation from the skeleton. Variation in a skeletal indicator (tire wear) is not caused by the passage of time *per se,* but rather by the sum of biomechanical and physiological processes (road friction) that themselves are imperfectly and indirectly associated with calendar time. Individuals are constantly subjecting their joint surfaces to mechanical stress, but the degree and nature of that stress (and the resulting strain experienced by the bones) varies considerably depending on the size and muscularity of the individual, their activity levels (which change through the lifespan), the nature of the work they do, and inherent differences in the thickness and composition of the connective tissues that bind those joints. Furthermore, these biomechanical effects occur against a backdrop of both system-wide and local physiological processes that occur around-the-clock within the body, such as oxygen metabolism, nutrient absorption, excretion of waste products, repair of tissues, endocrine activity and hormone secretion, immune system activation, growth, and reproduction—processes that vary across the lifespan and differ between individuals. The real question, then, is not why chronological age at death is so poorly correlated with skeletal morphology—rather, it is more valid to wonder why chronological age is correlated with skeletal morphology *at all* in the face of these incredibly complex, highly variable phenomena!

Therefore, chronological age is simply a proxy for understanding or summarizing the complexity of biological and biomechanical phenomena that result in skeletal growth early in life and in skeletal degeneration ("wear and tear") later in life. Arguably, biological anthropologists are really more interested in *these* processes than in some imperfect shorthand proxy that by its very nature involves substantial estimation error. Unfortunately, we do not have the biological equivalent of an odometer in the human body. So why bother estimating chronological age at death from the skeleton at all? Certainly, there are circumstances when the anthropologist can avoid the transformation entirely and yet still examine meaningful relationships between biological and cultural phenomena. It is common for researchers studying prehistoric populations to automatically transform biological age into an estimated chronological age for each individual, and then use these estimated ages to search for relationships with, say, susceptibility to disease, indicators of social class, or personal wealth. But biological age can be used instead of chronological age just as easily, with none of the associated transformation error. For example, one could examine the relationship between the amount of grave goods and pubic symphysis phase for individuals within a cemetery in an attempt to determine whether those with more advanced phases tended to have greater wealth or social status. Theoretically, this method, a form of "seriation" (ranking), should give a more accurate picture of accumulated "personal wear and tear" than chronological age would, particularly considering that the society in question may not have measured chronological age in the same way (or given it the same level of significance) that we do today in the industrialized world.

In bioarcheological settings, the anthropologist is generally more interested in elucidating broader, group-level phenomena than in extrapolating individual age estimates for each skeleton *per se*. Not only can the actual chronological ages for the decedents never be known in most cases because of the lack of historical documentation, but it can be argued that such individualizing information is not as important for the questions being asked. Does knowing that Decedent Y's age at death was 47.5 years old rather than 52.4 years old really help us to understand the prevalence and spread of communicable diseases after European contact, or how older adults contributed to the group economy? Instead, would knowing that a disproportionate number of individuals in a cemetery display heavy osteoarthritis on 50 percent of their synovial limb joints be enough to say something meaningful about their involvement in strenuous horticultural activities? The former approach entails an unnecessary transformation of biological age into a precise chronological age estimate that may carry no additional information and provide no analytical benefits. The latter approach uses untransformed biological age descriptions that may be sufficient, in a theoretical sense, to address the questions posed by the anthropologist. In other words, biological age descriptions are well-suited for *population-level* analyses and comparisons in which individual data are not the focus, while, as we shall see, chronological age estimates are more important when the analysis is focused on specific questions involving specific *individuals.*

There are, of course, practical advantages to transforming biological age into a chronological age estimate even in ancient samples. While it may be fairly straightforward to assign a phase descriptor to the pubic symphysis and then another to the auricular surface, it is more difficult to combine those different descriptors into a single, summary descriptor of overall biological age. For instance, what is the biological age of someone with a Phase II pubic symphysis and 8.2 mm of tooth root transparency? The scores from the different indicators are not necessarily additive, and the separate indicators may correlate too poorly to allow any one of them to stand as a proxy for the others. Each indicator may reflect its own unique life history of biomechanical and physiological events, despite being present in the same body. Furthermore, osteologists frequently face a situation where not all indicators are present and observable in each and every skeleton, forcing numerous tedious comparisons of each individual indicator to the relevant biocultural variables being examined.

While it may be possible to combine the indicators into a valid summary biological age, historically such methods have not been developed or used by osteologists, probably because individual chronological age estimates can be averaged across indicators easily. It is a simple matter to take the predicted age for a Phase II pubic symphysis and average it with the predicted age for a given measure of root transparency, producing a single summary value for the decedent that can be used in subsequent analyses. Thus the practical appeal of using estimated chronological ages has probably discouraged more complex methods of seriating biological ages, although the former entails estimation error that would be avoided in the latter.

In modern industrialized settings, forensic anthropologists face a different set of issues with respect to the estimation of chronological age. Calendar age is not only recorded very precisely, with careful documentation of the date and even the minute of birth, but it is used as a gatekeeper to certain significant rights and privileges (driving, drinking, age of consent, voting, retirement) and also as one of the components of a *legal identification*. A person's birth date is as important to their legal identity as their name, sex, eye color, and fingerprint pattern. Because a forensic anthropologist is charged with helping the medicolegal system identify unknown human remains, s/he cannot stop with the description of biological age. In other words, explaining that an individual has a Phase II pubic symphysis is not useful in a police missing person report. An estimate of the chronological age at death (and thus the decedent's presumed birth date) is needed to facilitate the identification process.

In forensic casework, the focus is not on making statements about the nature of life within a group or population, or to test broad theories regarding relationships between biocultural variables. Rather, the focus is narrowed to making statements about the life and death of a *specific individual*. These statements are hypotheses that can be tested when and if the individual is positively identified and when the exact nature of their death is confirmed through other investigatory means. Therefore, the transformation of the biological age description for a skeleton into a chronological age estimate is a necessary evil, and full cognizance of the likely error is crucial. If the error interval is too narrow, the medicolegal investigators may exclude the actual decedent from consideration. If the error interval is too broad, it will include irrelevant candidates. Anthropologists must understand how to construct the error interval and the factors that can influence its magnitude. The rest of this chapter examines issues related to the detection and understanding of error in predicting chronological age.

HOW MUCH ERROR?

Washburn's quotation at the beginning of this chapter suggests that anthropologists have had a tendency to underestimate the normal range of error associated with chronological age estimates. Indeed, a perusal of the recent literature indicates that the situation has probably not changed much in the past 50 years. The anthropological literature contains numerous examples of investigators underestimating or underappreciating the normal range of variation in skeletal indicators, constructing inappropriately-narrow error intervals, misapplying basic statistical tests, and deriving overly-specific interpretations from small and poorly-balanced samples. As a result, it is difficult for the typical practitioner to know exactly which studies, if any, can be used securely when estimating chronological age of unidentified decedents.

In their classic work on the age-related metamorphosis of the auricular surface, Lovejoy et al. (1985b) present 5-year-wide age brackets for each of the first six phases, a reflection of the sampling strategy they employed in defining the phases. In many subsequent human osteology texts that have reprinted the technique (e.g., White, 2000:359; Schwartz, 2007:239–40; Ubelaker, 1999:81–82), the 5-year intervals are published without explanation as if they represent actual error ranges for each phase, and this writer has witnessed numerous instances when both bioarcheologists and forensic anthropologists have accepted them uncritically as statistically valid ranges. Indeed, it has been demonstrated that appropriately-constructed error intervals for the auricular surface are significantly broader, ranging from 10 to 60 years (Osborne et al., 2004).

Other phase methods fare equally poorly. For example, the "95 percent" intervals given by Îscan et al. (1984) for the sternal extremity of the rib were constructed incorrectly and underestimate the true error intervals by a factor of at least 2 or 3 (Nawrocki and Osborne, 2000). The actual 95 percent intervals are similar to those obtained for the auricular surface. In fact, sample sizes are so small for some rib phases that no reliable error intervals can be constructed from them.

Correctly constructed error ranges for adult indicators are rarely less than 15 to 20 years per phase, and they may be considerably larger. For example, pubic symphysis error intervals, based on some of the largest and best-documented samples ever used in age-estimation studies of the skeleton (Brooks and Suchey, 1990; Guthrie, 2008), can be 50 years wide. Ironically, some anthropologists claim that they would rather use the rib method developed by Îscan and colleagues than the Suchey-Brooks pubic symphysis method because the latter is more "error-prone" than the former, as reflected by the published error intervals. However, Brooks and Suchey's (1990) published error intervals are some of the few that were produced in consultation with a statistician and are therefore correctly calculated. These intervals reflect biological reality. Simply put, *chronological age estimation from any single indicator is highly inaccurate in adults.*

Methods based on continuous indicators have the potential to fare better than discrete phase methods. The variance in a continuous indicator trait is spread more evenly across the entire age span, allowing the resulting regression line to "dial in" an age estimate more precisely, which should reduce overall error. Discrete phase methods, in contrast, partition the age span into a smaller number of fairly wide segments, each of which covers a large age interval. For example, in six-phase systems like the Suchey-Brooks pubic symphysis or Osborne auricular surface methods, only six possible estimated ages are available to assign to an unidentified adult, who could be anywhere from 20 to 110 years old. This arrangement necessarily results in higher errors and wider error intervals, because all individuals within any given phase are assigned the same "target age" (the mean age for all specimens in the original study that displayed that phase), and many of those individuals are much younger or much older than that target age. Methods using continuous traits are more *precise* because they allow the investigator to assign many possible target ages rather than just six or eight, and so any given prediction is likely to be closer to the actual chronological age of the decedent. Theoretically, if it were possible to score discrete phases more precisely on a continuous scale, as some have tried (Pasquier et al., 1999; Telmon et al., 2005; Nawrocki, 1998), one should observe an increase in accuracy and a reduction in estimation error. The degenerative changes that occur at joint surfaces should be continuous, occurring in small (but not necessarily regular) increments throughout the lifespan. However, it is difficult to measure those changes on a precise scale, and so anthropologists have tended to develop phase descriptors for them.

Studies of bone histomorphometry (microscopic structure of osteons), because they are based on continuous measurements, have generally reported smaller overall error intervals than phase methods (see Robling and Stout, 2008 for a review). For example, Kerley (1965) obtained ranges as small as 11 years for the fibula, while equations generated for non-weight-bearing bones such as the cranium (Curtis, 2003) are about twice as large (26 years). Most authorities report variation in the 15 to 20-year range (based on doubled standard errors; Robling and Stout, 2008). However, small sample sizes can produce artificially low error rates in regression formulae, and many of the early histomorphometric studies in particular were based on small numbers (Curtis, 2003). Furthermore, some studies using continuous traits commit a form of "statistical incest" by including multiple specimens from the same individual in one equation. Due to an autocorrelation effect, this practice artificially reduces error, increasing the appearance of accuracy.

Even for the more precise continuous indicators, the error intervals for chronological age estimation in adults are still unsettlingly wide. Why, then, do aging indicators perform so poorly? Analysis of covariance studies of phase indicators have repeatedly shown that age at death, while clearly affecting the appearance of the skeletal indicators more than sex, ancestry, or any other variables tested, still only accounts for *less than half* of the total variance in those skeletal indicators, meaning that the majority of the variation is attributable to *factor(s) other than age or biological grouping*. For the cranial sutures, between 35 and 51 percent of the variance is due to age (Zambrano, 2005; Nawrocki, 1998); for the pubic symphysis, 45 to 49 percent (Uhl, 2007, Guthrie, 2008); for the auricular surface, 34 to 37 percent (Osborne et al., 2004; Uhl, 2007); for the sternal extremity of the ribs, 44 percent (Uhl, 2007). Clearly, many factors other than age influence joint degeneration in adults, again supporting the idea that the accumulated biomechanical and physiological effects are only indirectly affected by the passage of calendar time. As a result, the error ranges associated with any particular skeletal indicator are likely to be very large.

For subadults the situation is more optimistic. For example, in Smith's (2005) study of Midwest American children between the ages of 5 and 15 years, nearly 90 percent of the variance in dental development was attributable to the combination of age at examination and sex, meaning that very little of the variance was unexplained. Undoubtedly, the rapid growth of the teeth during childhood and the richness of detail of the scoring method makes age estimation much more precise in subadults. Even so, the error ranges for each dental stage were from 3 to 5 years, which seems large considering the significant changes in body size, social development, and intellectual ability that occur yearly in growing children. In other words, we know that an 8-year-old and a 13-year-old are very different, but for an anthropologist predicting chronological age from dental status, s/he would have to acknowledge the statistical fact that a set of teeth at a given stage could reasonably belong to either individual. The variability seen in adult aging, therefore, has its roots in childhood development, and while the absolute error may be smaller in the latter, the relative size of the error ranges with respect to overall age *may be just as large*. Childhood is just a microcosmic reflection of what is to come in later years.

THE TRAJECTORY EFFECT

One aging phenomenon that seems obvious but which is consistently ignored by osteologists is the tendency for aging error ranges to increase with increasing age. As explained above, subadult aging errors are absolutely smaller than adult aging errors. Even within subadults, however, aging errors increase from birth to the attainment of skeletal and dental adulthood in the late teens. In adults, this trend even more apparent. For example, the error ranges for pubic symphysis phases in males begin at 9 years for Phase I and gradually reach 52 years by Phase 6 (Brooks and Suchey, 1990). Similar effects are present for most other adult aging indicators scored on a phase basis (Uhl, 2007).

Figure 6.1 illustrates this phenomenon, which I call the "trajectory effect." It can be explained with a simple analogy. Imagine throwing a ball at a target. Very minor changes in the angle of release magnify across the distance the ball travels and can make the ball miss its target. If the distance to the target is short, this discrepancy is small and the ball will miss only by inches. If the distance is long, the discrepancy grows, making the ball miss its target by many feet even though the angle of release was the same. In other words, the trajectory of the ball is set at the moment of release, and how widely it misses is a function of how close you were standing to the target when you threw.

The accumulated biomechanical and physiological forces that result in changes to the skeletal indicators seem to follow different trajectories in different individuals. At conception, the angle and speed of the release is set. Over the years and decades, slight differences magnify to produce large differences in the appearance of the skeletal indicators even for individuals of the same chronological age. As a result, the error intervals for each indicator become increasingly broad as one moves through the lifespan. Making the matter more complex is the possibility that the angle or speed may actually change during an individual's lifetime, with alterations in biomechanical activity or physiological processes. Thus, an individual's trajectory may change, making chronological age prediction even more difficult.

The increase in error ranges with increasing chronological age can become so great that, in some cases, the skeletal indicator stops being correlated with age later in life. For example, Nawrocki (1990, 1998) found that the correlation between summed suture closure and age at death, while significant for individuals below the age of 50, drops to insignificance when examining just those individuals older than 50. This phenomenon does not necessarily mean that no age-related changes in the skeletal indicator are occurring after 50; minimally, it signifies that the process becomes so swamped by individual variation that it is no longer an easy task to detect the real trend statistically unless younger individuals are included in the mix.

FIGURE 6.1
THE "TRAJECTORY EFFECT" IN AGING. VARIATION IN ANY GIVEN SKELETAL
INDICATOR WILL INCREASE AS AGE INCREASES, RESULTING IN WIDER ERROR
INTERVALS FOR ANY AGING TECHNIQUE. THE DASED LINES REPRESENT
THE LIMITS OF VARIATION AT ANY GIVEN AGE, WHILE THE SOLID LINE
REPRESENTS THE MEAN VALUE AT THAT AGE.

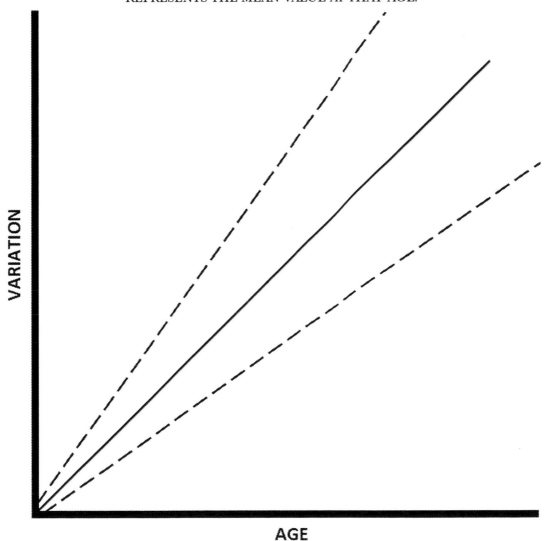

Unfortunately, ignorance of the trajectory effect has led to much confusion when testing or comparing aging methods. For example, not all researchers have carefully monitored the age at death distributions of their study samples. If a preponderance of older individuals is present in the sample, as is common in studies using cadaver or cemetery populations, one could come to the conclusion that a method is not particularly accurate because errors are greater in older samples. In contrast, if younger individuals dominate the sample, one could overestimate the accuracy of the method, which might falter when applied to a broader, more balanced population. A similar problem exists when researchers test existing methods using new, independent samples. For example, Megyesi et al. (2006) tested the Lamendin et al. (1992) dental aging technique using an historic British sample. Unfortunately, the mean ages of the British test sample and the original French sample were not provided by either set of authors. Megyesi and colleagues found that mean error for their British sample was about 6 years higher than that obtained by Lamendin and colleagues, but they did not recognize that some or all of this difference could have resulted from a lower mean age in the original French sample. In this situation, comparisons of mean error are entirely meaningless because crucial baseline information on the samples is unavailable.

Ideally, a test sample should have the same age at death distribution and the same mean age as the original study sample. Furthermore, any new method should use an even age distribution with approximately equal numbers of adult specimens from each decade or half-decade of life (Nawrocki, 1998), with smaller age intervals for subadults. Even a large study sample begins to thin when individuals are allocated into their separate decade and sex groups, producing cells with relatively few members. For example, a sample of 100 adult males and females distributed across an age span of 20 to 90 years averages only 7 individuals per cell (7 decades × 2 sexes = 14 cells), which may be too few to test hypotheses or establish an age-estimation method.

Linear regression using a continuous aging indicator has a tendency to mask the trajectory effect and thus the age-related increase in error. The least-squares regression line is fixed at the meanS for the x and y variables, and the line pivots around this point to best fit the scatterplot of observations. Just as the standard deviation is a measure of average error regardless of the exact distribution of ages in a phase, the standard error of the estimate in regression is averaged across the entire line regardless of whether some parts of the scatterplot are more highly variable (e.g., more dispersed) than others. Therefore, a confidence interval generated for a regression line can be artificially symmetrical. Assessing trends in error for both continuous and discrete skeletal indicators should commence by calculating error separately for each decade of the adult lifespan and for smaller intervals for subadults. In most cases, the older decades will display greater estimation error.

CONSTRUCTING ROBUST ERROR INTERVALS

How, then, should an investigator construct and report error intervals for a particular method? Several statistics have been used in the past for phase studies, and each has its own uses and advantages (Nawrocki & Osborne, 2000; Saunders et al., 1992). As for any set of observations, errors can be summarized in two ways–by describing their *central tendency* and by describing their *dispersion*. When analyzing an unidentified decedent, the anthropologist must have at least one measurement of central tendency to establish a predicted target age and at least one measurement of dispersion to construct an error interval.

Measures of central tendency include statistics such as the mean, mode, and median of the errors, and also their bias and inaccuracy (Lovejoy et al., 1985a), each of which summarizes an aspect of the *average degree of overall error* for each phase. For example, one could report that the mean error for a particular phase is 9.7 years, indicating that, on average, each specimen is misaged by that amount. Mean error is also known as the "inaccuracy" of a phase if the signs of the errors (positive or negative, reflecting overaging or underaging) are omitted. If the signs are included when the errors are averaged, the resulting statistic is called "bias," a measure that indicates whether the method has an overall tendency to overage or underage the specimens.

Measures of dispersion include the observed range of raw age values per phase (what is the difference between the youngest and oldest person noted for a phase?), the standard deviation of the mean age, and percentile prediction intervals (such as the 95% prediction interval), each of which summarizes the *spread of the errors*. For example, stating that most of the observed values for a particular phase varied from 26 to 51 years gives the investigator an idea of the diversity of scores that can be expected and thus a better appreciation for the accuracy or inaccuracy of a method.

Mean error (inaccuracy) is the most commonly reported measure of error used in the aging literature for both discrete and continuous indicators, probably because the statistic conveys how well the method performs *on average*. However, a study that calculates and provides multiple measures of both central tendency and dispersion of the errors is more valuable to the investigator using that data to predict the ages of unidentified individuals, for together they paint a broader picture of variation in the skeletal indicator and how well it tracks advancing age. Furthermore, multiple measures of error make it more likely that a study will be comparable to other, similar studies.

In forensic settings, the 95 percent prediction interval is an important measure of accuracy and should be published for each phase used in an aging method. The prediction interval (Hahn and Meeker, 1991; Osborne et al., 2004; Nawrocki and Osborne, 2000) is an estimate of the interval in which future individuals drawn from the same population as the original study sample will fall. For example, the 95 percent prediction interval for Phase IV pubic symphyses is 21 to 73 years (Guthrie, 2008:28), meaning that an unknown individual displaying a Phase IV pubis is 95 percent likely to fall within that particular age interval. Constructing the prediction interval requires the mean age, the standard deviation in years, and the sample size for each phase. While there are a number of conditions that must be satisfied for this statistic to be accurate (a large sample size, normal distribution of the errors in a phase, etc.), other measures of dispersion suffer from relatively greater problems. The observed range, for example, is dependent on sample size and is likely to underestimate the true dispersion of errors in the population if small numbers of individuals were used to construct each phase. The prediction interval corrects for sample size and is therefore the most appropriate benchmark for predicting a likely age interval for an unknown individual.

Why use a 95 percent prediction interval instead of a 50 percent or 75 percent interval? Some might argue that 95 percent represents an unnecessarily high level of generality that is not needed or desirable in forensic casework. After all, the resulting error intervals for an individual indicator can be so broad as to be nearly useless in distinguishing between potential decedents. However, the 95 percent figure is commonly accepted in scientific hypothesis testing as the corresponding alpha value threshold for determining statistical significance. In other words, with a 95 percent prediction interval the investigator knows (theoretically) that there is only a one in 20 chance that the decedent's actual chronological age falls outside that interval, and thus it is unlikely that the decedent will be excluded from consideration erroneously.

Understating an error interval can have other negative effects. Imagine a scenario where a forensic anthropologist is asked to justify an age estimate for a decedent after having used, say, the very narrow error intervals published for the sternal extremity of the ribs, in which a Phase V rib for white males has a reported interval of 34.4–42.2 years (Îscan et al., 1984). It is reasonably straightforward to calculate that this 8-year interval covers less than 50 percent of the ages of individuals likely to have a Phase V rib in the population. Therefore, on cross-examination, how would the anthropologist respond to the question "So Doctor, do you realize that your age interval is just as likely to be *wrong* as *right*?"?! Using the mean error as a guideline for estimating the accuracy of one's age estimate for a skeleton fails for the same reason: the estimate plus and minus the mean error will never approximate more than about 50 percent of the observed interval of ages obtained for a phase or for an estimate derived from a regression equation.

For regression equations using continuous data, measures of central tendency of the errors can be calculated as for phase methods. For measures of dispersion, one can calculate a standard error of the estimate for the entire regression line (analogous to the standard deviation for mean age for a phase) or a 95% confidence interval for an estimate (analogous to the 95 percent prediction interval for a phase–see Giles and Klepinger, 1988). In addition, one can calculate various measures of covariance, such as the correlation coefficient (r) and the coefficient of determination (r^2), which is the percentage of variance in the dependent variable (the continuous skeletal indicator) that is explained by variance in the independent variables (chronological age at death, sex, etc.). Measures of covariance provide an estimate of how accurate a method is but are not applicable in and of themselves when working with unknown individuals or when constructing error intervals.

UNUSUAL BIASES

Phase methods using discrete skeletal indicators as well as linear regression using continuous indicators necessarily produce some counterintuitive biases in chronological age estimation that can be misinterpreted by the investigator. For example, plotting mean error (inaccuracy) by decade for the auricular surface, error in the early decades (20s and 30s) averages about 13 years (Osborne et al., 2004, Table 10). In the middle decades (40s, 50s, & 60s), average error drops to about 10 years. Then in the oldest decades (70s and 80s), error climbs again to reach a high of 23 years. At first this trend seems to contradict the trajectory effect, in which error increases gradually with increasing age. However, age-estimation methods are simply ways of modeling the indirect and imperfect relationship between chronological age and the skeletal indicator, and this transformation can produce some odd results. In short, the process of adjusting an age-estimation method to reduce error results in systematic and predictable biases. For example, because individuals in their 20s and 60s are further from the mean target ages assigned for most phases (which are between 29 and 49 years for Phases III through VI for the 8-phase auricular surface system), their ages are estimated with higher error than individuals in their 40s. While the results will vary somewhat with the specific distributional characteristics of the sample, error trends from high to moderate to very high levels from young to middle to advanced decades. The trajectory effect does attenuate the errors slightly in the younger decades and magnifies the errors in the upper decades.

Ironically, then, it follows that increasing the number of young adults in a sample might actually inflate the overall error rate, just like (but perhaps not as much as) increasing the number of older adults! Conversely, samples that include many middle-aged adults, with lower numbers of young and old adults, would display lower-than-normal error rates. Clearly, sampling strategies can have important implications for the apparent accuracy of a method.

Another unusual bias occurs in both phase and regression studies. Recall that one can calculate mean error by retaining the signs of the errors instead of excluding them, which will reveal the tendency of a method to overage or underage the decedents regardless of the overall magnitude of the errors. This value (which, perhaps confusingly in this context, is called "bias") can be calculated by decade. For the auricular surface (Osborne et al., 2004, table 10), in the 20s bias is about 12 years, then decreases to zero years in the middle decades, then drops further to -27 years by the 80s. In other words, for young individuals, we tend to *overestimate* their ages, for middle-aged individuals we tend to overestimate and underestimate equally (reducing bias to zero), and for old individuals we systematically *underestimate* their ages. This pattern can be seen in numerous studies, and sometimes it is inappropriately attributed to the particular nature of the skeletal indicator rather than to the basic nature of the methods used.

So why not just adjust our aging methods so that they do not have these systematic biases? Remember that these are just *trends in the data*. The methods may have a *tendency* to overage young individuals, but there are still plenty of young decedents who will be *underaged*. The anthropologist cannot determine *a priori* when a skeleton arrives for analysis whether it will be overaged or underaged. Most aging methods, therefore, strike a balance between inaccuracy (absolute error) and bias (the tendency to overage or underage specific age groups), and to reduce one kind of error necessarily means that the other kind will increase. For a forensic anthropologist working over a career on isolated cases that are essentially randomly selected from the population at large, the optimal approach is to find a way to reduce the overall *inaccuracy* in estimation even though the resulting estimates may be slightly biased over the long run.

HOW MANY PHASES?

Most phase studies of adult age changes in specific skeletal indicators use subjective criteria to define the number of phases and their characteristics. Generally, these studies tend to identify more, rather than fewer, phases. For example, Todd's (1920) original study on the pubic symphysis identified ten phases; Lovejoy et al.'s (1985b) study of the auricular surface identified eight phases, as did Îscan et al.'s (1984) research on the sternal end of the fourth rib. Apparently, these authors believed that their observations of fine morphological gradations were valid reflections of biological reality, or that more phases provide more accurate age estimates, or both. Indeed, splitting up the adult age interval into more phases allows each phase to cover a narrower range of possible ages, reducing the error interval for each phase and increasing at least the appearance of accuracy and precision. But is it always statistically valid for an indicator to have many phases rather than fewer phases?

Katz and Suchey (1986), using a large sample of identified pubic symphyses, could not find justification for Todd's ten phases and therefore condensed Todd's method down to just six phases. Similarly, Osborne et al. (2004) discovered that the mean ages of some adjacent auricular surface phases were not significantly different. Their revised auricular surface scoring method identified only six phases. Nawrocki and Osborne's (2000) and Uhl's (2007) assessments of Îscan and colleagues' rib data also indicated that something fewer than eight phases was more appropriate.

It appears, then, that osteologists have tended to partition the variation of certain adult skeletal indicators into more phases than is statistically warranted. This conclusion does not necessarily suggest that morphological variation at these sites does not continuously grade across narrow intervals. Instead, it tells us that the degree of random variation not attributable to chronological age is so great that we cannot partition the lifespan precisely into numerous phases. In other words, the sizes of the phases are so great that small differences in mean age between the phases are swamped by within-phase variation.

It is interesting that a number of methods seem to be converging on six phases. If we consider the part of the human lifespan that is covered by most of these studies—specimens tend to be between 20 and 80 years at death, a 60-year range—then our ability to identify chronological age is no greater than about a decade per phase on average, being even less precise, of course, in later decades. In other words, osteologists should identify an adult decedent into nothing less than a 10-year predicted age interval.

CONFOUNDING VARIABLES

Many osteologists have wondered whether other biological variables, such as sex and ancestry, may have significant effects on the morphology of skeletal indicators independent of chronological age. If these variables do affect the aging process, we may be able to improve our age-estimation methods by controlling for them. Analysis of covariance (ANCOVA) is the most appropriate and robust procedure for testing hypotheses regarding the influence of other variables (Meindl and Lovejoy, 1985; Nawrocki, 1998; Osborne et al., 2004). The skeletal indicator is treated as the dependent variable that is affected by various possible independent variables, including sex, ancestry, and age at death. Sex and ancestry are categorical main effects, and age is a continuous covariate. The strength of this multivariate procedure lies in its ability to control for variance in several independent variables *at the same time*. In other words, if sex is determined to be significant during the analysis, then the investigator knows that sex affects the skeletal indicator independent of any other variable (such as age).

Unbalanced samples pose a considerable problem for univariate tests. For example, a t-test may reveal that the mean error for an age-estimation method is higher for males than for females. The researcher could conclude that different male physiology or activity levels leads to higher aging errors in that sex. However, if there are more older males in the sample than older females, the greater mean age at death for males could artificially increase their error rate. Fortunately, ANCOVA partitions the variance in the skeletal indicator and identifies the portions that are independently attributable to sex and age. Therefore, if the increased male error rate resulted from uneven sampling, the sex variable in the ANCOVA would not reach significance. This example underscores the importance of conducting basic hypothesis testing *before* generating the age-estimation method or constructing a regression. The researcher should first determine whether the indicator is affected by biological variables other than age at death. If none of these other variables are significant, the predictive model can be generated without them. Large, well-balanced samples with substantial numbers of individuals of both sex and ancestry groups in *each* decade are needed to facilitate strong *a priori* hypotheses testing.

Unfortunately, few researchers properly isolate the effects of sex and ancestry on age indicators, and so it is difficult to determine how relevant they are in the age-estimation process. Uhl (2007) and Nawrocki (1998) found significant ancestry effects on various aging indicators, and sex appeared to be less important. Guthrie's (2008) study of the pubic symphysis found no sex or ancestry effects, although Zambrano's (2005) study of cranial suture closure found significant sex effects. However, in all of these studies, the variance explained by sex or ancestry is *very small,* on the order of a few percent, so although the effects are *statistically* significant, they are *practically* irrelevant and have little measurable effect on the age-estimation process. When the range of variation in a specific phase is 35 years, the year or so of added variability contributed by ancestry does not seem very important.

DOES AVERAGING HELP?

So far the discussion has centered on errors inherent in single skeletal indicators. However, osteologists recognize the importance of considering multiple indicators simultaneously in age estimation, as they do when determining sex and ancestry. Unfortunately, the best method of combining those indicators is not always clear. Should one weigh some indicators more than others? Under what circumstances should an indicator be discounted? To make matters more complex, an argument could be made that combining indicators may actually hurt the estimation process. If the different skeletal indicators have different correlations with chronological age and different error rates, then some will be more accurate than others. Combining or averaging an inaccurate indicator with an accurate indicator coud reduce the predictive quality of the latter (Saunders et al., 1992). Instead, a better approach might be to employ the single best indicator with the lowest error rates and use it exclusively.

Early studies combining multiple skeletal indicators by way of complex "multifactorial analysis" (Lovejoy et al., 1985a) were promising, but, because of the way they worked, could not be applied to individual forensic cases. Some studies comparing the effectiveness of single indicators versus the simple averaging of multiple indicators have shown that averaging modestly increases the accuracy of chronological age estimation and reduces aging errors (Uhl, 2007). Despite the different accuracies of individual indicators, each appears to "track" its own unique aspect of the aging process. When combined, these different measures are better predictors of chronological age in much the same way that multiple skeletal measurements are better predictors of sex or ancestry than single measurements in discriminant analysis, or how regression formulae using multiple limb bones are better estimators of stature than those using a single bone. In other words, each indicator accounts for a different portion of the overall variance in aging, and so even a "poor" indicator may have something significant to contribute.

An annoying problem with simple averaging is that there is no obvious way to construct a prediction interval for an estimated age at death for a specific skeleton, because the errors for each individual indicator are not additive. Ways around this problem include overlapping the error intervals for different methods and using regression to combine the individual indicators even if they are discrete (Uhl, 2007; Nawrocki, 1998).

CONCLUSION: THE ART OF AGE ESTIMATION

Experienced anthropologists understand that skeletal analysis is as much art as it is science. While there are numerous objective and numerical methods for the estimation of chronological age at death, how one applies and combines those methods, and the confidence that one places in them, differs according to the situation. For example, the osteologist will frequently encounter an "atypical" age marker that seems to have experienced either a retarded or an accelerated rate of growth or degeneration relative to other age indicators in that skeleton. The decision whether to reject or include an atypical marker hinges on the analyst's experience and the ability to discern unusual causes of the aberration (trauma, unusual activity levels, congenital malformation, etc.). Unfortunately, it can be difficult to distinguish atypical causes of skeletal morphology from normal variability.

The importance of individual experience and the need for intuitive decision-making suggests that it is unlikely that precise, standardized protocols can be developed for age estimation in forensic anthropology. As other fields of forensic science attempt to increase their precision and admissibility in court by carefully defining "best practice" standards for the acceptance and interpretation of their particular brand of forensic evidence, anthropology may find this task unrealistic. How can one "standardize" an approach that includes so much intuitive and subjective assessment? How can we decide which method or combination of methods is best when none of them are able to account for more than 50 percent of the variability in the skeletal indicators? Perhaps the best that we can do is to make sure that our individual methods are statistically valid and educate ourselves regarding their systematic biases.

Some broad generalizations can be made. First, the estimation of chronological age at death entails significant transformation error. This error is absolutely lower for subadults and increases during adulthood. While methods using continuous indicators can be more precise than those using discrete indicators, all indicators perform rather poorly when measured with the same yardstick. Therefore, it is unlikely that estimates of chronological age will ever be very accurate.

Second, the pattern and distribution of the errors is not random but is shaped by the particular methods we employ. Inaccuracy (absolute mean error) tends to be distributed in a U-shaped fashion, with the highest rates in the oldest decades. Bias trends from positive to a high negative value, resulting in systematic overestimation of younger individuals and underestimation of older individuals. Therefore, the structure of our study samples can dramatically affect our interpretations of the efficacy of a method quite independently of how well the skeletal marker actually tracks age. Furthermore, subsequent tests of existing methods must take into account the sample structure of the original study.

Third, error intervals for both phase studies and regression equations must be constructed using sound statistical methodology, as researchers have chronically underestimated actual rangeS of variation in the skeletal markers being studied. Because of the widths of these error intervals, it is more difficult to demonstrate significant differences between morphological phases than to create them in the first place, and so some classic studies using 8 or 10 phases have been reduced to about 6 phases in revision studies. These results suggest that our ability to estimate chronological age at death in adults cannot be resolved to intervals smaller than about 10 years.

Fourth, multivariate hypothesis testing methods must be used to assess the effects of sex and ancestry on aging indicators; unbalanced samples can invalidate univariate tests and fail to account for complex interactions between the variables. Even when analysts have discovered significant effects for sex or ancestry, the magnitude of those effects is always small and easily overwhelmed by random variation in the skeletal indicator. Therefore, corrections for sex and ancestry may not be practical or necessary when estimating age at death. A more reasonable strategy may be to combine biological groups to construct robust samples from which overall aging trends can be determined more effectively. Methods based on these robust samples are more likely to be applicable in a wider array of situations than current methods that are (unnecessarily) tailored to specific subgroups.

Finally, averaging the results from multiple skeletal indicators is more accurate than using single indicators, but the degree of improvement is not substantial. The problem with averaging is that it is difficult to construct an appropriate error interval for the target estimate. Hopefully, advanced multi-variate methods will assist future investigations in the same way that computerized discriminant analysis has improved the determination of sex and ancestry. This approach will require the synthesis of large, shared databases on skeletal aging against which the investigator can compare individual cases as they are encountered.

REFERENCES

Brooks, S., & Suchey, J. (1990). Skeletal age determination based on the os pubis: A comparison of the Acsadi-Nemeskeri and Suchey-Brooks methods. *Human Evolution 53:* 227–238.

Curtis, J. M. (2003). Estimation of age at death from the microscopic appearance of the frontal bone. Master's thesis, Department of Biology, University of Indianapolis.

Fazekas, I., & Kosa, K. (1978). *Forensic fetal osteology.* Akademiai Kiado, Budapest.

Giles, E., & Klepinger, L. (1988). Confidence intervals for estimates based on linear regression in forensic anthropology. *Journal of Forensic Sciences 335:*1218–1222.

Guthrie, E. (2008). The effects of sex and ancestry on pubic symphysis morphology. Master's thesis, Department of Biology, University of Indianapolis.

Hahn, G., & Meeker, W. (1991). *Statistical intervals: A guide for practitioners.* Hoboken, NJ: Wiley.

Îscan, Y., Loth, S., & Wright, R. (1984). Age estimation from the rib by phase analysis: White males. *Journal of Forensic Sciences 294:*1094–1104.

Katz, D., & Suchey, J. (1986). Age determination of the male os pubis. *American Journal of Physical Anthropology 69:*427–435.

Kerley, E. (1965). The microscopic determination of age in human bone. *American Journal of Physical Anthropology 23:*149–164.

Lamendin, H., Baccino, E., Humbert J., Tavernier J., Nossintchouk R., & Zerilli A. (1992). A simple technique for age estimation in adult corpses: The two criteria dental method. *Journal of Forensic Sciences 375:*1373–1379.

Lovejoy, O., Meindl, R., Mensforth, R., & Barton, T. (1985a). Multifactorial determination of skeletal age at death: A method and blind tests of its accuracy. *American Journal of Physical Anthropology 68:*1–14.

Lovejoy, O., Meindl, R., Pryzbeck, T., & Mensforth, R. (1985b). Chronological metamorphosis of the auricular surface of the ilium: A new method for the determination of adult skeletal age at death. *American Journal of Physical Anthropology 68:*15–28.

McKern, T., & Stewart, T. (1957). Skeletal age changes in young American males. Quartermaster Research & Development Center, U.S. Army, Natick Massachusetts, Technical Report EP-45.

Megyesi, M., Ubelaker, D., & Sauer, N. (2006). Test of the Lamendin aging method on two historic skeletal samples. *American Journal of Physical Anthropology 131:*363–367.

Mendel, R., & Lovejoy O. (1985). Ectocranial suture closure: A revised method for the determination of skeletal age at death based on the lateral anterior sutures. *American Journal of*

*Physical Anthropology 68:*57–66.

Nawrocki, S. (1990). Regression formulae for estimating age at death from cranial suture closure: A test of Meindl & Lovejoy's method. Paper presented at the 6th Northeast Forensic Anthropology Association Conference, York PA.

Nawrocki, S. (1998). Regression formulae for estimating age at death from cranial suture closure. In K. J. Reichs (Ed.), *Forensic osteology: Advances in the identification of human remains* (2nd ed.), pp. 276–291. Springfield, IL: Charles C Thomas.

Nawrocki, S., & Osborne, D. (2000). Serious problems in the estimation of age from human skeletal remains. Paper presented at the 7th Midwest Bioarcheology & Forensic Anthropology Association Conference, Columbia, MO.

Osborne, D., Simmons, T., & Nawrocki, S. (2004). Reconsidering the auricular surface as an indicator of age at death. *Journal of Forensic Sciences 495:*905–911.

Pasquier, E., Pernot, L., Burdin, V., Mounayer, C., Le Rest, C., Colin, D., Mottier, D., Roux, C., & Baccino, E. (1999). Determination of age at death: Assessment of an algorithm of age prediction using numerical three-dimensional CT data from pubic bones. *American Journal of Physical Anthropology 108:*261–268.

Robling, A., & Stout, S. (2008). Histomorphometry of human cortical bone: Applications to age estimation. In M. A. Katzenberg & S. R. Saunders (Eds.), *Biological anthropology of the human skeleton*, pp. 187–213. New York: Wiley-Liss.

Saunders, S., Fitzgerald, C., Rogers, T., Dudar, C., & McKillop, H. (1992). A test of several methods of skeletal age estimation using a documented archaeological sample. *Canadian Society of Forensic Sciences Journal 25*(2): 97–118.

Schwartz, J. (2007). *Skeleton keys.* New York: Oxford University Press.

Smith, E. (2005). A test of Ubelaker's method of estimating subadult age from the dentition. Master's Thesis, Department of Biology, University of Indianapolis.

Stewart, T. (1979). *Essentials of forensic anthropology.* Springfield, IL: Charles C Thomas.

Telmon, N., Gaston, A., Chemla, P., Blanc, A., Joffre, F., & Rouge, D. (2005). Application of the Suchey-Brooks method to three-dimensional imaging of the pubic symphysis. *Journal of Forensic Sciences, 503:*507–512.

Todd, W. (1920). Age changes in the pubic bone I: The male white pubis. *American Journal of Physical Anthropology 3:*285–334.

Ubelaker, D. (1999). *Human skeletal remains.* Washington: Taraxacum.

Uhl, N. (2007). Multifactorial determination of age at death from the human skeleton. Master's Thesis, Department of Biology, University of Indianapolis.

Washburn, S. (1958). Review of "Skeletal age changes in young American males," by T. McKern & T. Stewart. *American Antiquity 242:*198–199.

White, T. (2000). *Human osteology* (2nd ed.). San Diego: Academic Press.

Zambrano, C. (2005). Evaluation of regression equations used to estimate age at death from cranial suture closure. Master's Thesis, Department of Biology, University of Indianapolis.

Chapter 7

APPLICATIONS OF THE HUMAN SACRUM IN AGE AT DEATH ESTIMATION

Nicholas V. Passalacqua

I n order to estimate chronological age as accurately as possible, multiple indicators of age at death are required. The development of additional age at death estimation techniques should enhance the precision (absolute mean age estimate versus actual age error) and accuracy (confidence interval width) of an age prediction. Further, while reliable aging techniques are available for many different anatomical regions of the human skeleton, depending on contextual circumstances one or more of these diagnostic areas may not be available for analysis. Thus, developing methods for different anatomical structures allows the practitioner to better predict the age of an individual in more contexts.

The sacrum is particularly useful for age at death estimation research because it allows for a completely independent structure to be analyzed. Further, a number of clearly defined developmental and degenerative changes are well documented (Bollow et al., 1997; McKern and Stewart, 1957; Sashin, 1930; Scheuer and Black, 2000; Shibata et al., 2002). The method described herein incorporates components of a number of previously described methodologies and morphological traits to different regions of the sacrum, resulting in an assemblage of criteria for estimating age in one osseous structure.

This paper will (1) describe a macromorphoscopic method of age at death estimation of the human sacrum as originally developed by Passalacqua (2009), (2) illustrate the utility of the method in comparison to other indicators of skeletal age at death, and (3) propose and describe applications of the sacrum in multifactorial age at death estimation.

102

AGE AT DEATH ESTIMATION USING THE SACRUM

Materials and Methods

In the construction of this sacral aging method, a sample of 384 paired ilia and sacra were chosen from the Hamann-Todd collection (Cleveland Museum of Natural History) and 249 specimens from the W. M. Bass collection (University of Tennessee, Knoxville). Both males and females of European and African ancestry were sampled with ages ranging from 10–96 years. Following the development of phases and marker morphologies on the Hamann-Todd collection, an independent sample of 249 individuals from a modern forensic skeletal series was used to test the efficacy of the new aging technique. Using percent correct and absolute mean error (AME) (defined below) to evaluate methodological performance and validate a method for forensic usage, no differences for sex or ancestry were found. Thus a pooled sample of 633 individuals was used to create the final comparative sample.

MORPHOLOGIC TRAITS ANALYZED AND CHARACTER STATE DEFINITIONS

Surface Changes

Billows are morphologies similar to those found on the pubic symphyseal surface (Suchey and Katz, 1998). They can be manifested as very shallow ridges and furrows but usually are characterized by an uneven undulating surface (Figure 7.1). They appear on the sacral auricular surface early in life and are observable until a small plate-like epiphysis fuses to the surface usually in mid to late teens (Lovejoy et al., 1985).

Surface Changes Scoring

- 0 = Billowing is present on the sacral auricular surface. Note the lack of fusion between the sacral bodies (Figure 7.1 A).
- 1 = No billowing is present on the sacral auricular surface. The surface is generally smooth (Figure 7.1 B).

Vertebral Ring Fusion and Absorption (S1 Ring Fusion)

Vertebral ring fusion and absorption is scored by the degree of fusion or absorption between the superior vertebral epiphysis and the vertebral body

FIGURE 7.1
LATERAL VIEW ILLUSTRATING STAGES OF
SACRAL AURICULAR SURFACE CHANGES

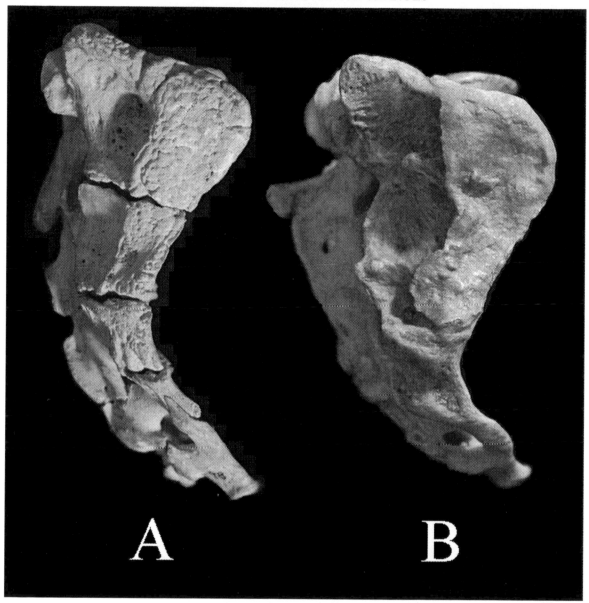

(Figure 7.2). This is noted for either the first sacral vertebra or a sacralized fifth lumbar vertebra.

FIGURE 7.2
SUPERIOR VIEW ILLUSTRATING STAGES OF SACRAL VERTEBRAL BODY

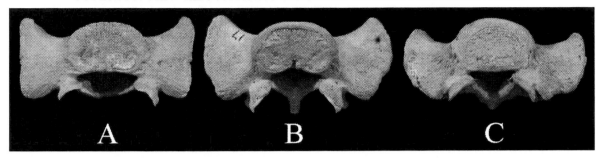

S1 Ring Fusion Scoring

- 1 = Incomplete Fusion. No border on ring. May show a cracked appearance on anterior surface where ring will fuse (Figure 7.2 A).
- 2 = Fused. Raised border present on anterior aspect of ring with epiphysis completely fused to vertebral body (Figure 7.2 B).
- 3 = Absorbed. Border no longer raised from surface. The ring has a flattened and or compressed appearance (Figure 7.2 C).

Microporosity

Microporosity is defined as pits or holes on the subchondral auricular surface with a diameter less than 1millimeter (mm) (Figure 7.3) (Buckberry and Chamberlain, 2002).

Microporosity (Micro) Scoring

- 1 = No Microporosity is present.
- 2 = Microporosity is present (Figure 7.3 A).

Macroporosity

Macroporosity is defined as cortical auricular surface pits or holes with a diameter of *more than* 1mm (Buckberry and Chamberlain, 2002).

Macroporosity (Macro) Scoring

- 1 = No Macroporosity is present.
- 2 = Macroporosity is present (Figure 7.3 B).

FIGURE 7.3
LATERAL VIEW ILLUSTRATING SACRAL AURICULAR SURFACE POROSITY

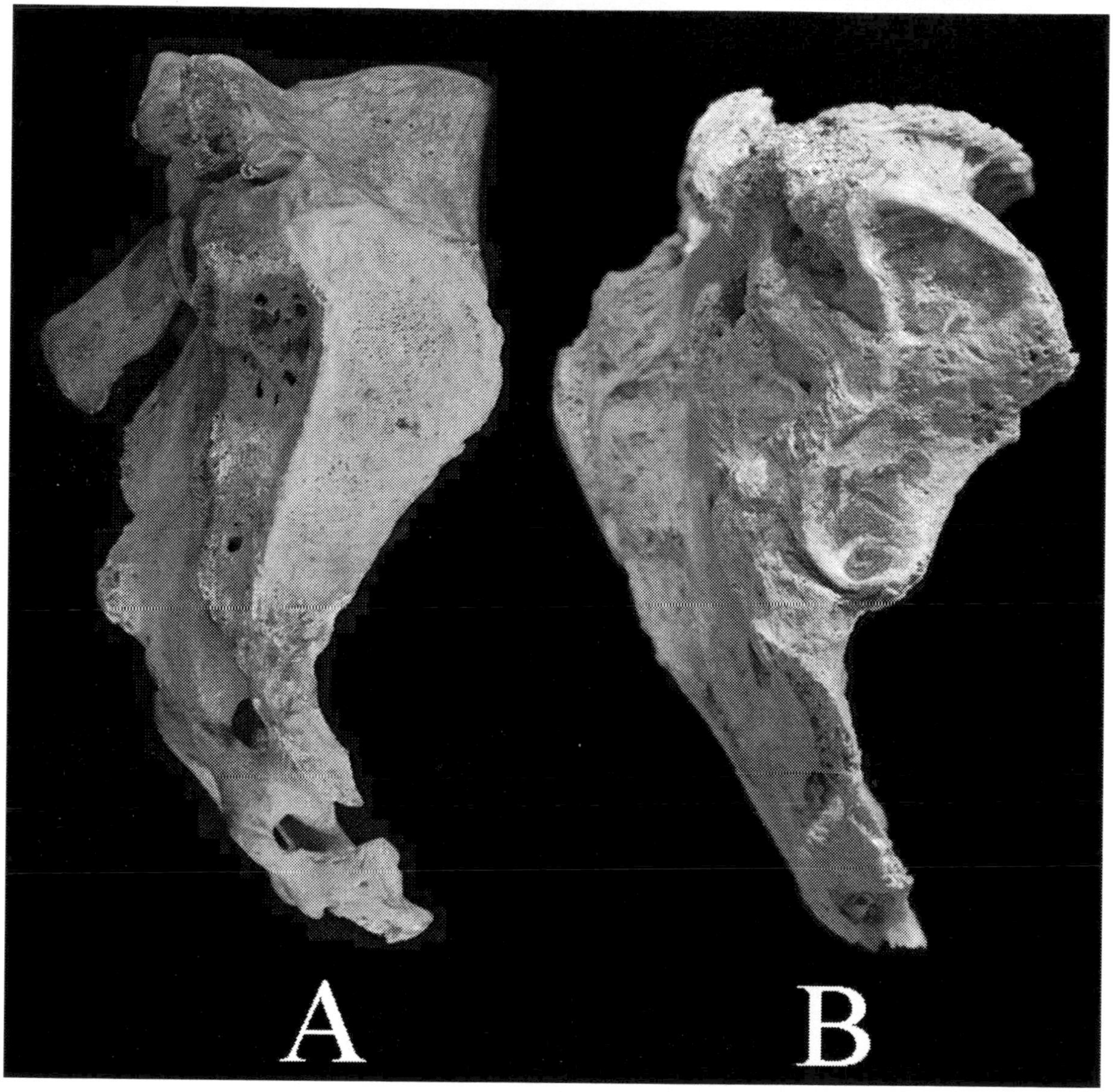

Osteoarthritic Auricular Apical Lipping (Apical Changes)

Osteoarthritic auricular apical lipping refers to the osteophytic activity which occurs around the rim of the sacral auricular surface due primarily to arthritic modification but may also be attributed to enhanced activity levels (Figure 7.4). Females tend to show more extreme degrees of apical growth

FIGURE 7.4
LATERAL VIEW ILLUSTRATING STAGES OF OSTEOARTHRITIC
SACRAL AURICULAR SURFACE APICAL CHANGES

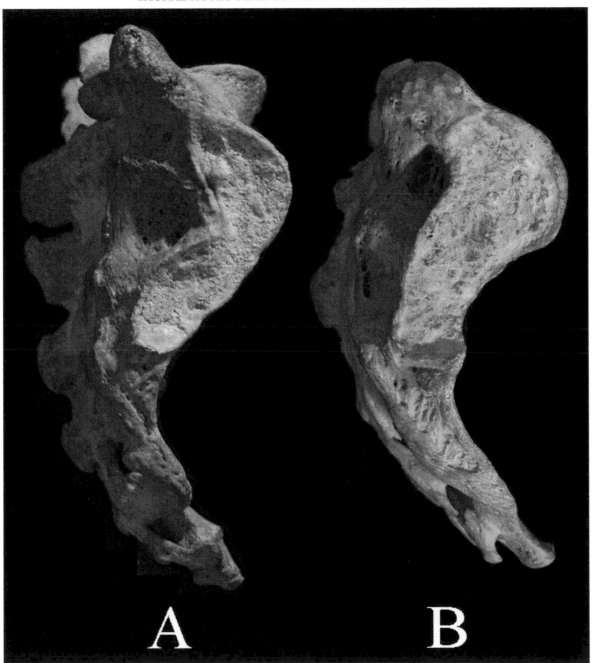

than males, especially at the anterior apex.

Apical Changes Scoring

- 1 = Anterior apex is sharp and distinct (Figure 7.4 A).
- 2 = Lipping and or irregularity is present at the apexes. The auricular surface is slightly depressed to the rim (Figure 7.4 B).

Sacral Vertebral Body (S1/S2 and S2/S3) Fusion

Sacral vertebral body fusion is the developmental fusion of the sacral vertebral elements (sacrabrae) to adjacent vertebral bodies to form the single sacral bone (Figure 7.5).

Second and Third Sacral Segment Vertebral Fusion (S2/S3 F) Scoring

- 1 =Incomplete fusion. Refers to any lack of fusion, particularly located on the anterior body or lateral alae (Figure 7.5 A-B).
- 2 = Completely fused (Figure 7.5 C-D).

First and Second Sacral Segment Vertebral Fusion (S1/S2 F) Scoring

- 1 = Incomplete fusion (see above). (Figure 7.5 A-C).
- 2 = Completely fused (Figure 7.5 D).

Component System Development

Based on the results of the above trait correlations with age, the seven aging criteria were sequentially arranged to reflect the differential timing of significant aging events. This aging sequence was then patterned, creating a sequential coding component system. This system creates a dummy variable using the scores for each of the seven traits. The order of appearance of each trait within the seven-digit code was calculated to maximize the Spearman's rank correlation coefficient of the code with age (Table 7.1). Rank order statistics were selected in order to obtain a coding system in which a higher score in the seven-digit code corresponds more frequently to an older individual. Each unique seven-digit component code was then translated into a verbal description of the combination of morphological traits (morphological stage) and associated with the appropriate statistically-validated chronological confidence interval (68% and 95% probabilities) (Table 7.2).

FIGURE 7.5
ANTERIOR VIEW ILLUSTRATING STAGES OF SACRAL BODY FUSION PATTERN

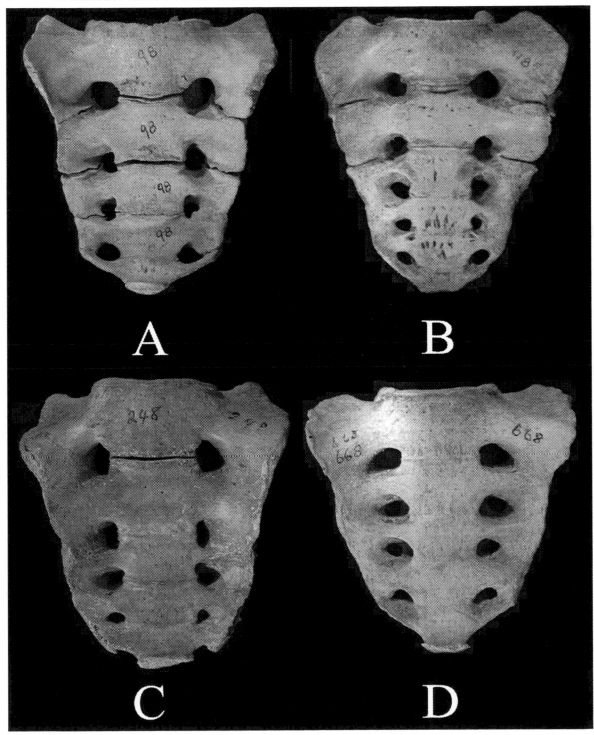

TABLE 7.1
PHASE, UNIQUE CODE AND DESCRIPTION OF TRAITS
ASSOCIATED WITH EACH PHASE

Phase	Code*	Trait Appearance
1	1011111	No porosity, lipping, or complete fusions.
2	2111211	S2/S3 fusion complete, auricular plate fused, S1 ring fused.
3	2121211	S1/S2 fusion complete.
4	2122211	Lipping present on apex.
4	2122221	Microporosity present.
5	2122311	S1 ring absorbed, no porosity.
6	2122321	S1 ring absorbed, microporosity present.
6	2122322	S1 ring absorbed, macroporosity present.

*Trait Coding Order: S2/S3 F, Surface Changes, S1/S2 F, Apical Changes, S1 Fusion, Micro, Macro

TABLE 7.2
AGE ESTIMATES BY PHASE

Phase	Mean Age	68% Range	95% Range	n	S	Median Age	Min Age	Max Age	AME
1	16.11	13–16	9–23	19	3.38	17	10	24	2.63
2	23.05	20–26	17–29	22	3.05	23	19	29	2.6
3	27.96	19–37	10–46	56	9.23	26.5	16	71	6.6
4	45.39	31–45	16–75	142	14.89	43.5	18	93	12.09
5	50.82	36–67	21–81	66	15.09	47.5	24	96	12.39
6	62.79	49–77	36–91	328	14.04	63	30	97	11.57

THE SACRUM IN MULTIFACTORIAL AGE AT DEATH ESTIMATION

Materials

The following combined age at death estimation methods were developed from a primary sample of European American males (n = 107) from the Bass Collection (University of Tennessee, Knoxville, TN) and then tested on an equivalent independent sample of European American males (n = 49) from the Hamann-Todd Collection (Cleveland Museum of Natural History, OH). Four age at death techniques were applied to each individual: Suchey and Katz (1998), Îscan et al. (1984, 1985), Lovejoy et al. (1985), and Passalacqua (2009). The three comparative techniques were chosen due to their wide scale usage in forensic anthropology. While age changes between individual techniques are likely correlated, the goals here are to both compare the performance of each individual aging technique as well as their performances together in multifactorial methods, not to further validate the sacrum method; thus the assumption is that any resulting bias would be minor. In addition, all these individuals were included in the development of the sacrum method (Passalacqua, 2009), thus it is possible the error rates determined here could be biased.

Data Preparation

The presentations of data in each of the applied methodologies differ in many ways; the most glaring being the construction of the confidence intervals. Suchey and Katz (1998) and Passalacqua (2009) both use standard deviation ranges, along with statistical means, while Lovejoy et al. (1985a) uses a categorical range (and thus also lack true mean ages), and Îscan et al. (1984, 1985) have small sample sizes which do not truly account for 95 percent of the variation in the phase. In cases where statistical confidence intervals were needed, but only categorical ranges were available, or when means were used, and no mean ages per phase were presented, these data were calculated based on the original data presented. The categorical confidence intervals presented were used as 1 standard deviation (68% confidence interval, 1S) ranges and then doubled to create two standard deviation (95% confidence interval, 2S) ranges. In the case of open-ended confidence intervals such as 60+, individuals falling into these phases were excluded from the test sample to avoid possible errors.

Methodological Comparisons

Each of the combined methods will be based on the primary Bass Collection sample then, when applicable, tested on the smaller, independent, Hamann-Todd sample. These combined methods will be compared using three main categories: percent correct, method bias, and method inaccuracy. Percent correct is defined as the percentage of individuals contained within the confidence interval of the phase into which they classify. Method Bias is defined as the average difference between the predicted (phase mean) age and actual age (residual value). Absolute Mean error (sometimes referred to as Inaccuracy) is defined as the absolute difference between the predicted (phase mean) age and actual age (absolute residual value) (Lovejoy et al., 1985b).

TABLE 7.3
STAND-ALONE TECHNIQUE SPEARMAN CORRELATIONS

Samples	Îscan et al.	Lovejoy et al.	Suchey and Katz	Passalacqua	n
Bass Collection	0.51	0.24	0.50	0.29	107
Hamann-Todd Collection	0.70	0.35	0.73	0.60	49
Pooled Collections	0.68	0.38	0.67	0.47	156

TABLE 7.4
STAND-ALONE TECHNIQUE PERFORMANCES

Method	% Correct 1 S	% Correct 2 S	Bias	AME
Îscan et al.	10%	35%	-9.17	11.38
Lovejoy et al.	22%	37%	-3.38	10.75
Passalacqua	45%	91%	8.99	13.45
Suchey and Katz	69%	94%	-4.65	8.40

TABLE 7.5
MULTIFACTORIAL METHOD PERFORMANCES

Method	% Correct 1 S	% Correct 2 S	Bias	AME
PCA Forward Stepwise Linear Regression Method	39%	83%	16.22	17.24
Component Method	55%	81%	-4.71	10.73
Decision Tree Regression	37%	58%	0.69	10.12
Decision Tree Regression (with V-Fold cross-validation)	43%	73%	0.29	9.76
Linear Regression Method	74%	91%	-3.87	8.90

Multifactorial Methods and Results

Original Technique Performances

Spearman correlations between age and phase for each technique were cal-culated on the Bass sample, the Hamann-Todd sample and the pooled sam-ple (Table 7.3). Performance data for these techniques are presented in Table 7.4. The performances of each of the multifactorial methods (presented below) are displayed in Table 7.5.

TABLE 7.6
COMPONENT METHOD PHASE DATA

Phase	Summed Phase Score	Mean Age	S	68% Range	95% Range	n
1	<21	31	4.88	26–36	21–41	6
2	22	50	6.19	43–56	37–62	6
3	23&24	52	11.59	41–64	29–76	33
4	25&26	68	13.83	54–81	40–95	43
5	27&28	73	12.35	61–85	48–98	16
6	29	75	7.62	67–83	60–90	5

Component System

The Component System method involves using the phase scores for each of the four age estimation techniques as a summing variable. In this method the phase scores are summed to reach a total score, this total then corresponds to a new phase score associated with new mean ages and confidence intervals (Table 7.6).

Decision Tree Regression

This method uses decision tree regression predictive modeling. Here, the four age at death estimation techniques act as independent (predictor) variables and age acts as the dependant (target) variable. Each split picks the best variables in attempt to halve the sample. In order to read these models, each node presents the sample size and standard deviation contained within the phases listed. One should begin by looking at the top node (node 1) and then follow the flow chart down. These analyses were preformed using the program DTREG (Sherrod, 2003), presented in Figure 7.6. Due to some programmatic complexities, a single individual in the test sample is completely misclassified because they have phase scores lower than anyone in the reference sample. Because of this, data is presented without the outlying individual.

Decision Tree Regression (With Cross-Validation)

This is the same method as the regular decision tree regression except the data is cross-validated using V-Fold cross-validation (similar to K-Fold cross-validation). In this case the cross-validation limited the tree size to the minimum standard error. These analyses were preformed using the program DTREG (Sherrod, 2003) presented in Figure 7.7.

FIGURE 7.6

DECISION TREE REGRESSION MODEL WITHOUT CROSS-VALIDATION

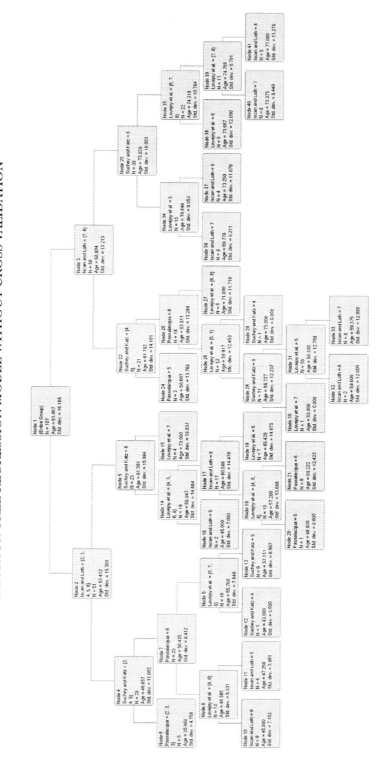

FIGURE 7.7
DECISION TREE REGRESSION MODEL WITH V-FOLD
CROSS-VALIDATION TO MINIMUM STANDARD ERROR

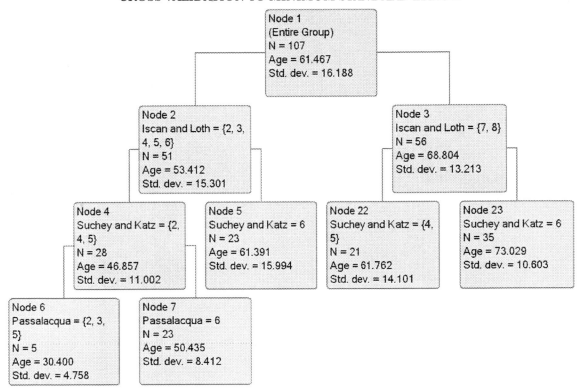

Linear Regression

A simple linear regression was calculated using the four age at death estimation techniques as independent variables and age as the dependant variable.

Principle Components Analysis

This method begins with a principle components analysis of the four age at death estimation techniques (Table 7.7). These data are then used to create a linear forward stepwise regression using age as the dependant variable. The forward stepwise analysis excluded the third and fourth principal components.

TABLE 7.7
COMMUNALITIES FOR PC 1

Method	Pearson r^2
Passalacqua	0.83
Îscan et al.	0.82
Suchey and Katz	0.73
Lovejoy et al.	0.56

Discussion/Conclusions

From comparisons to other single age at death techniques, the sacrum performs competitively (see Table 7.4). These results indicate the utility of the sacrum is comparable to other tested age at death estimation techniques and thus the sacrum can be recommended as a tool to estimate age at death using the Passalacqua method (2009). Concerning multifactorial age estimation, the sacrum holds the greatest potential in the later developmental stages of early adulthood as demonstrated by the terminal nodes of the decision-tree method with cross validation (see Figure 7.7). From the multifactorial age at death estimation methods presented here, the Linear Regression Method performed with the smallest amounts of error overall, as is congruent with the results of Uhl (2007). However, decision-tree regression (with cross-validation) may be another avenue of future age at death research as it presented low results for both bias and inaccuracy (see Table 7.5). The ability to generate predictive models has potential in both single trait based age at death techniques and multifactorial combinatory methods and should not be discounted.

ACKNOWLEDGMENTS

The author would like to thank the collection managers, specifically: Mr. Lyman Jellema of the Cleveland Museum of Natural History and Dr. Lee Meadows Jantz of the University of Tennessee, Knoxville. Additional thanks to Mr. Luis L. Cabo, Dr. Dennis C. Dirkmaat, Dr. Steven A. Symes, Dr. Krista Latham, Dr. Michael Finnegan, Dr. Joseph T. Hefner, Ms. Natalie M. Uhl and Mr. Christopher W. Rainwater for their contributions to this research.

REFERENCES

Bollow, M., Braun, J., Kannenberg, J., Biedermann, T., Schauer-Petrowskaja, C., Paris, S., Mutze, S., & Hamm, B. (1997). Normal morphology of sacroiliac joints in children: Magnetic resonance studies related to age and sex. *Skeletal Radiology 26:*697–704.

Buckberry, J. L., & Chamberlain, A. T. (2002). Age estimation from the auricular surface of the ilium: A revised method. *American Journal of Physical Anthropology 119:*231–239.

Îscan, M. Y., Loth, S. R., & Wright, R. K. (1984). Age estimation from the rib by phase analysis: white males. *Journal of Forensic Sciences 29:*1094–1104.

Îscan. M. Y., Loth, S. R., & Wright, R. K. (1985). Age estimation from the rib by phase analysis: White females. *Journal of Forensic Sciences 30:*853–863.

Lovejoy, C. O., Meindl, R. S., Mensforth, R. P., & Barton, T. J. (1985b). Multifactorial determination of skeletal age at death: A method and blind tests of its accuracy. *American Journal of Physical Anthropology 68*(1):1–14.

Lovejoy, C. O., Meindl, R. S., Pryzbeck, T. R., & Mensforth, R. P. (1985a). Chronological metamorphosis of the auricular surface of the ilium: A new method for determination of adult skeletal age at death. *American Journal of Physical Anthropology 68*(1):15–28.

McKern, T. W., & Stewart, T. D. (1957). Skeletal age changes in young American males. Quartermaster Research and Development Command Technical Report EP-45, Natick, MA.

Passalacqua, N. V. (2009). Forensic Age-at-death estimation from the human sacrum. *Journal of Forensic Science 54*(2):255–262

Sashin, D. (1930). A critical analysis of the anatomy and pathologic changes of the sacro-iliac joints. *Journal of Bone and Joint Surgery 12:*891–910.

Scheuer, L., & Black, S. (2000).   *Developmental juvenile osteology.* San Diego: Academic Press.

Sherrod, P. H. (2003). DTREG Classification and regression trees and support vector machines for predictive modeling and forecasting. www.dtreg.com

Shibata, Y., Shirai, Y., & Miyamoto, M. (2002). The aging process in the sacroiliac joint: Helical computed tomography analysis. *Journal of Orthopedic Science 7:*12–18.

Suchey, J. M, & Katz, D. (1998). Applications of pubic age determination in a forensic setting. In Kathleen J. Reichs (Ed.), *Forensic osteology: Advances in the identification of human remains,* pp. 204–236. Springfield, IL: Charles C Thomas.

Uhl, N. M. (2007). Multifactorial determination of age-at-death from the human skeleton. MS Thesis. University of Indianapolis.

Chapter 8

LIMITATIONS OF CARTILAGE OSSIFICATION AS AN INDICATOR OF AGE AT DEATH

HEATHER M. GARVIN

A major task of forensic anthropologists involves the analysis of dry skeletal remains. However, this role has expanded over the past 20 years and many cases now involve decomposing, burned, or otherwise altered remains which can no longer provide fingerprints or visual identification, yet would require extensive processing before the skeletal remains could be grossly examined. A radiographic analysis can provide an immediate preview of the remains, expediting the investigation until a more thorough skeletal examination is completed.

Although radiographic analysis is a popular means for positive identification, it remains relatively underutilized in determining biological profiles. The research summarized below investigates the use of radiographic analysis of cartilage ossification as an indicator of chronological age. It should be noted that changes in cartilage are referred within this study as "ossification," while other studies may use the terms "calcification" or "mineralization." There are in fact, differences among the terms, however, these processes can only be differentiated histologically, and in many studies are used interchangeably (Senac et al., 1985).

SAMPLE

Both the larynx and the anterior thoracic chest plate are routinely removed at autopsy and can be easily radiographed without interfering with standard

FIGURE 8.1
AGE DISTRIBUTION OF AUTOPSY SAMPLE

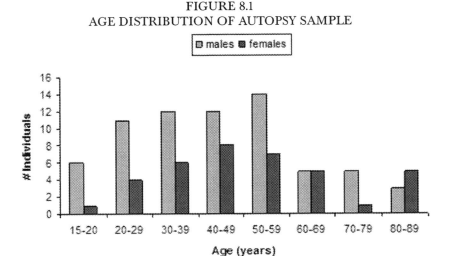

autopsy procedures. In this study 106 laryngeal structures and chest plates removed during autopsy at the Broward County Medical Examiner's Office, FL, were radiographed in an antero-posterior orientation with a *UX Universal Uni-Matic* 325 open x-ray machine (Universal/Allied Inc., Franklin Park, IL), at 50 amps, 40 kilovolt peaks, for a duration of 0.5 seconds. The sample consisted of male and female individuals of African-American and European-American ancestry, ranging from 15–89 years of age (Figure 8.1).

THYROID CARTILAGE

Previous Research

As early as 1958, studies have suggested the cartilaginous structures of the larynx tend to ossify with age (Yoshikawa, 1958). Most studies are descriptive but do not provide any standards for age estimation (Ajmani et al., 1980; O'Halloran and Lundy, 1987; Mupparapu and Vuppalapati, 2004). Still others suggest that cartilage ossification is not significantly correlated with age (Jurik, 1984; Scheuer and Black, 2000). Many articles that do discuss ossification correlations with specific ages are published in non-indexed or foreign language journals, and therefore are either inaccessible or require translation for use by most U.S. forensic anthropologists (Vlcek, 1980; Jurik, 1984; Strek et al., 1993). One study by Černy (1983) summarizes many of these foreign works and presents ossification of the thyroid cartilage as an accurate age determination method in the forensic context. While Černy's (1983) original article is published in Czech, the results of his study have been reproduced in a popular forensic anthropological text (Krogman and Îscan, 1986), and therefore is a common reference in the forensic field. Unfortunately, as pointed out by Scheuer and Black (2000), Černy's own observations have been based on a white male sample of five thyroid cartilages. Furthermore, the discrete narrow age ranges presented by Černy are not accompanied by any descriptive statistics necessary to comply with Daubert standards (Christiansen, 2004). For these reasons, the accuracy of Černy's (1983) method was tested on laryngeal radiographs from a modern forensic sample. While a summary of the research follows, the full results of the evaluation of laryngeal ossification are presented in Garvin (2008).*

Because the current sample is examined radiographically, as compared to the gross examination in previous studies, the possibility of methodological bias must be considered. Ideally, both a gross and radiographic examination would have been completed and the correlation of the results documented, however, time constraints in the medical examiner setting did not allow for processing of gross specimens. A literature search for similar studies documenting the correlation between observed radiographic and gross ossification was unsuccessful. Given that the soft tissue structures, such as muscle and cartilage were observed on the radiographs and the borders of the ossified regions were clearly demarcated, it is not expected that the degree of ossification would be underrepresented in the films. This study focused on the presence and absence of ossification in various thyroid cartilage regions, and not the magnitude of ossification. Therefore, even if there is any loss of radiodensity due to attenuation factors or overlying soft tissue, it should not affect the results and the method is equally applicable to radiographic and gross specimens. It is more likely that the radiographic technique would more accurately represent the true age related changes, allowing for *in situ* observation of ossification areas, which given the fragility of the laryngeal structures, could easily become damaged or reduced during subsequent processing.

Testing Černy's Phase Method

Černy's phase descriptions were applied to 104 laryngeal radiographs and each individual assigned a phase. Based on the age ranges provided for each

---

*The research completed by Garvin (2008) was awarded the 2008 J. Lawrence Angel Award by the American Academy of Forensic Sciences.

TABLE 8.1
PERCENT OF INDIVIDUALS CORRECTLY CLASSIFIED BY ČERNY'S PHASES

Sex *Ancestry*	*Females*	*Males*	*Ancestry Total*
"White"	10.34%	28.84%	22.22%
"Black"	14.29%	18.75%	17.39%
Sex Total	11.11%	26.47%	21.15%

phase, the percent of individuals correctly classified were calculated (Table 8.1). Overall, 21.15 percent of individuals were correctly classified and "white" males had the highest accuracy of 28.84 percent. Percent correct values calculated per phase displayed similarly low values, with the exception of phase 9 (66.67%) in which individuals with almost complete ossification were predicted to be at least 57 years old. To account for sample size, a binomial distribution model was used to calculate different theoretic correct classification rates with a larger sample and results indicated that given the narrow age ranges, even with larger sample sizes probabilities of percent correct classifi-

FIGURE 8.2
ČERNY AGE RANGES (BLACK) AND OBSERVED AGE RANGES (GREY) PER PHASE

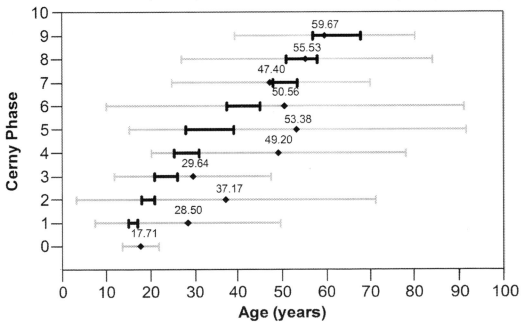

cation were below standards. The parameters of actual age distribution, including 68 and 95 percent confidence intervals, were estimated for each phase (Figure 8.2) (Garvin, 2008). In comparison to Černy's documented age ranges, the new age ranges overlapped highly and spanned up to 80 years. Even mean ages did not sequentially increase with each phase.

Ossification Trends

Anatomical regions of the thyroid cartilage as defined by Scheuer and Black (2000) were independently scored ("0" = no ossification, "1" = incomplete ossification, "2" = complete ossification) to analyze the progression of ossification (Table 8.2). As depicted by the darkest regions in Figure 8.3, the posterior triangles were always the first region to ossify and were observed in individuals as young as 19 years of age. The inferior horns and posterior borders were always the next regions to ossify. The remaining regions were more variable, occurring relatively concurrently, but the anterior midline tongue was always the last region to begin ossification and was not ossified in individuals younger than 30 years of age. The complete ossification of the laminae and cranial branch were not observed in individuals younger than 39 years. While a consistent pattern in the sequence of ossification was determined, ages at which each pattern of ossification were displayed varied highly per individual, and if two standard deviations were applied would span 35 to 84 years.

Certain demographic patterns in ossification were also observed. None of the females displayed complete ossification of the laminae, cranial branches, or anterior midline tongue despite comparable ages with the males. This is consistent with previous reports of increased male ossification compared to females (Ajmani et al., 1980; Jurik, 1984; Mupparapu and Vuppalapati, 2004; Pufe et al., 2004; Filho et al., 2005). Interestingly, similar to the females, none of the "black" males displayed ossification of the cranial branch and only four displayed any signs of ossification in the laminae. While these effects may be excused by sample sizes, other considerations such as the effects of menopause, hormones, vitamin D and calcium deficiencies should be investigated.

TABLE 8.2
OBSERVED TRENDS IN THYROID CARTILAGE OSSIFICATION

FEATURE	*TREND*
Any ossification	If any ossification > 18 years
Posterior triangles, posterior borders, and inferior horns	If not completely ossified < 37 years
Laminae and cranial branch	If completely ossified > 39 years
Midline tongue	If ossified > 30 years
Cricoid cartilage	If ossified > 25 years

FIGURE 8.3
REGIONAL PROGRESSION (DARK TO LIGHT) OF THYROID

A – ant midline tongue

B – cranial branch

C – sup horn

D – lamina

E – posterior border

F – posterior triangle

G – inf horn

H – caudal branch

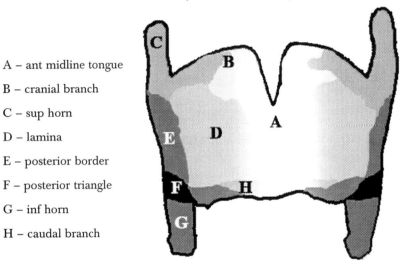

SUMMARY

The results of this study suggested that Černy's (1983) method does not meet forensic standards when applied to a modern sample. While a consistent progression of ossification exists with age, due to high degrees of variations between individuals, it is not strongly correlated with specific ages. This suggests that individual factors affect cartilage ossification, and ossification is not solely the result of the aging process. Based on observations in this study, ossification of the thyroid cartilage is extremely limited for forensic age at death estimation. The presence of ossification can be used as an indication of an adult. Lack of ossification of the posterior borders, inferior horns, and posterior triangles indicates an age less than 37 years, while ossification of the midline tongue suggests at least 30 years of age. Besides these general principles, degree of thyroid ossification cannot be applied in the forensic context without further investigation into variables affecting the ossification process.

COSTAL CARTILAGE

Previous Research

The ossification of costal cartilage has been well documented to occur with advancing age (e.g., King, 1939; Eichelberger and Roma, 1954; Semine and Damon, 1975; McCormick, 1980; Stewart and McCormick, 1984; McCormick and Stewart, 1988; Barrés et al., 1989; Barchilon et al., 1996). Some of the most well-known studies in costal cartilage ossification have been completed by McCormick and Stewart (McCormick, 1980; McCormick and Stewart, 1983, 1988; Stewart and McCormick, 1984) in which costal cartilage "mineralization" is discussed in terms of age-related changes. However, age estimations are limited to general descriptions of the expected ossification changes by decade. These trends were determined by scoring areas of ossification on a nine point scale (0–4+). Because of the noted variation in ossification patterns, each chest plate was also assigned to one of eight (A–H) more specific ossification patterns. The paradoxical combination of a complex categorical scoring system with simplified age estimation descriptions and statistical parameters, is not practical for forensic application.

A more recent approach by Barrés et al. (1989) similarly applied a qualitative scoring method (scale of 1–5) to bone demineralization, fusion of the manubrium to the sternal body, cartilage-to-sternum attachment changes, cartilage "mineralization," and rib to cartilage attachment changes. A photo-template was provided by the authors to help standardize scoring methods. The scores were then applied to a regression formula to estimate an individual's age with a standard error of ± 8.4 years. However, their results suggest relatively low correlation (r) values between age at death and scored traits, and high inter-observer errors. Some correlations were as low as 0.02 suggesting absolutely no correlation, while other values were strongly negative suggesting a *decrease* in ossification with age. In the case of the ossification of the cartilage-to-sternum attachment sites of females, the first judge had a correlation value of -0.27, the second judge a value of +0.02, and the third +0.58. This high variability in correlation of traits with age suggests this method is unreliable.

A closer look at the presented methods reveals many possible sources of these errors. First of all, the sample size was small, consisting of a total of 55 individuals. Secondly the photographic template provided was of overall poor quality. There were inconsistencies between terminology used in the text and on the template (e.g., the text referred to fusion of the manubrium, while the template displayed fusion of the sternal body). No written descriptions of the scoring characteristics were provided to resolve these discrepancies. The template also did not differentiate between male and female ossification patterns, despite extensive documentation of sexually dimorphic patterns (Elkeles, 1966; Sanders, 1966; Navani et al., 1970; McCormick and Stewart, 1983; Stewart and McCormick, 1984; McCormick et al., 1985; Rao and Pai, 1988). Finally, the regression equation provided placed the majority of weight (0.89) on ossification of cartilage-to-sternum attachment while all other scored traits were weighted 0.03 or less. For the example provided by the authors, this meant that for an individual estimated at 31.15 years, cartilage-to-sternum attachment accounted for 26.7 years while all other traits combined contributed 4.65 years of the estimate. In a method that presents a standard error of ± 8.4 years (approximately ± 17 years with a 95 percent confidence interval), the added 4.65 years seems trivial.

Testing the Barrés et al. Method

When the Barrés et al. (1989) method was applied to the forensic sample of chest plate radiographs, the predicted age fell within one standard deviation in 43 percent of the sample, and within two standard deviations in 78 percent of the sample. While these accuracy rates are acceptable, recall that two standard deviations span a broad 34 years. A plot of actual age versus estimated age suggests that this technique tends to overage individuals under 48 years of age and underages those above. ANCOVA results show male and female slopes are not significantly different, while intercepts are different. This pattern makes sense, given that McCormick (1980) concluded that females show a delayed pattern of ossification, and corroborates that standards should be sex specific. Furthermore, when logistic and linear regressions were created for total and sex specific radiograph scores, bone demineralization and cartilage mineralization were consistently the only significant variables. Given that these traits were given minimal weight in the Barrés et al. equation, these results were unexpected.

Ossification Trends

In an attempt to simplify scoring methods and create a practical method for estimating chronological age, the radiographs collected at autopsy were scored binomially (being assigned a "1" if changes were absent, and a "2" if any changes were present) on the following features (Figure 8.4):

a. Costal cartilage ossification of any of the sternal rib ends
b. Costal cartilage ossification peri-sternally
c. Costal cartilage ossification centri-chondrally (mid-costal cartilage)
d. Irregularity of cartilage ossification to the costal manubrium notch
e. Irregularity (evidence of flaring, cupping, bony extensions, or bone degradation) of the sternal rib ends
f. Complete fusion of the sternal body
g. Any bony fusion of the xiphoid to the sternal body
h. Any bony fusion of the manubrium to the sternal body

Using a binomial scale of presence or absence should minimize inter-observer error and increase replicability.

Minimum ages at which these changes occurred and maximum ages lacking changes were noted for each feature (Table 8.3). Complete fusion of the sternal body was documented in all individuals older than 21 years and fusion of the manubrium or xiphoid to the sternum indicated at least 25 years of age. Changes to the costal manubrium notch typically occurred first, followed by peri-sternal ossification. Because all individuals displayed changes in these two regions by the fifth or sixth decade of life, both presence and absence of these traits can be used to indicate general age estimations. Centri-chondral ossification was more variable and did not develop in all individuals, therefore only its presence could be utilized, and indicated an individual was least 30 years of age. Although only general age groups can be predicted from this information, the trends in timing of ossification presented in Table 8.3 would be useful in narrowing age estimation obtained from other forensic techniques.

A New Practical Method

For a more statistical approach, each individual's eight presence/absence scores were summed to create a total composite score (dummy variable) of the chest plate changes. Descriptive statistics, including two standard deviations and observed ranges are provided for each composite score in Table 8.4.

FIGURE 8.4
EXAMPLE OF A CHEST PLATE RADIOGRAPH SCORED
USING THE MODIFIED BINOMIAL METHOD

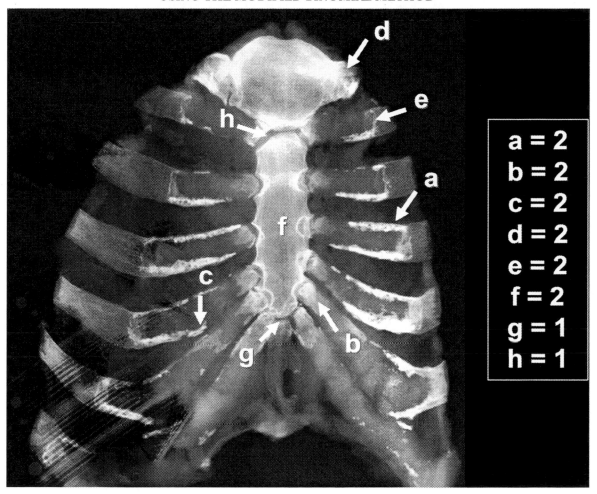

Spearman rank correlation of the composite scores and age revealed a significant positive correlation ($p < 0.01$), with a correlation coefficient $r = 0.78$. The relationship between age and composite score appeared non-linear, leveling off around the fifth decade of life since at this age presence of changes in all the scored regions is most likely (Figure 8.5). There were no apparent sexual differences in the relationship of composite score and age, since scores were based on presence not degree of ossification.

TABLE 8.3
OBSERVED TRENDS IN COSTAL CARTILAGE OSSIFICATION

FEATURE	*TREND*
Costal cartilage ossification of any of the sternal rib ends	If ossified > 26 years
Costal cartilage ossification peri-sternally	If ossified > 23 years If lacks any ossification < 42 years
Costal cartilage ossification centri-chondrally	If ossified > 30 years
Irregularity or cartilage ossification to the costal manubrium notch	If irregular or ossified > 19 years If lacks irregularity or ossification < 58 years
Irregularity of sternal rib ends	If lacks irregularity < 27 years
Complete fusion of the sternal body	If fused > 17 years If unfused < 21 years
Any bony fusion of the xiphoid to the sternal body	If fused > 25 years
Any bony fusion of the manubrium to the sternal body	If fused > 25 years

FIGURE 8.5
DISTRIBUTION OF COMPOSITE CHEST PLATE SCORES BY AGE

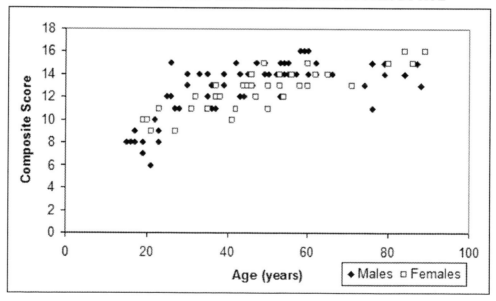

TABLE 8.4
OBSERVED AGE RANGES AND DESCRIPTIVE STATISTICS
FOR CHEST PLATE COMPOSITE SCORES

Composite Score	n	Min Age	Mean Age	Max Age	1 sd	2 sd	Observed Range
8	5	15	18.6	23	3.1	6.2	15–31
9	5	17	21.8	27	3.6	7.2	15–36
10	4	19	25.5	41	10.4	20.8	15–30
11	11	23	37.8	76	14.7	29.4	15–46
12	13	25	39	54	8.3	16.6	22–61
13	16	30	51.3	88	15.5	31	20–72
14	24	30	53.3	84	13	26	27–81
15	18	26	58.4	87	16.9	33.8	25–83
16	6	58	73.2	89	15.6	31.2	42–89+

SUMMARY

While the studies by McCormick and Stewart (McCormick, 1980; Stewart and McCormick, 1984; McCormick and Stewart, 1988) were thorough, their methodologies were not practical for forensic application. The method by Barrés et al. (1989) attempted to simplify and quantify scores of degree of ossification, but inconsistencies, lack of consideration of sex differences, and lack of detailed descriptions resulted in high inter-observer errors. By applying a binomial scoring method (presence/absence) and creating composite scores, the author was able to obtain accurate and reliable age estimations regardless of sex. Reducing the subjectivity of the scoring method simplifies the method, decreasing inter-observer error rates. Still, age at which changes to the chest plate occurs remains highly variable between individuals, and when the necessary standard deviations are applied the result is broad age estimations.

CONCLUSION

Černy's (1983) method of determining age from thyroid cartilage ossification and the Barrés et al. (1989) method using ossification and changes to the chest plate, did not provide accurate results when applied to a modern forensic sample. Reasons for these discrepancies in accuracy may include: lack of statistical descriptions, small sample sizes, or inadequate methodological approaches in these studies. Differences in sample distributions or possible secular changes in the modern forensic sample could also lead to lower accuracy rates. Regardless, these results convey the necessity to continually test the accuracy of previous studies on contemporary samples to verify that they meet the present forensic and statistical standards.

An investigation into the progression of ossification of the thyroid and costal cartilages concluded that degree and frequency of ossification does increase with advancing age. In both cases, successive patterns of ossification were documented revealing specific trends in the sequence of regional ossification. These trends can be used to discriminate general age groups such as young, middle, and older adults (Tables 8.2–8.4). However, individual ages at which these patterns were observed were highly variable, making narrow age range estimates not possible. The presented modified methods in estimating age from cartilage ossification are practical and provide all the necessary statistics for evaluation. Testing and including data from various additional, and larger samples may narrow the current estimated age ranges and are encouraged to assess method reliability and constraints.

Overall cartilage ossification is extremely limited as a forensic indicator of age, but not useless. Although age ranges from the modified cartilage ossification methods are broad, they are highly accurate, and may be used in conjunction with other skeletal age analyses to narrow original age ranges. When presented with remains that would require extensive processing before evaluation, methods investigating the radiographic appearance of cartilage ossification can provide immediate preliminary age ranges for the initial investigation. The results of this study are in agreement with McCormick's (1980: 736) that "the ease, rapidity, and relative inexpensiveness of this procedure on intact or partially decomposed bodies recommends its use."

UNDERSTANDING CARTILAGE OSSIFICATION

Although it was concluded that the scores obtained from the Černy (1983) and Barrés et al. (1989) methods were not correlated with age, these scores should still be an accurate account of the degree of ossification present. Since radiographs of both regions were obtained from the same individuals, correlations between degree of ossification in the thyroid and costal cartilages were analyzed. Spearman rank correlation between the Černy method scores and

Barrés et al. scores revealed that degree of ossification between the two regions was not significantly correlated (p > 0.05).

On one hand, this is expected because neither pattern was found to be highly correlated with age. In contrast, it suggests that at least some influences responsible for the ossification of the thyroid cartilage are independent of those affecting the costal cartilage. Attention should then be drawn to regionally dependent influences, such as mechanical stress from muscle attachments. Interestingly, in the thyroid cartilage the first regions to ossify, such as the posterior borders and caudal branch, are areas where the intrinsic and extrinsic laryngeal and pharyngeal muscles attach. Similarly with costal cartilage, the typical male pattern involves linear ossifications from the superior and inferior costal margins (Elkeles, 1966; Sanders, 1966; Navani et al., 1970; McCormick and Stewart, 1983; Stewart and McCormick, 1984; McCormick et al., 1985; Rao and Pai, 1988) where all of the intercostal muscles attach (Moore and Agur, 2002; Netter, 2003). This evidence may suggest that as supportive properties of cartilage deteriorate with age that ossification of areas of muscle attachments may be necessary for reinforcement. The changes in structure and composition of costal cartilage with age have been documented (Hukins et al., 1976; Mallinger and Stockinger, 1988). Lau et al. (2007) investigated changes in the mechanical properties of costal cartilage due to ossification; however, the focus of their study was the affect on frontal impact in car crashes, not whether the structural changes in the cartilage induce the ossification.

While this study provides evidence that regionally dependent variables are important in cartilage ossification, it does not rule out systemic influences. Besides mechanical stress, other factors that have been suggested to induce ossification include pathology, nutrition, hormones, and genetics (Vastine et al., 1948; Eichelberger and Roma, 1954; Vlcek, 1980; Wobst et al., 1980; Senac et al., 1985; Classen and Werner, 2004; Pufe et al., 2004). But overall the specific mechanism and causes of cartilage ossification remain unknown, possibly due to a lack of clinical importance. Isolating the effects of these various environmental influences would be challenging, but besides larger sample sizes, may be the only way to accurately narrow estimated age ranges.

ACKNOWLEDGMENTS

The author would like to thank the Broward County Medical Examiner's Office for the opportunity to radiographically study the specimens. The assistance provided by student intern, Ana Del Alamo, and all of the autopsy technicians is greatly appreciated.

REFERENCES

Ajmani, M. L., Jain, S. P., & Saxena, S. K. (1980). A metrical study of laryngeal cartilages and their ossification. *Anatomimscher Anzeiger 148*:42–8.

Barchilon, V., Hershkovitz, I., Rothschild, B., Wish-Baratz, S., Latimer, B., Jellema, L., Hallel, T., & Arensburg, B. (1996). Factors affecting the rate and pattern of the first costal cartilage ossification. *The American Journal of Forensic Medicine and Pathology 17*:239–247.

Barrés, D. R., Durigon, M., & Paraire, F. (1989). Age estimation from quantification of features of "chest plate" x-rays. *Journal of Forensic Sciences 34*(1): 28–233.

Cerny, M. (1983). Our experience with estimation of an indvidual's age from skeletal remains of the degree of thyroid cartilage ossification. *Acta Universitatis Palackianae Olomucensis 3*:121–44.

Christensen, A. M. (2004). The impact of daubert: Implications for testimony and research in forensic anthropology (and the use of frontal sinuses in personal identification). *Journal of Forensic Sciences 49*:1–4.

Classen, H., & Werner, J. (2004). Gender-specific distribution of glycosaminoglycans during cartilage mineralization of human thyroid cartilage. *Journal of Anatomy 205*:371–380.

Eichelberger, L., & Roma, M. (1954). Effects of age on the histochemical characterization of costal cartilage. *American Journal of Physiology 178*:296–304.

Elkeles, A. (1966). Sex differences in the calcification of the costal cartilages. *Journal of the American Geriatrics Society 14*:456–462.

Filho, J. A. X., Bohadana, S. C., Perazzio, A. F., Tsuji, D. H., & Sennes, L. U. (2005). Anatomy of the cricothyroid articulation: differences between men and women. *Ann Otol Rhinol Laryngal 114*:250–2.

Garvin, H. M. (2008). Ossification of laryngeal structures as indicators of age. *Journal of Forensic Sciences 53*:1023–1027.

Hukins, D. W., Knight, D. P., & Woodhead-Galloway, J. (1976). Amianthoid change: Orientation of naormal collagen fibrils during aging. *Science 194*:622–624.

Jurik, A. G. (1984). Ossification and calcification of the laryngeal skeleton. *Acta Radiologica Diagnosis 25*:17–22.

King, J. B. (1939). Calcification of the costal cartilages. *The British Journal of Radiology 12*:2–12.

Krogman, W. M., & Îscan, M. Y. (1986). *The human skeleton in forensic medicine.* Springfield, IL: Charles C Thomas.

Lau, A., Oyen, M. L., Kent, R. W., Murakami, D., & Torigaki, T. 2007. Indentation stiffness of aging human costal cartilage. *Acta Biomateriala 3*:97–103.

Mallinger, R., & Stockinger, L. (1988). Amianthoid (abestoid) transformation: Electron mircoscopical studies on aging human costal cartilage. *American Journal of Anatomy 181*:23–32.

McCormick, W. F. (1980). Mineralization of the costal cartilages as an indicator of age: Preliminary observations. *Journal of Forensic Sciences 25*:736–741.

McCormick, W. F., & Stewart, J. H. (1983). Ossification patterns of costal cartilages as an indicator of sex. *Archives of Pathology and Laboratory Medicine 107*:206–210.

McCormick, W. F., Stewart, J. H., & Langford, L. A. (1985). Sex determination from chest plate roentgenograms. *American Journal of Physical Anthropology 68:*173–195.

McCormick, W. F., & Stewart, J. H. (1988). Age related changes in the human plastron: A roentgenographic and morphologic study. *Journal of Forensic Sciences 33:*100–120.

Moore, K. L., & Agur, A. M. (2002). *Essential clinical anatomy.* Baltimore, MD: Lippincott, Williams and Wilkins.

Mupparapu, M., & Vuppalapati, A. (2004). Ossification of laryngeal cartilages on lateral cephalometric radiographs. *The Angle Orthodontist 75:*196–201.

Navani, S., Shah, J. R., & Levy, P. S. (1970). Determination of sex by costal cartilage calcification. *American Journal of Roentgenology and Radium Therapy 108:*771–774.

Netter, F. H. (2003). *Atlas of human anatomy.* Teterboro, NJ: Icon Learning Systems.

O'Halloran, R. L., & Lundy, J. K. (1987). Age and ossification of the hyoid bone: Forensic implications. *Journal of Forensic Sciences 32*(6):1655–9.

Pufe, T., Mentlein, R., Tsokos, M., Steven, P., Varoga, D., Goldring, M. B., Tillmann, B. N., & Paulsen, F. P. (2004). VEGF expression in adult permanent thyroid cartilage: Implications for lack of cartilage ossification. *Bone 35:*543–52.

Rao, N. G., & Pai, L. M. (1988). Costal cartilage calcification pattern—A clue for establishing sex identity. *Forensic Science International 38:*193–202.

Sanders, C. J. (1966). Sexing by costal cartilage calcification. *The British Journal of Radiology 39:*233–234.

Scheuer, L., & Black, S. (2000). *Developmental juvenile osteology.* London, UK: Elsevier Ltd.

Semine, A. A., & Damon, A. (1975). Costochondral ossification and aging in five populations. *Human Biology 47(1):*182–8.

Senac, M. O., Lee, F. A., & Gilsanz, V. (1985). Early costochondral calcification in adolescent hyperthyroidism. *Radiology 156:*375–377.

Stewart, J. H., & McCormick, W. F. (1984). A sex- and age-limited ossification pattern in human costal cartilages. *American Journal of Clinical Pathology 81:*765–769.

Strek, P., Nowogrodzka-Zagorska, M., Skawina, A., & Olszewski, E. (1993). Ossification of human thyroid cartilage: Scanning electron microscopic study. *Folia Morphologica 52:*47–56.

Vastine, J. H., Vastine, M. F., & Arango, O. (1948). Genetic influence of osseus development with particular reference to the deposition of calcium in the costal cartilages. *The American Journal of Roentgenology and Radium Therapy 59*(2):213–221.

Vlcek, E. (1980). Estimation of age from skeletal material based on the degree of thyroid cartilage ossification. *Soudni lekarstvi 25:*6–11.

Wobst, R., Hommel, G., & Sames, K. (1980). Morphological and histochemical studies in human rib cartilage chondrons of different age groups. *Gerontology 26:*311–320.

Yoshikawa, E. (1958). Changes of the laryngeal cartilages during the life and their application of determination of the probable age. *Japanese Journal of Legal Medicine 12:*1–40.

Chapter 9

DETERMINATION OF AGE AT DEATH USING THE ACETABULUM OF THE OS COXA

Kyra E. Stull and Dustin M. James

D etermining chronological age at death from human skeletal remains is one of the primary goals of the forensic anthropologist. Age estimates are essential for narrowing the list of potential victims to aid in the identification process, as well as allowing for demographic reconstructions in an archaeological context. In medicolegal work, the age at death estimate is very crucial considering a wide range will include excess individuals and a narrow range may inadvertently remove the missing individual from the list. For this purpose it is important that chronological age estimates be both precise and accurate.

Numerous skeletal elements can be used to assess age at death in adults, such as the pubic symphysis, the iliac auricular surface, sternal rib ends, and cranial sutures (Îscan et al., 1984; Krogman and Îscan, 1986; Îscan, 1989; Schmitt et al., 2002). Certain osseous regions are more frequently available for analysis in bioarchaeological and forensic contexts considering differing tendencies in preservation rates (Lovejoy et al., 1985; Brooks and Suchey, 1990; Rouge-Maillart et al., 2004). Due to its concave shape and the thickness of surrounding soft tissue, the acetabulum of the *os coxa* is protected from many destructive taphonomic processes and is frequently preserved long after other osseous regions are compromised. Due to its durability it has become an asset in both fields of archaeology and forensics for creating appropriate demographic data. Most commonly, the acetabulum has been used for sex determination through both metric and nonmetric analysis (Rissech and Malgosa, 1997; Rissech et al., 2003; Rissech and Malgosa, 2005;

Benazzi et al., 2008). More recently the acetabulum is an increasingly growing area of interest in the orthopedic community, stemming from the necessity for replacements and surgical implants (Konrath et al., 1998; Rissech et al., 2001; Milz et al., 2001; Daniel et al., 2005). The pattern of acetabular formation, growth, and degeneration has been discussed in publications from many different scientific fields, although its utility as an age at death indicator was not first observed until 2004 by Rouge-Maillart and colleagues. The original study consisted of 30 male *os coxae,* of which twenty-one were Spanish subjects buried in Granolers cemetery and nine were white individuals from forensic autopsies in Toulouse, France (2004). Rouge-Maillart et al. (2004) described four different skeletal features for examination: the acetabular rim, the acetabular fossa, the lunate surface, and apical activity. The authors then broke each skeletal feature into degenerative morphological stages, with each feature having a different number of stages. The objective of the preliminary research conducted by the current authors was to test the techniques and criteria proposed by Rouge-Maillart et al. (2004) and determine the accuracy, reliability, and repeatability of their research.

Two main problems with the Rouge-Maillart study were discovered after the preliminary research was conducted by the current authors: (1) some stage descriptions were too ambiguous to be replicable, and (2) morphological changes to the lunate surface of the acetabulum did not correlate with chronological age. The overall results of the preliminary study clearly depicted that the techniques Rouge-Maillart et al. (2004) proposed were not applicable to the field of forensic anthropology. The current study revises the Rouge-Maillart et al. (2004) method by only focusing on three age-related features as well as providing revised descriptions of each stage originally proposed by Rouge-Maillart et al. (2004). The effectiveness of the revised technique was then tested on a modern skeletal collection.

MATERIALS AND METHODS

The sample consists of 405 completely fused left *os coxae* from white and black males and females ranging in known age from 16 to 100 years (Figure 9.1).

The majority of the sample (361 specimens, 89%) was acquired from the William M. Bass Donated and Forensic Skeletal Collection, both housed at the University of Tennessee, Knoxville, TN. The remaining 11 percent (44 specimens) of the sample were drawn from the skeletal collection at the

FIGURE 9.1
AGE DISTRIBUTION REPRESENTING THE INDIVIDUALS USED WITHIN THE STUDY

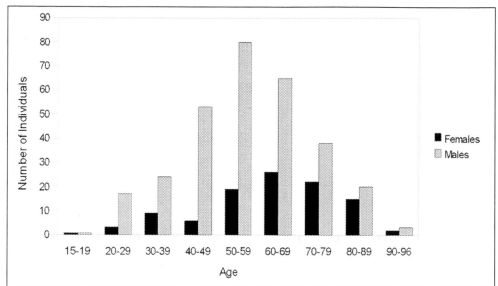

Hamilton County Medical Examiner's Office, Chattanooga, TN. Any specimen exhibiting pathological or morphologically abnormal features was not included. However, individuals illustrating signs of non-inflammatory osteoarthritis or diffuse idiopathic skeletal hyperostosis (DISH) were included in the study, as these conditions are associated with age (Rouge-Maillart et al., 2007).

Following the revised method of Rouge-Maillart et al. (2004), three regions of the acetabulum, the acetabular rim (Figure 9.2), the acetabular fossa (Figure 9.3), and the apical region (Figure 9.4) were individually and macroscopically examined by one of the authors (KS). The pubic symphyses and iliac auricular surfaces were concealed from the observer to prevent any biases. Each region was assigned a score ranging from 1 to 4 depending on the exhibited morphology, 1 being the least and 4 being the most degenerated.

Age distributions incorporating two standard deviations were calculated for each stage of each feature to properly incorporate 95 percent of the population (Figure 9.5). Spearman rank correlations between the feature scores and age were calculated, as well as each area tested by sex and ancestral group for between-stage differences in mean age through a series of Kruskal-Wallis tests (with Bonferroni correction).

FIGURE 9.2
MORPHOLOGICAL STAGES ASSOCIATED WITH THE ACETABULAR RIM

Stage	Observation	Description
1	No Activity	Blunt and smooth edge; no osteophytes; no sign of activity
2	Rim Definition	Blunt or Sharp defined rim
3	Lip formation or Elongation of Rim	Lip formed on articular surface or posterior border Elongation of the rim with a pinched effect Beginning presence of osteophytes and degeneration on rim (not destruction)
4	Destruction of Rim or Bone Growth	Destruction of rim by either microporosity or macroporosity causing a resorbtion like appearance of bone Nonuniform bone growth causing an irregular appearance Appearance of Porosity is the major factor

Stage 1   Stage 2 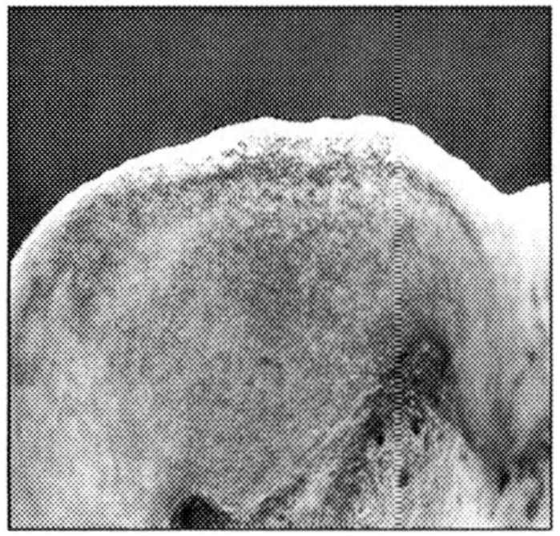   Stage 3 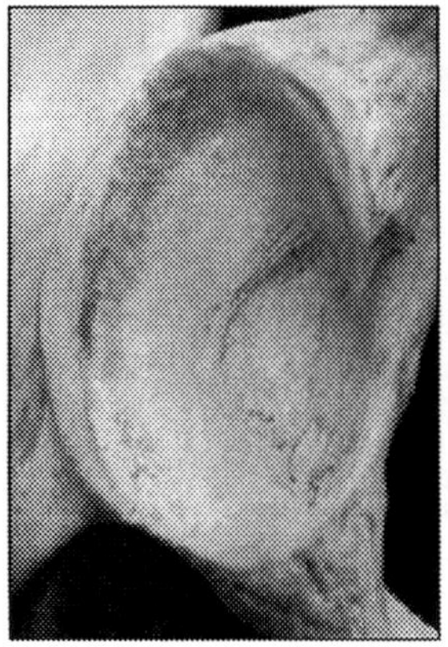   Stage 4

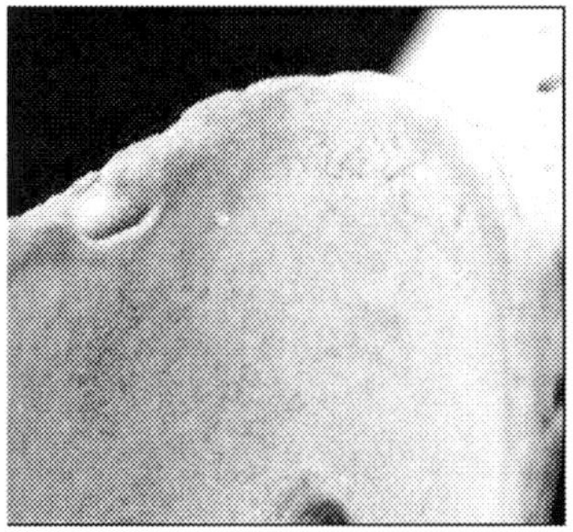

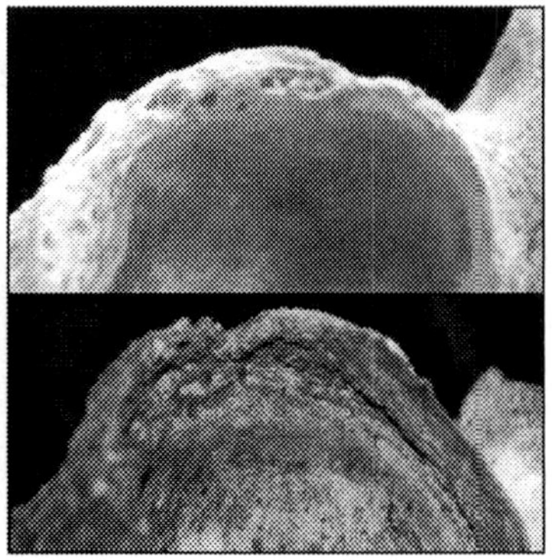

FIGURE 9.3

MORPHOLOGICAL STAGES ASSOCIATED WITH THE ACETABULAR FOSSA

Stage	Observation	Description
1	Dense*	Dense with peripheral macroporosity
2	Microporosity*	Formation of Microporosity
3	Trabecular Bone*	Appearance of Trabecular Bone**
4	Extensive Macroporosity	Extensive macroporosity throughout

*In the event that activity is only occurring on the peripheral portion of the fossa, still classify it in the corresponding stage

**In numerous cases specimens skip stage 3 and go straight to stage 4   Possibility of macroporosity caused by microporosity.

Stage 1

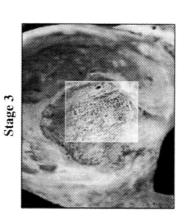

Stage 2

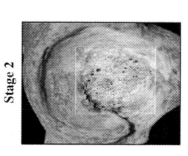

Stage 3

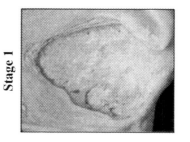

Stage 4

FIGURE 9.4
MORPHOLOGICAL STAGES ASSOCIATED WITH THE APICAL

Stage	Observation	Description
1	Blunt	Blunt and smooth appearance
2	Rim Formation	Formation of the rim and sharper appearance
3	Moderate Activity	Pointed apex (somewhat triangular in shape) OR Broadening in width
4	Osteophyte Activity	Possible appearance of osteophyte activity

Bottom 1/3rd of articular surface of acetabulum

Stage 1   Stage 2 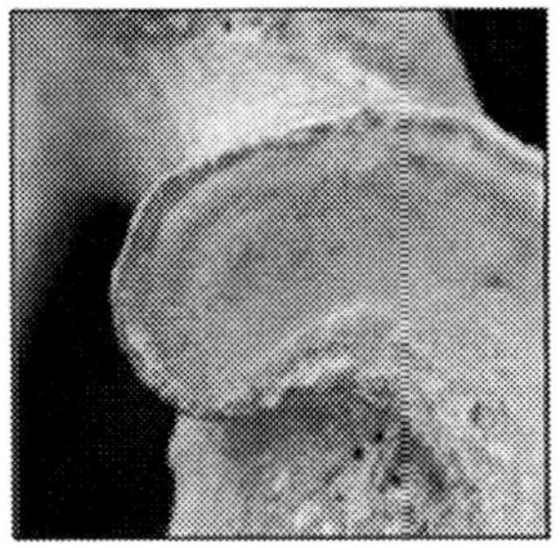   Stage 3 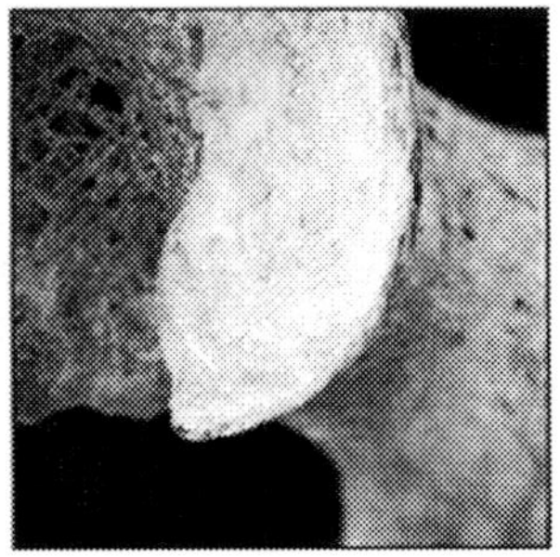   Stage 4

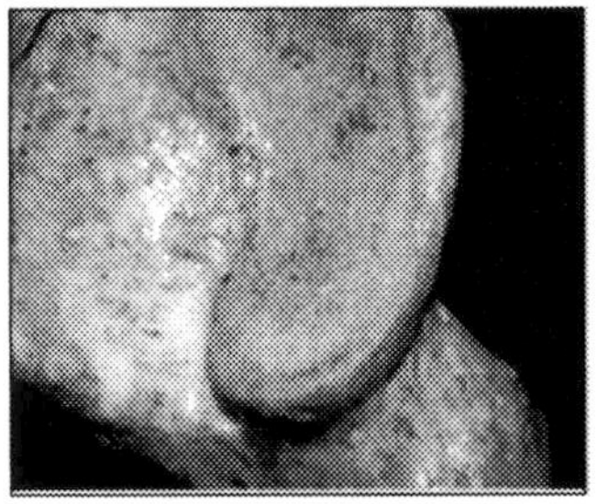

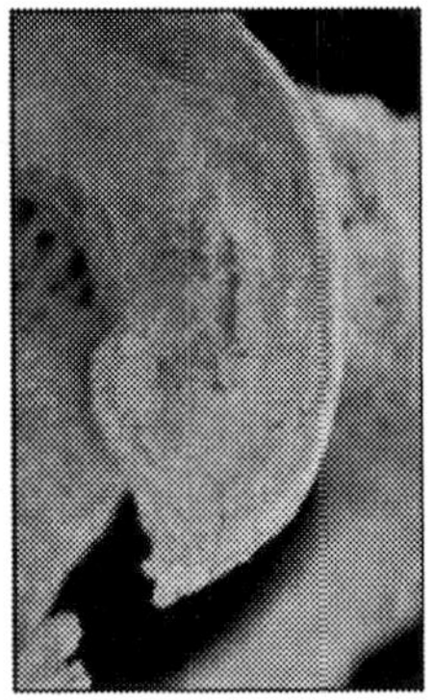

FIGURE 8.5
DISTRIBUTION OF COMPOSITE CHEST PLATE SCORES BY AGE

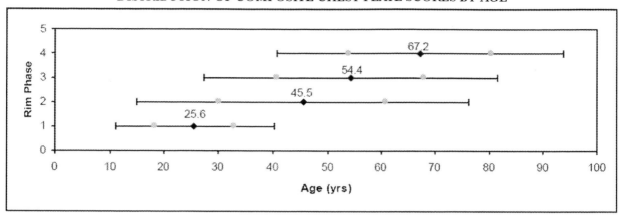

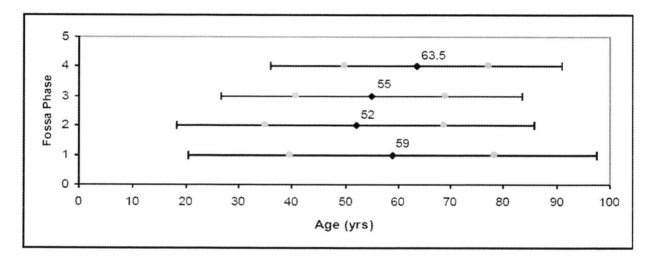

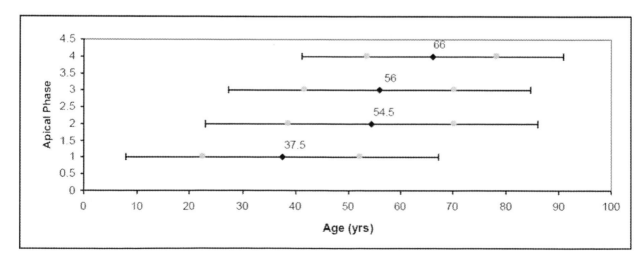

TABLE 9.1
SPEARMAN RANK CORRELATIONS FOR ALL FEATURES

Correlations

			Rim	*Fossa*	*Apical*	*Age*
Spearman's Rho	Rim	Correlation Coefficient	1.000	.295**	.436**	.516**
		Sig. (2-tailed)	.	.000	.000	.000
		N	406	406	406	405
	Fossa	Correlation Coefficient	.295**	1.000	.167**	.247**
		Sig. (2-tailed)	.000	.	.001	.000
		N	406	406	406	405
	Apical	Correlation Coefficient	.436**	.167**	1.000	.386**
		Sig. (2-tailed)	.000	.001	.	.000
		N	406	406	406	405
	Age	Correlation Coefficient	.516**	.247**	.386**	1.000
		Sig. (2-tailed)	.000	.000	.000	.
		N	405	405	405	405

**Correlation is significant at the 0.01 level (2-tailed).

RESULTS

All three features are significantly correlated with age (p = 0.01) as shown by Spearman rank correlations (Table 9.1). Although significant, the correlations are low overall, with the acetabular rim exhibiting the highest correlation (r = 0.519). The Kruskal-Wallis statistical analysis reveals a substantial overlap between stages for the acetabular fossa (p-value = 0.339) and apical region (p-value = 0.040), and demonstrates that only the acetabular rim (p-value = 0.000) shows stage differences for white males.

An ANOVA two-way analysis then demonstrated that there was no interaction between the skeletal features being observed and sex of the individual. As a result, the authors decided to pool males and females to increase the overall sample sizes, allowing for more analyses to be performed. Prior to the ANOVA results, white males were the only group with an adequate sample size (272 specimens). MANOVA was then completed on all three features with age as the dependent variable and sex/feature as the grouping factors. Once the sexes were pooled, the results showed much better stage delineations.

The acetabular rim displays a positive linear manner allowing for discrete standard deviations and between-stage differences (Figure 9.6). When exam-

FIGURE 9.6
AGE DISTRIBUTION BY RIM STAGE

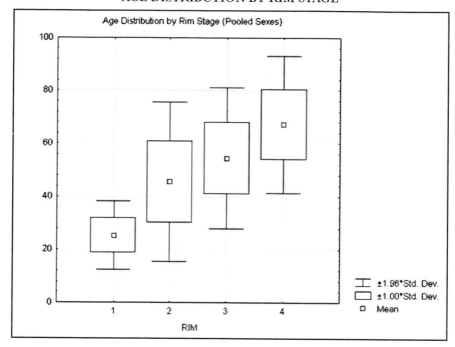

FIGURE 9.7
AGE DISTRIBUTION FOR FOSSA STAGES GROUPED BY SEX

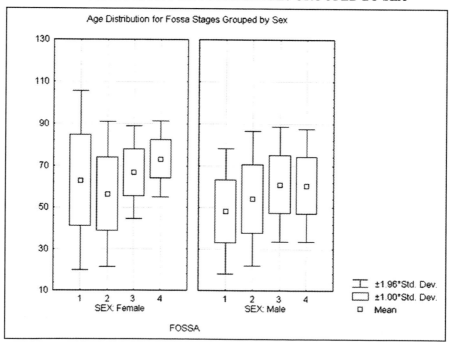

FIGURE 9.8
AGE DISTRIBUTION FOR APICAL STAGES GROUPED BY SEX

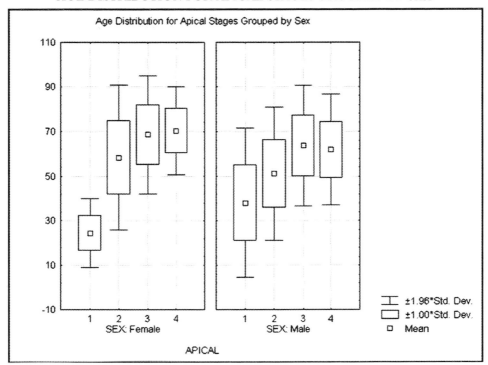

ining the ANOVA two-way with pooled-sexes for the acetabular fossa, the results suggest stages 1 and 2, and stages 3 and 4, should be collapsed into the same groups (Figure 9.7).

In light of these results, a binomial scoring system for the acetabular fossa will help produce a more accurate age range estimate. Until a new scoring technique is derived, the standard deviations should be grouped for acetabular fossa stages 1 and 2, and stages 3 and 4. The results for the apical region showed the most non-patterning age ranges associated with each stage (Figure 9.8). ANOVA two-way did show differences between stages, but these results were difficult to interpret. Currently, stage 2 demonstrates the largest problem with a differential average mean despite a large standard deviation. An immediate solution would be to collapse stages 3 and 4 since their average mean is very similar and stage 3 encompasses the standard deviation area for stage 4. However, the ideal solution for the convoluted results would be to create a new coding system associated with the apical region.

DISCUSSION AND CONCLUSIONS

Methods involving the iliac auricular surface (Lovejoy et al., 1985; Buckberry and Chamberlain, 2002; Mulhern and Jones, 2005; Osborne et al., 2004) and pubic symphysis (Todd, 1921; Brooks, 1955; Osborne et al., 2004) have been used for decades and continue to be the basis for numerous macroscopic age at death estimates. The method proposed here takes the same approach applied to the aforementioned areas of the *os coxa* and employs them to the patterns of degeneration associated with the acetabulum. The acetabulum, as with any bone, displays a general formation and breakdown in correspondence with age (Schmitt et al., 2002). Using the acetabulum as an age at death technique combined with other methods of aging can aid in age at death estimation of unknown human skeletal remains.

The acetabular rim displayed the strongest correlation with chronological age when compared to the other two features. Additionally, the acetabular rim was the only skeletal feature that displayed significant mean age differences between stages, resulting in the acetabular rim being the most promising area acting as an age at death indicator. These results demonstrated that when estimating a chronological age range morphological assessments of the acetabular fossa and apical region do not increase the precision of age estimates which can be obtained from the acetabular rim. For the acetabular fossa and the apical region to be considered useful as age predictors, the acetabular fossa stages must become binomial, and a new coding system should be derived for the apical region. Currently, these two features offer no further assistance in predicting a chronological age range.

Kruskal-Wallis results indicate that all stages per feature reveal very broad confidence intervals, making the revised method too imprecise for use in forensic settings as a stand alone technique. However, the revised technique would be functional in archaeological settings. Research has been performed in which the acetabular and auricular aging methods were combined with some success (Rouge-Maillart et al., 2004). As with most non-metric analyses used in forensic settings, employing multiple aging techniques eliminates bias and is more statistically significant (Lovejoy, 1985; Bedford et al., 1993).

The current study demonstrates that the acetabulum has potential and should be considered as an age at death indicator. Further research should be concerned with elucidating a better coding system for the stages of the fossa and apical region using a modern known sample, with results including percent correct classifications to check the accuracy and examine its capability as an age at death estimation technique.

ACKNOWLEDGMENTS

This research could not be completed without the support and guidance of Dr. Lee Meadows-Jantz of the University of Tennessee; Drs. Dennis Dirkmaat and Steve Symes of Mercyhurst College; and Dr. Joseph Hefner. Thank you to the University of Tennessee, Knoxville and the Hamilton County Medical Examiners Office for granting the authors access to their skeletal collections. We are endlessly grateful for the statistical assistance from Luis Cabo-Perez, and editorial comments from Stephanie Super and Chris Rainwater.

REFERENCES

Bedford, M. E., Russel, K. F., Lovejoy, C. O., Meindl, R. S., Simpson, S. W., & Stuart-Macadam, P. L. (1993). Test of the multifactorial aging method using skeletons with known age-at-death from the Gran collection. *American Journal of Physical Anthropology 91*:287–9.

Benazzi, S., Maestri, C., Parisini, S., Vecchi, F., & Gruppioni, G. (2008). Sex assessment from the acetabular rim by means of image analysis. *Forensic Science International 180*.

Brooks, S. T. (1955). Skeletal age at death. The reliability of cranial and pubic age indicators. *American Journal of Physical Anthropology 13*:567–59.

Brooks, S., & Suchey, J. M. (1990). Skeletal age determination based on the os pubis: a comparison of the Ascádi-Nemeskeri and Suchey-Brooks methods. *Human Evolution 5*(3):227–38.

Buckberry, J. L., & Chamberlain, A. T. (2002). Age estimation from the auricular surface of the ilium: A revised method. *American Journal of Physical Anthropology 119*:231–9.

Daniel, M., Iglic, A., & Kralj-Iglic, V. (2005). The shape of acetabular cartilage optimizes hip contact stress distribution. *Journal of Anatomy 207*:85–91.

Îscan, M. Y., Loth, S. R., & Wright, R. K. (1984). Metamorphosis at the sternal rib end: a new method to estimate age at death in white males. *American Journal of Physical Anthropology 65*(2):147–56.

Îscan, M. Y. (1989). *Age markers in human skeleton.* Springfield, IL: Charles C Thomas.

Konrath, G. A., Hamel, A. J., Olson, S. A., Bay, B., & Sharkey, N. A. (1998). The role of the acetabular labrum and transverse acetabular ligament in load transmission in the hip. *Journal of Bone and Joint Surgery 80*:1781–88.

Krogman, W. M., & Îscan M. Y. (1986). *The human skeleton in forensic medicine* (1st ed.). Springfield, IL; Charles C Thomas.

Lovejoy, C. O., Meindl, R. S., Pryzbeck, T. R., & Mensforth, R. P. (1985). Chronological metamporphosis of the auricular surface of the ilium: A new method for the determination of adult skeletal age at death. *American Journal of Physical Anthropology 68*:15–28.

Lovejoy, C. O., Meindl, R. S., Mensforth, R. P., & Barton, T. J. (1985). Multifactorial age determination of skeletal age at death: A method and blind tests of its accuracy. *American Journal of Physical Anthropology 68*:1–14.

Milz, S., Valassis, G., Büttner, A., Maier, M., Putz, R., James, R. R., & Benjamin, M. (2001).

Fibrocartilage in the transverse ligament of the human acetabulum. *Journal of Anatomy 198:*223–28.

Mulhern, D. M., & Jones, E. B. (2005). Test of revised method of age estimation from the auricular surface of the ilium. *American Journal of Forensic Science 126:*61–65.

Osborne, D. L., Simmons, T. L., & Nawrocki, S. P. (2004). Reconsidering the auricular surface as an indicator of age at death. *Journal of Forensic Sciences 49:*905–11.

Rissech, C., & Malgosa, A. (1997). Sex prediction by discriminate function with central portion measures of innominate bones. *Homo 48*(1):22–32.

Rissech, C., Sañudo, J. R., & Malgosa, A. (2001). The acetabular point: A morphological and ontogenetic study. *Journal of Anatomy 198:*743–48.

Rissech, C., Garcia, M. M., & Malgosa, A. (2003). Sex and age diagnosis by ischium morphometric analysis. *Forensic Science International 135:*188–96.

Rissech, C., & Malgosa, A. (2005). Ilium growth study: Applicability in sex and age diagnosis. *Forensic Science International 147:*165–74.

Rouge-Maillart, C., Telmon, N., Rissech, C., Malgosa, A., & Rouge, D. (2004). The determination of male adult age at death by central and posterior coxal analysis–A preliminary study. *Journal of Forensic Sciences 49*(2).

Rouge-Maillart, C., Jousset, N., Vielle, B., Gaudin, A., & Telmon, N. (2007). Contribution of the study of the acetabulum for the estimation of adult subjects. *Forensic Science International 171:*103–110.

Schmitt, A., Murail, P., Cunha, E., & Rouge, D. (2002). Variability of the pattern of aging on the human skeleton: Evidence from bone indicators and implications on age at death estimation. *Journal of Forensic Sciences 47:*1203–09.

Todd, T. W. (1921). Age changes in the pubic bone: The male white pubis. *Am J Phy Anthropol 3:*285–339.

Chapter 10

ESTIMATION OF AGE FROM FETAL REMAINS

ANGIE K. HUXLEY

INTRODUCTION

As forensic science expands and diversification occurs, forensic specialists need to be apprised of the changes in each of the subspecialties. One may be asked to generally assess for populational affiliation, sex, age, pathologies, anomalies and traumata to assist in positive identification of fetal remains that are submitted to the Medical Examiner's Office. These remains may take a variety of forms from a completely developed fetus to a partial calcined diaphysis for analysis. Forensic fetal remains are those that are encountered within the medicolegal sphere and so rare that senior forensic anthropologists may only see a few cases over the course of several years. Expertise in forensic fetal osteology is typically gained by a medline search or referring to the only book on the topic–Fazekas and Kósa's, *Forensic Fetal Osteology*–which has not been available in print since 1978. For scientists who seek a deeper appreciation of fetal remains, collections exist at the U.S. National Museum of Natural History Smithsonian Institution, and the Albert Szent-Györgyi Medical University, Department of Forensic Pathology in Szeged, Hungary. An extensive background in neonatal, juvenile and adult skeletal anatomy provides the framework for understanding some of the variability that will be encountered case to case.

TABLE 10.1
LUNAR MONTHS TO GESTATIONAL MONTHS CONVERSION

Mois Lunaires (Lunar Months)	*Mois Civils (Civil or Gestational Months)*
4 ¼	3.8
4 ½	4.0
4 ¾	4.3
5	4.5
5 ¼	4.7
5 ½	5.0
5 ¾	5.2
6	5.4
6 ¼	5.6
6 ½	5.8
6 ¾	6.1
7	6.3
7 ¼	6.5
7 ½	6.8
7 ¾	7.0
8	7.2
8 ¼	7.4
8 ½	7.6
8 ¾	7.9
9	8.1
9 ¼	8.3
9 ½	8.5
9 ¾	8.8
10	9

DETERMINATION OF AGE

Determination of fetal age has changed with the advancement of technology. There are two ages that can be determined for the fetus–lunar age and gestational age–depending on the study that one uses for comparison. Olivier and Pineau (1958) were the first to tabulate the difference between the 10 lunar months and the 9 civil or gestational months assigned to the fetus (Table 10.1). Huxley and Angevine (1998) later published these data for the purposes of conversion between lunar age derived from Fazekas and Kósa (1978) and Olivier and Pineau (1958, 1960) to gestational age for medicolegal purposes.

At the turn of the century, aging techniques may have included external measurements on the fetus (e.g., cephalic region, torso and appendages, crown-heel length (CHL) or crown-rump length), the presence or absence of

TABLE 10.2
REGRESSION FORMULAE FOR THE DETERMINATION OF FETAL HEIGHT
IN CM FROM DIAPHYSEAL LENGTH (OLIVIER AND PINEAU 1960)

7.92 (length of humerus) -0.32 ± 1.8 cm (r = 0.9878)
13.8 (length of radius) -2.85 ± 1.82 cm (r = 0.9875)
8.73 (length of ulna) -1.07 ± 1.59 cm (r = 0.9905)
8.29 (length of femur) +4.42 ± 1.82 cm (r = 0.9875)
7.39 (length of tibia) +3.55 ± 1.92 cm (r = 0.9861)
7.85 (length of fibula) +2.78 ± 1.65 (r = 0.9897)

specific external features (i.e., lanugo), ossification centers and combinations thereof. Numerous references by Schultz (1926, 1929), Mall (1906, 1907), Scammons and Calkins (1929), Streeter (1920) and others can be used to assign dates to the fetuses found in the late 1800s and early 1900s. Medical standards for the determination of age have changed since the early 1900's, although under some circumstances these older techniques may be useful. If one finds a partial torso or an appendage—an ear, hand or foot—then these studies may be beneficial. Moreover, there are also new studies available based on aborted fetuses, such as sonographic measurements and post-partum neonates discussed below (Amato et al., 1991; Mercer et al., 1987; Kumar and Kumar, 1993; Goldstein et al., 1988).

In the early 1900s, Balthazard and Dervieux (1921) developed formulae to estimate crown-heel height (and in a separate regression formulae, age) from the humerus, femur, and tibia, but not the radius, ulna, or fibula stating that it was impossible to identify these bones in the fetus. Later, Olivier and Pineau (1958, 1960) clarified that the radius, ulna and fibula could be identified based on morphology, and developed regression formulae for all long bones. They concluded that identification may need to be assessed on partial remains, and that any long bone diaphysis may be useful. There is a linear relationship between diaphyseal length and fetal length for calculation of age; however, each diaphysis grows at a different rate. They note that using a single long bone for calculation of age may be problematic as there is considerable variability in determined age (refer to Table 10.2 for their formulae).

The subsequent determination of fetal age was based on comparison to average fetal length at a given age by means of the regression equation found in Olivier and Pineau (1960): Log Age = 0.01148 height + 0.4258 cm, as well as Log Age = 0.039/weight +0.433gr. Their estimates are based on a diaphyseal shrinkage rate of 2 percent from wet to dry bone. In the 1990s, Huxley and Jimenez (1996) published an article demonstrating that the radial regres-

TABLE 10.3
HASSE'S RULE DEMONSTRATING RELATIONSHIP BETWEEN
AGE AND CROWN-HEEL LENGTH (FAZEKAS AND KOSA, 1978)

1 LM, length of fetus	1.1 = 1 cm
2 LM. length of fetus	2.2 = 4 cm
3 LM, length of fetus	3.3 = 9 cm
4 LM, length of fetus	4.4 = 16 cm
5 LM, length of fetus	5.5 = 25 cm
6 LM, length of fetus	6.5 = 30 cm
7 LM, length of fetus	7.5 = 35 cm
8 LM, length of fetus	8.5 = 40 cm
9 LM, length of fetus	9.5 = 45 cm
10 LM, length of fetus	10.5 = 50 cm

sion formula gives an inaccurate calculation of crown-heel length (stature), and therefore lunar age. Using their radial regression formulae, age calculated from a case fetus was three months greater than that of other diaphyses, and therefore should not be used in medicolegal cases.

Fazekas and Kósa (1978) collected fetal remains for legal investigation from Szeged and the surrounding countryside after the end of WW II to present. These materials are thought to represent illegally aborted fetuses as abortion was outlawed at that time, and maternal/fetal demise was reported to the forensic pathologist. A total of 138 fetal skeletons of Eastern European descent composed of 71 males and 67 females between the ages of three lunar months and full-term newborns were collected, autopsied, macerated, measured and housed in the Department of Forensic Medicine. The morphometric data for each fetus are listed by order of cases (e.g, order of cases "128" in table 26 is the same fetus as "128" in table 43) throughout the book. Autopsy records are available for maternal health and circumstances of delivery. Lunar age, however, is not always available for all of the fetuses, which is one of the limitations of this collection. One would have to pull all of the autopsy records to record which of the fetuses are of known lunar age, and which fetuses had lunar age calculated through Haase's rule (Table 10.3). Moreover, this collection dates prior to the 1960s and 1970s, which is another limitation. The environmental and social constraints placed upon this population at the end of WW II to present may have impacted fetal growth and development. Modern methods for calculation of lunar age were not well established.

More recent studies in age estimation from this collection arise from Kósa and colleagues, who are attempting to estimate age from individual bones. For instance Castellana and Kósa (1999, 2001) have published 3 studies in the last 10 years. They assessed individual ossification centers for the cervical spine and found that the dens of the axis may be useful to assess fetal maturity. This study was later expanded to include the description to identify and classify cervical, thoracic and lumbar vertebral ossification centers of 107 fetuses with subsequent regression formulae for the determination of fetal age (Kósa and Castellana, 2005).

Currently, a number of modalities may be utilized depending on the nature of the forensic remains. If the remains are fresh with fully intact diaphyseal length, it may be possible to compare fetal diaphyseal measurements obtained on healthy, living, modern fetuses *in utero* from ultrasound. Ultrasonography is conducted on a fetus in utero for the purposes of obtaining measurements, which provide the most accurate estimation of gestational age (Jones et al., 1991; Wagner and Calhoun, 1998; Degani, 2001). These standards were developed and used for gestational age calculation; any variation in growth and development may possibly represent pathological or anomalous states (Chitty and Pandya, 1997; Sen, 2001; Snijders, 2001). Three measurements were found to be beneficial–biparietal diameter (BPD), abdominal circumference (AC) and femoral length (FL). Two of these measurements (BPD, AC) are not readily available in mummified, decomposed or osseous forensic fetal cases. Femoral length (FL) must be converted from wet, living bone length to dry length, which will create significant shrinkage to the diaphysis (Huxley, 1998a). The wet bone measurements conducted by Petersohn and Köhler (1965) were taken from fetuses in excellent condition and does not represent measurements taken from forensic cases or pathological specimens that may have been altered from freezing, cooling or placement in formalin. Comparison of sonographic data derived from living fetuses to dry diaphyseal length from forensic cases is subject to error without correction between the estimation techniques.

Measurements on sonographic fetal portions (e.g., the ear, hand, foot) may be used to determine gestational age. In some publications, measurements were obtained by ultrasound *in utero;* in others taken from aborted or premature fetuses. Such studies are valuable if there is no shrinkage in the fetal remains, and direct comparisons can be made to the data from the medical literature. In a study by Huxley (1998b), foot length from a known aborted fetus in a criminal case was used to determine age from four different studies (Amato et al., 1991; Mercer et al., 1987; Kumar and Kumar, 1993; Goldstein et al., 1988) in comparison to age derived from Fazekas and Kósa's (1978) regression formulae. Each of these research groups had a different sample size, material modality and country of origination, yet all were accurate within 3 weeks of known age (Huxley, 1998b). This study suggests that other appendages (e.g., ear, hand or foot) may be beneficial.

Another type of methodology includes radiographic measurements from intact spontaneous or therapeutically aborted and stillborn fetuses. For example, Warren (1999) took radiographs of all long bones from 252 aborted and stillborn fetuses of European descent of known crown-heel length (CHL), then developed regression formulae for estimating CHL from radiographic measurements from the six long bones (R2 = 0.8375, p < 0.05). The article states that "one measurable long bone diaphysis" must be present, so the sample size for each diaphyseal regression formulae is unknown. He was attempting to develop a normative sample for gestational age determination from a U.S. population.

Moreover, Adalian et al. (2001) used femoral ultrasound measurements from fetuses to validate postmortem radiographic measurements that included the epiphysis on intact fetuses. In a later study, these authors clarified the difference between radiographic and anatomical measurements by dissecting 30 pairs of fetal femora. The difference between the two modalities was 4.03 percent (p < 0.001). They increased the sample size to 60 femora, then analyzed the data with a bootstrap technique and developed a regression formula with an r2 of 99 percent (SE 0.252 mm, CI confidence interval with limits of -0.35 and 0.657 mm). This difference did not entail any significant differences (p = 0.498), and therefore, they concluded that with the proposed correction, radiographic measurements could easily be used by forensic specialists to establish new growth standards to fit their population of interest (Piercecchi et al., 2002).

When analyzing postmortem radiographic images, the following items need to be considered: the specimens need to be placed in an anteroposterior (AP) or posteroanterior (PA) position; placed as close to the film plate as possible to avoid parallax errors or projection cone artifacts; the calcified ends of the diaphyses need to be clarified; and an absolute scale needs to be placed directly on the film for measurement.

To review, several modalities have been used to determine fetal age. The use of these modalities are dependent upon the nature of the remains—intact, partially macerated, dried, carbonized, calcined—and the type of analysis available to the researcher. For instance, if a calcined fetus was found in a crematorium during a forensic investigation, then Huxley's work with Petersohn and Köhler's data would be the most appropriate. Or, if a partially macerated fetus was found in a dumpster then one may consider either radiographic imaging if the fetus needed to remain intact for comparison of dry bone length with Fazekas and Kósa's collection and/or measurement with comparison to external morphometrics (i.e., the ear, hand or foot). It is important to understand that analysis of healthy therapeutically aborted fetuses would provide the best standard for analysis with intact fetuses, as spontaneously aborted or stillborn fetuses may have undiagnosed pathological conditions that may not be apparent prior to use in this study. Moreover, even a chromosomal analysis of the remains will not exclude other variables that affect fetal growth and development, such as TORCES (Toxoplasmosis, Other (varicella, mumps, parvovirus, HIV), Rubella, Cytomegalovirus, Syphilis) and other conditions (Chalmers et al., 1989; Wright et al., 1996; Barr, 1997; Johnson, 2004).

DETERMINATION OF AGE FROM FETAL REMAINS WITH PERI- AND POSTMORTEM ARTIFACT

While there are no published case reports on peri- and post-mortem damage caused by natural flora and fauna, there are numerous studies on the effects of heat on the human fetus. In the 1960s, Petersohn and Köhler assessed the degree of shrinkage from fresh and dry, carbonized and calcined fetuses. Using these data, studies were undertaken to facilitate age calculation by systematically re-evaluating diaphyseal shrinkage and determine shrinkage rates from wet to dry, carbonized and calcined states. Average shrinkage for all long bones with standard deviation, minimum and maximum values was calculated for each diaphysis and then for all diaphyses between 4–10 lunar months (LM) and for newborns (Table 10.4). These findings suggest that percent shrinkage due to drying, carbonization and calcination is greatest in the earliest age groups, decreasing substantially with advancing age. The rates of shrinkage, however, vary by the burning process utilized and age group studied. These general findings are similar to those of Petersohn and Köhler; yet specific values for percent shrinkage vary greatly from values cited in this analysis. These data provide a means to assess the degree of shrinkage that occurs for each diaphysis for each given age group. As the rate of diaphyseal shrinkage decreased with age, age estimation will be more accurate the later states of gestation (Huxley and Kósa, 1999).

TABLE 10.4
THESE PERCENTAGES REFLECT SHRINKAGE FROM WET TO DRY,
CARBONIZED AND CALCINED STATES USING AN AVERAGE OF
ALL LONG BONES (HUXLEY, 1998A; HUXLEY AND KOSA, 1999)

	Dry Diaphyses	*Carbonized Diaphyses*	*Calcined Diaphyses*
4 LM	10.09% ± 2.67%	32.50% ± 12.12%	40.11% ± 17.51%
5 LM	5.74% ± 0.84%	14.01% ± 4.44%	18.29% ± 4.42%
6 LM	3.48% ± 0.49%	6.78% ± 1.06%	9.84% ± 1.27%
7 LM	2.32% ± 0.16%	4.18% ± 0.31%	9.82% ± 0.51%
8 LM	2.18% ± 0.51%	3.47% ± 0.42%	9.42% ± 0.72%
9 LM	1.76% ± 0.14%	3.05% ± 0.18%	9.45% ± 0.33%
10 LM	1.90% ± 0.59%	2.46% ± 0.67%	8.94% ± 0.37%
Newborns	1.28% ± 0.55%	2.16% ± 0.29%	8.96% ± 0.49%

ERRORS ON AGE ESTIMATION USING
FORENSIC FETAL COLLECTIONS

With limited references available, the field of forensic fetal osteology has much potential for study and growth. There are two commonly known fetal collections–the fetal collection at the National Museum of Natural History (NMNH), Smithsonian Institution in Washington D.C., U.S.A., and the Hungarian Fetal Collection in Szeged, Hungary. These collections have a number of differences in the composition, and acquisition process that provided inherent bias for subsequent study. As discussed below, these two collections represent the *only* available skeletal fetal collections in the world.

The fetal collections at the NMNH are antiquated, dating between the late 1800s and early 1900s. In all cases, these fetuses were collected primarily by physicians and researchers at Armed Forces Institute of Pathology (AFIP), John Hopkins, The University of Maryland Medical Center, Howard University Medical School and District of Columbia (D.C.) County Morgue without written consent of the patient, in standard methods of acquisition for the time. The fetal remains are thought to come from lower socioeconomic groups in Baltimore, Maryland and Washington, D.C. areas. Dr. Aleš Hrdlička then curated the fetuses into the Smithsonian fetal collection between 1903 and 1917 (Gindhart, 1989). This collection is composed of a total of 271 fetuses, with 120 white and 151 black, mixed as "mulatto," "quadroon" or "octoroon" fetuses. This collection can be further subdivided into 119 males and 94 females between three lunar months and neonates and newborns. Pertinent acquisition information was placed in a card catalog, which may have included ancestry, phenotypic sex, lunar age and a few external measurements. Age assessments were made by F. P. Mall, J. H. Smith, D. S. Lamb, E. L. Morgan, G. B. Poole, J. F. McKaig, S. R. Karpele, T. C. Smith, T. F. Lane, W. R. Buchanon, and others. Maternal medical history was unknown by comparison to today's health care standards, and certainly fetal care was limited. Presumably this collection mostly represents fetuses from spontaneous abortions, and may be biased by anomalous or pathological materials that have inherent inaccuracies in gestational age estimation (Sherwood et al., 2000; Sims and Collins, 2001). The political and socioeconomic environment of the time suggests that black fetuses were under different environmental constraints than white fetuses *in utero* and postpartum (Almond, 2002, 2003). Individuals of black and admixed ancestry may have had less opportunity for health care creating higher rates of maternal and fetal morbidity and mortality (Shearer, 1989).

As mentioned above, part of the inherent bias in the collection is the possibility of inaccuracy of assigned fetal age at the time of acquisition. In a study by Huxley (2005), a total of 78 fetuses from the National Museum of Natural History (N.M.N.H) were used to compare age assigned from the card catalog to that obtained from diaphyseal length using Fazekas and Kósa (1978) to assess discrepancies between lunar age assignments. A total of 38 fetuses were taken based on ethnic affiliation, sex and age so that cell composition is more nearly equal for both blacks and whites across all lunar age groups. This sample is composed of 8 white males, 1 white female, 13 black males, 13 black females and 3 "mulatto" males.

Age-discrepancy was calculated by comparing age listed on the card catalog and age calculated from comparison for Fazekas and Kósa's fetal collection. These calculations revealed that 20 (52.63%) showed no difference in age; 11 (28.95%) had a one-month difference; 6 (15.79%) had a two-month discrepancy and 1 (2.63%) had a five-month divergence. The sum total of the discrepancy rate is 18 (47.37%) of the studied fetuses. The average difference between lunar age from diaphyseal length and lunar age from external morphology is 0.74 + 1.03 months, reflecting a nearly three-week difference between the two ages. When these data were sorted by pathologists to assess for inter-observer error, F.P. Mall had a discrepancy in 13 out of 25 cases. Age estimation from seven fetuses diverged by one month and six fetuses by two months. When these data are then grouped by ethnic affiliation, there were 2 white, 15 black, and 1 mulatto fetus. When examined by sex, 12 of these were male and 6 were female. Thus, black males are misclassified more than any other grouping in this sample.

Moreover, age is also estimated for many of the fetuses representing the Hungarian collection. As mentioned previously, these remains were partially collected for legal investigation from areas around Szeged after the end of WWII to the present. The materials are composed of illegally aborted fetuses, spontaneously aborted fetuses, and/or maternal and fetal demise. Some of the autopsy records are available to researchers for maternal health, the circumstances of delivery and fetal/newborn morphometric data; however, lunar age may not always be available on all fetuses. Indeed, one would have to pull all of the autopsy records to document which of the fetuses are of known lunar age, and which of the fetuses had lunar age calculated through Haase's rule.

When comparing the two collections, the NMNH collection may be limited by a part of the collection having inaccurate lunar age assessments. Yet, the NMNH collection represents the only easily accessible collection in the U.S, compared to the Hungarian collection which is accessible at the Department of Anatomy and Pathology at the Albert Szent-Györgyi Medical University in Szeged, Hungary. The two collections are not completely comparable since the NMNH fetuses are of both black and white descent, and the Hungarian fetal collection is of Eastern European descent. If one were to use the NMNH collection, it is necessary for lunar age to be independently confirmed and discrepancies assessed before testing other variables, such as differences in growth and development due to ethnicity and sex.

Thus, the NMNH fetal skeletal collection is the only one of known ethnicity, known sex, and in over half of the materials tested known and confirmed lunar age. While this collection may have limitations, given this information, one can calculate lunar age and compare it to that given in the card catalog. Finally, these two collections stored at NMNH and Szeged, Hungary allow for a rare opportunity to study fetal materials that are not readily available elsewhere. Little research has been done on either collection, especially the pathological materials in the NMNH. Because fetal materials are not easily obtainable and so few collections are available, these materials provide a wealth of data for comparative research purposes.

DISCUSSION

The type of forensic fetal case that is submitted to the investigator will dictate the type of approach taken for gestational age estimation. If the remains are ossified, then perhaps those standards derived from museum collections would be most appropriate (Fazekas and Kósa, 1978; Huxley, 1998a; Petersohn and Köhler, 1965). Whereas, if the remains are intact with minimal shrinkage or preservation artifact, then perhaps radiological studies would be better for comparison (Adalian et al., 2001; Warren, 1999). While there are inherent limitations involved in using museum collections or even autopsy specimens (i.e., materials may be pathological or anomalous), the fact that there are no other collections easily available necessitates their usage. Currently there is no "one" perfect dataset that utilizes healthy therapeutically aborted fetal remains for all of the contexts—healthy intact, decomposed, mummified, osseous, burnt and calcined—that one may access to determine gestational age. Such data may be useful to develop fetal profiles for forensic cases and thus determine fetal viability at the time of maternal and/or fetal demise.

Forensic anthropologists rarely come across forensic fetal remains, yet these remains present a challenge with so little access and availability for study and comparison. When considering the parameters of our field, determination of population affiliation and sex are difficult (nearly impossible) from bone and teeth, while determination of age may be possible. As stated previously, these remains may take a variety of forms from a completely formed fetus to a partial calcined diaphysis for analysis. A variety of techniques are available for this assessment depending upon the overall condition of the remains. If one uses traditional forensic anthropological sources, then age is calculated in lunar months; if one uses other sources—embryological and sonographic—then age is reported as gestational weeks. For comparison between ages derived from these various studies, especially in cases involving age assessments of incomplete fetal remains that may be partially damaged by taphonomic factors, it is necessary to convert between lunar age and gestational age. This information is useful for developing a forensic profile at any gestational age as well as providing a means to assess the probability of viability at the time of death.

ACKNOWLEDGMENTS

Much gratitude is given to Ferenc Kósa, M.D., Ph.D. for discussions of the Hungarian fetal collection. Travel to Szeged, Hungary for direct collaborations with Dr. Ferenc Kósa was made possible through a Lucas Research Grant awarded to AKH by the Forensic Science Foundation. Great appreciation is given to David Hunt, Ph.D., Curator of NMNH for access to the fetal skeletal remains and photocopies of card catalog data. Funding for travel to the Smithsonian was awarded to AKH by the Department of Anthropology and the Graduate College at The University of Arizona. Sincerest thanks are given to J. B. Angevine, Ph.D., Professor Emeritus, Department of Cell Biology and Anatomy, Arizona Health Sciences Center, The University of Arizona for editorial assistance over the years. This chapter is dedicated to W. H. Birkby, Ph.D., D-A.B.F.A., Professor Emeritus, Forensic Science Center, Pima County Arizona for forensic training and encouragement at the Human Identification Laboratory. Dr. Birkby formally retired December 11, 2009 after spending 44 years practicing forensic osteology.

REFERENCES

Adalian, P., Piercecchi-Marti, M. D., Bourliere-Najean, B., Panuel, M., Fredouille, C., Dutour, O., & Leonetti, G. (2001). Postmortem assessment of fetal diaphyseal femoral length: Validation of a radiographic methodology. *Journal of Forensic Sciences 46*(2):215–219.

Almond, D. V. (2002). Cohort differences in health: A duration analysis using the National Longitudinal Mortality Study. Available at: http://www.src.uchicago.edu/prc/pdfs/ almond02.pdf. Accessed October 1, 2004.

Almond, D. V. (2003). Is the 1918 influenza pandemic over? Long-term effects of *in utero* influenza exposure in the post-1940 U.S. population. Available at: http://www.nber.org ~almond/jmp2.pdf. Accessed October 1, 2004.

Amato, M., Huppi, P., & Claus, R. (1991). Rapid biometric assessment of gestational age in very low birth weight infants. *Journal of Perinatal Medicine 19*:367–371.

Balthazard, T., & Dervieux. (1921). Etudes anthropologiques sur le foetus humain. *Annals De Médicine Légale* 37–42.

Barr, M. (1997). Growth as a manifestation of teratogenesis: lessons from human fetal pathology. *Reproductive Toxicology 11*(4):583–587.

Castellana, C., & Kósa, F. (1999). Morphology of the cervical vertebrae in the fetal-neonatal human skeleton. *Journal of Anatomy 194* (Pt 1):147–152.

Castellana, C., & Kósa, F. (2001). Estimation of fetal age from dimensions of atlas and axis ossification centers. *Forensic Science International 1*:117(1-2):31–43.

Chalmers, I., Enkin, M., & Keirse, M. J. C. (1989). *Effective care in pregnancy and childbirth.* Oxford, England: Oxford University Press.

Chitty, L. S., & Pandya, P. P. (1997). Ultrasound screening for fetal abnormalities in the first trimester. *Prenatal Diagnosis 17*(13):1269–81.

Degani, S. (2001). Fetal biometry: Clinical, pathological, and technical considerations. *Obstetric Gynecology Survey. 56*(3):159–67.

Fazekas, I. G., & Kósa, F. (1978). *Forensic fetal osteology.* Budapest, Hungary: Akademiai Kiado.

Gindhart, P. S. (1989). An early twentieth-century skeleton collection. *Journal Forensic Sciences 34*(4):887–893.

Goldstein, I., Reece, E., & Hobbins, J. (1988). Sonographic appearance of the fetal heel ossification centers and foot length measurements provide independent markers for gestational age estimation. *American Journal of Obstetrics and Gynecology 159*:923–926.

Huxley, A. K., & Jimenez, S. B. (1996). Technical note: Error in Olivier and Pineau's regression formulae for calculation of stature and lunar age from radial diaphyseal length in forensic fetal remains. *American Journal of Physical Anthropology 100*(3):435–7.

Huxley, A. K. (1998a). Analysis of shrinkage in human fetal diaphyseal lengths from fresh to dry bone using Petersohn and Köhler's data. *Journal of Forensic Sciences 43*(2):423–426.

Huxley, A. K. (1998b). Comparability of gestational age values derived from diaphyseal length and foot length from known forensic foetal remains. *Medicine, Science and the Law 38*(1):42–51.

Huxley, A. K., & Angevine, J. B. (1998). Determination of gestational age from lunar age assessments in human fetal remains. *Journal Forensic Sciences 43*(6):1254.

Huxley, A. K., & Kósa, F. (1999). Calculation of percent shrinkage in human fetal diaphyseal lengths from fresh bone to carbonized and calcined bone using Petersohn and Köhler's data. *Journal Forensic Sciences 44*(3):577–583.

Huxley, A. K. (2005). Gestational age discrepancies due to acquisition artifact in the forensic fetal osteology collection at the National Museum of Natural History, Smithsonian Institution, USA. *American Journal of Forensic Medicine and Pathology 26*(3):216–20.

Johnson, K. E. Overview of TORCH infections. [UpToDate website]. 2004. Available at: http://www.utdol.com/application/topic.asp?file=neonatol/11894&type=A&selectedTitle =1~8. Accessed October 8, 2004.

Jones, T. B., Wolfe, H. M., & Zador, I. E. (1991). Biparietal diameter and femur length discrepancies: Are maternal characteristics important? *Ultrasound in Obstetrics and Gynecology 1*(6):405–9.

Kósa, F., & Castellana, C. (2005). New forensic anthropological approachment for the age determination of human fetal skeletons on the base of morphology of vertebral column. *Forensic Science International 147* Suppl:S69–74.

Kumar, G. P., & Kumar, U. K. (1993). Estimation of gestational age from hand and foot length. *Medicine, Science and the Law 33*:48–50.

Mall, F. P. (1906). On ossification centers in human embryos less than one hundred days old. *American Journal of Anatomy V*(32):434–458.

Mall, F. P. (1907). On measuring human embryos. *Anatomical Record 1*:129–140.

Mercer, B., Sklar, S., Shariatmadar, A., Gillieson, M., & D'Alton, M. (1987). Fetal foot length as a predictor of gestational age. *American Journal of Obstetrics and Gynecology 156*:350–355.

Olivier, G., & Pineau, H. (1958). Determination de l'age du foetus et de l'embryon. *Archives D'Anatomie (La Semaine des Hospitaux) 6*:21.

Olivier, G., & Pineau, H. (1960). Nouvelle détermination de la taille foetale d'après les longeuers diaphysaires des os longs. *Annales de Medicine Legale 40:*141.

Petersohn, F., & Köhler, J. (1965). Die bedeutung der veränderungen an fetalen röhrenknochen nach trocknung und hitzeeinwirkung für die forensische begutachtung der fruchtsgrösse. *Archiv fur Kriminologie 134:*143.

Piercecchi-Marti, M. D., Adalian, P., Bourliere-Najean, B., Gouvernet, J., Mczel, M., Dutour, O., & Leonetti, G. (2002). Validation of a radiographic method to establish new fetal growth standards: Radio-anatomical correlation. *Journal of Forensic Sciences 47*(2):328–331.

Scammons, R. E., & Calkins, L. A. (1929). *The development and growth of the external dimensions of the human body in the fetal period.* Minneapolis, MN: The University of Minnesota Press.

Schultz, A. H. (1929). The techniques of measuring the outer body of human fetuses and of primates in general. Publ Carnegie Instit, Washington No. 394, *Contributions in Embryology 117:*213–257.

Schultz, A. H. (1926). Fetal growth in man and other primates. *Quarterly Review of Biology 1:*465–521.

Sen, C. (2001). The use of first trimester ultrasound in routine practice. *Journal of Perinatal Medicine 29*(3):212–21.

Shearer, M. H. (1989). Maternity patients' movements in the United States 1820–1985. In I. Chalmers & M. Enkin (Eds.), *Effective care in pregnancy and childbirth.* Oxford England, Oxford University Press.

Sherwood, R. J., Meindl, R. S., Robinson, H. B., & May, R. L. (2000). Fetal age: methods of estimation and effects of pathology. *American Journal of Physical Anthropology 113*(3):305–315.

Sims, M. A., & Collins, K. A. (2001). Fetal death. A 10-year retrospective study. *American Journal of Forensic Medicine and Pathology 22*(3):261–265.

Snijders, R. (2001). First-trimester ultrasound. *Clinics in Perinatology 28*(2):333–52.

Streeter, G. L. (1920). Weight, sitting height, head size, foot length, and menstrual age of the human embryo. Publ Carnegie Instit, Washington, No. 274, *Contributions in Embryology 55:*143–170.

Wagner, R. K., & Calhoun, B. C. (1998). The routine obstetric ultrasound examination. *Obstetrics and Gynecology Clinics of North America 25*(3):451–63.

Warren, M. (1999). Radiographic determination of developmental age in fetuses and stillborns. *Journal of Forensic Sciences 44*(4):708–712.

Wright, C., Hinchliffe, S. A., & Taylor, C. (1996). Fetal pathology in intrauterine death due to parvovirus B19 infections. *British Journal of Obstetrics and Gynaecology 103*(2):133–136.

Chapter 11

REVISITING McKERN AND STEWART (1957): A COMPARISON OF PUBIC SYMPHYSIS METHODS AT THE JPAC-CIL

CARRIE A. BROWN

INTRODUCTION

Dirkmaat and colleagues (2008) suggested that forensic anthropology is developing in new directions and becoming increasingly interdisciplinary, incorporating, amongst other areas, taphonomy and archaeology. However, the more "traditional" pursuits of forensic anthropologists, such as the construction of the biological profile, continue to provide ample research opportunities. Age estimation falls into this second category and is an important component not only of the biological profile in forensic applications, but of paleodemographic and bioarchaeological studies as well. The persistent quest for accurate and precise skeletal age estimation methods is essential to many subfields of physical anthropology.

This chapter will compare pubic symphyseal methods employed to estimate age at death from the adult skeleton by using over three decades of data from the Joint POW/MIA Accounting Command Central Identification Laboratory's (JPAC-CIL) archives of identified individuals. These methods include: Todd, McKern-Stewart, and Suchey-Brooks. The goal of this chapter is to examine the age estimates produced by these methods in terms of error and discuss their applicability to casework at the JPAC-CIL specifically, and expand the discussion to all osteolgical uses within the field of physical anthropology.

THE LEGACY OF McKERN AND STEWART (1957)

The current day military skeletal identification laboratory–the JPAC-CIL–rests on a strong legacy of anthropological research, including, notably, the work of Thomas W. McKern and T. Dale Stewart in the identification of a large number of Korean War dead. "Operation Glory" involved the repatriation and identification of remains of American soldiers from North Korea in 1954 and provided an unprecedented opportunity to further the understanding of skeletal age indicators on a large sample of identified males (McKern and Stewart, 1957). The report that was produced as a result of this operation–McKern and Stewart's *Skeletal Age Changes in Young American Males* (1957)–was the first comprehensive study of age-related skeletal changes that was based on a modern skeletal series and not an anatomical collection (Bass, 2005). The sample size for this study was 450 individuals, including individuals who were prisoners of war (POW) and 75 individuals who were never identified.

The research conducted by McKern and Stewart (1957:2) had the dual goals of better understanding the range of human variation in aging and providing better training for anthropologists undertaking age estimation from the human skeleton. Additionally, the study provides useful historical perspectives on skeletal age estimation, standardization for certain skeletal elements, and even new methods, including the component scoring system for the pubic symphysis. McKern and Stewart (1957) describe the overall pattern of skeletal maturation in the final chapter of their report, and they also briefly enumerate the skeletal elements that are the best indicators of age. Of these, the innominates (*os coxae*) were identified as the most "critical area" for age estimation (McKern and Stewart 1957:171).

Age estimation methods outlined in McKern and Stewart (1957) are still used at the JPAC-CIL. These methods include: stages of epiphyseal fusion of the long bones, medial clavicle, vertebrae, iliac crest, and sacrum, the component system for the pubic symphysis, cranial suture closure, and third molar eruption. The continued use of these methods is attributable to the similarity in composition of the McKern-Stewart sample and the JPAC-CIL sample: largely young, white males of military age. Many of these skeletal indicators are employed successfully (i.e., with low error) at the JPAC-CIL (Brown, 2009), as will be demonstrated below with the pubic symphysis.

PUBIC SYMPHYSIS AGE ESTIMATION

The pubic symphysis is now recognized as the most frequently used (Aykroyd et al., 1999) and most reliable (Meindl and Lovejoy, 1989) adult age estimation technique. The first formal method using the pubic symphysis as an indicator of age was developed by T. Wingate Todd and his colleagues at Case Western Reserve University in the 1920s (Todd, 1920, 1921). Subsequent work served to further refine the ten-phase method developed by Todd. For example, Brooks (1955) found that the Todd pubic symphysis system overaged both males and females and therefore proposed modifications to the phase age intervals.

Contemporary to the work by Brooks, McKern and Stewart developed a pubic symphysis age estimation method for males based on features originally described by Todd: dorsal plateau, ventral rampart, and symphyseal rim. These three components were found to best represent the variability seen in age-related changes of the pubic symphysis. The components are scored separately (from zero to five) to arrive at a composite score and final mean age estimate. Casts of the different component scores are available for comparison and the statistics for composite scores are available in McKern and Stewart (1957). Gilbert and McKern (1973) also developed a component system for females. Their work demonstrated that females undergo somewhat different age-related changes of the pubic symphyseal face when compared to males. However, Suchey (1979) found the method difficult to apply and not at all accurate.

Potential problems with both the Todd and McKern-Stewart methods (i.e., age intervals per phase, sample biases) led to the continued investigation of age estimation based on the pubic symphysis by Suchey and colleagues. A large sample of male pubic bones was analyzed and the Todd ten-phase system was modified to a six-phase system by combining several of the original phases (Katz and Suchey, 1986). Casts for each of the six phases for males were then made available, followed shortly after by casts and phases for females. In 1990, Brooks and Suchey published unisex descriptions that focused primarily on major age-related changes for each of the six phases. The Suchey-Brooks system describes the average expression of age-related changes for each of the six phases, as opposed to the analysis of several different features by assigning numerical scores.

Two separate lineages of pubic symphysis age estimation diverged from the Todd method: techniques based on the McKern-Stewart component system and techniques that led to the development of the Suchey-Brooks phase system. Comments concerning the McKern-Stewart sample include its basis on an entirely male and limited age range sample, as well as a lack of testing on another population (Meindl et al., 1985). And while Suchey-Brooks is recognized as the most widely used pubic symphysis age estimation method, it too has come under criticism, mainly for the large age intervals associated with each of the six phases (e.g., Saunders et al., 1992).

MATERIALS AND METHODS

Pubic symphysis age estimation was analyzed by comparing the known age at death to the mean or median age per component score or phase for individuals identified at the JPAC-CIL between 1972 and 31 July 2008. The JPAC-CIL keeps an archive of all identified individuals, and each case file includes military records, CIL-produced reports, analytical notes, and additional identification media. Of individuals identified, 979 files had adequate information on both known age at death and methods used by CIL analysts to estimate age at death. Individual age estimation methods were then analyzed from the sample of 979 individuals. It is important to note that very few case reports written before 1988 were used in this study because most did not contain adequate information on age estimation (i.e., specific methods were not cited). Additionally, use of the Suchey-Brooks method was inherently limited to case reports written after 1986 since the method was not published before this year.

The Todd phase system was used for 10 individuals, the McKern-Stewart component system for the pubic symphysis was used for 79 individuals, and the Suchey-Brooks phase system was used for 93 individuals. Descriptive statistics for the entire sample and each pubic symphysis method are given in Table 11.1. The mean ages at death for all three of the method samples did not differ significantly from the total known age at death sample of 979 individuals or from one another (ANOVA with Bonferroni correction, $p < 0.05$). The samples for each method are not necessarily mutually exclusive, since it is possible that multiple methods could have been used to estimate the age at death of a single individual, even though this usage is not supported by current JPAC-CIL standard operating procedures (SOPs).[1] A chi-square (χ^2) test

---

1. SOP 3.4 of the JPAC-CIL Laboratory Manual stipulates the use of the McKern-Stewart system for those males believed to have died before 1960 and the use of the Suchey-Brooks system for all males believed to have died after 1960 as well as all females regardless of time period of death (JPAC-CIL, 2008); Todd is not a SOP-approved age estimation method. The applicability of methods to certain groups is based on an assumption of secular change. The current laboratory manual was instituted as part of the move towards ASCLD/LAB accreditation; these SOPs have only been applicable to CIL casework since 2003.

TABLE 11.1
DESCRIPTIVE STATISTICS FOR THE AGE DISTRIBUTIONS OF
THE TOTAL SAMPLE AND EACH PUBIC SYMPHYSIS METHOD

Method	N	Mean	Median	Min	Max	Range	Standard Deviation	Variance
All	979	27.24	26	17	59	42	6.59	43.39
Todd	10	31.10	31	24	41	17	6.51	42.32
McKern-Stewart	79	26.34	25	18	53	35	5.81	33.79
Suchey-Brooks	93	29.14	27	19	54	35	7.48	56.21

of significance was conducted in order to determine if a relationship existed between the method employed (McKern-Stewart or Suchey-Brooks) and associated conflict (World War I, World War II, Korea, Southeast Asia).

Analyses began with the calculation of descriptive statistics of known age at death distributions and correct and incorrect classifications for each method. Descriptive statistics were calculated using Microsoft Excel. Correct and incorrect classification involved a tally of the number of individuals who were correctly assigned to an age group based on their known age at death. A percentage was then developed by dividing the number of individuals correctly (or incorrectly) classified by the total sample size for that method. This portion of data analysis included multiple phase designations (e.g., the CIL analyst placed the individual in phases two and three of the Suchey-Brooks method). These calculations serve as a general measure of method performance.

Further analyses eliminated multiple phase designations, thereby slightly reducing the sample size for each method. This step was necessary because it was not possible to compare the estimated mean age at death to the known age at death for the McKern-Stewart or Suchey-Brooks samples because statistics for multiple categories are not included in the original publications. The midpoint of the assigned phase, including multiple phases, was used for the Todd method, but the overall sample size was so small for this method that little comparable information was gleaned. Error was mathematically calculated in two ways: bias, the directionality of error indicated by positive or negative values, positive meaning a tendency to overage, negative a tendency to underage, and inaccuracy, the average error given in years. The equations are as follows:

$$\text{Bias} = \Sigma \, (\text{estimated age-actual age})/N$$
$$\text{Inaccuracy} = \Sigma |\text{estimated age-actual age}|/N$$

Additionally, Pearson's r and r² were computed in order to determine the strength of the relationship between known (X) and estimated (Y) age at death for each method and the amount of variation in estimated age that was due to known age. The linear relationship was tested statistically with ANOVA. Results for all three methods are given first, followed by breakdowns of component scores or phases per method, and, finally, a detailed comparison of the Suchey-Brooks and McKern-Stewart methods. Again, the Todd method was eliminated from this comparison because of the overall small sample size.

RESULTS

Descriptive statistics for each pubic symphysis method are given in Table 11.1 (see Materials and Methods, above). The Todd method has the highest mean age at death but also the smallest range. The McKern-Stewart sample has the youngest ages for all values. The Suchey-Brooks sample is similar in composition to the McKern-Stewart sample, but is made up of more individuals between the ages of 30 and 40. The sample size for the Todd method is much smaller than either the McKern-Stewart or Suchey-Brooks samples and will be compared only briefly.

The Suchey-Brooks method has the highest correct classification of all three pubic symphysis methods (Table 11.2). The Todd method fares the poorest of the three, with the lowest correct classification at 70.0 percent. However, the Todd method has the lowest error (bias, inaccuracy) as seen in Table 11.3. This method has a small tendency to overage and an average error of 1.80 years. The McKern-Stewart method generally underages, with an average error of 2.68 years, while Suchey-Brooks overages, with an average error of 3.72 years.

TABLE 11.2
CORRECT AND INCORRECT CLASSIFICATIONS
FOR EACH PUBIC SYMPHYSIS METHOD

Method	*N*	*# Correct*	*% Correct*	*# Incorrect*	*% Incorrect*
Todd	10	7	70.0	3	30.0
McKern-Stewart	79	65	82.3	14	17.7
Suchey-Brooks	93	91	97.9	2	2.2

TABLE 11.3
ERROR FOR EACH PUBIC SYMPHYSIS METHOD

Method	N	Bias (Σ)	Inaccuracy (Σ)
Todd	10	0.10	1.80
McKern-Stewart	73	-1.07	2.68
Suchey-Brooks	86	0.76	3.72

TABLE 11.4
PEARSON'S R AND R² FOR EACH PUBIC SYMPHYSIS METHOD

Method	N	r	r²	Standard Error (in years)	P-value (ANOVA)
Todd	10	0.95	0.90	2.38	0.000
McKern-Stewart	73	0.79	0.63	3.04	0.000
Suchey-Brooks	86	0.80	0.63	4.55	0.000

All three pubic symphysis methods employed at the JPAC-CIL have statistically significant linear relationships between known and estimated age at death (Table 11.4). The Todd method has the highest correlation between known and estimated age at death as well as the lowest standard error. The McKern-Stewart and Suchey-Brooks methods have comparable r and r² values, while Suchey-Brooks has a higher standard error.

Because the Todd method was only used for ten individuals over a 36-year time span, results for this method will not be compared to the McKern-Stewart or Suchey-Brooks methods. It is important to point out that of the ten individuals aged with this method, half of them were assigned to multiple phases, and those individuals that were incorrectly classified were never misclassified by more than four years (Brown, 2009). The highest error values for individuals aged with the Todd method were found for individuals incorrectly classified (see Appendix A, Table A.1).

The McKern-Stewart method has an overall correct classification rate of 82.3 percent. Figure 11.1 displays the distribution of known ages for individuals aged with this method superimposed over the age intervals per composite score group as given in the original publication. Diamonds represent the mean age for each composite score group. The only composite score group with no incorrect classifications is composite score group three. All composite score groups underage, with the exception of groups ten and 15 (Figure 11.2).

FIGURE 11.1
KNOWN AGES OF IDENTIFIED MALES SUPERIMPOSED OVER THE McKERN-
STEWART AGE INTERVALS FOR EACH COMPOSITE SCORE GROUP. DIAMONDS
REPRESENT THE MEAN AGE FOR EACH GROUP (FROM BROWN 2009:113)

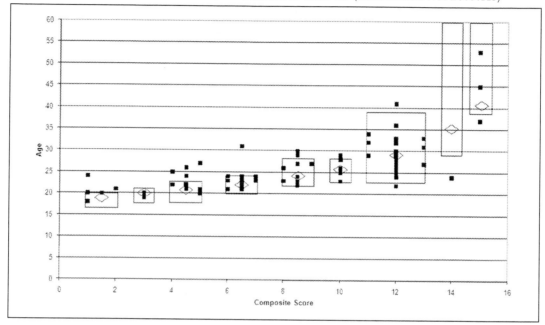

FIGURE 11.2
ERROR VALUES FOR COMPOSITE SCORE GROUPS
OF THE McKERN-STEWART METHODS

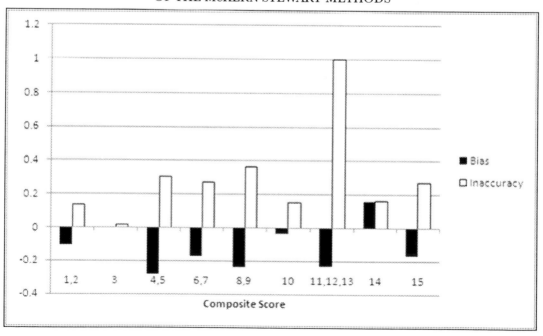

The highest average error in years for the McKern-Stewart method is 9.28 years for composite score 15, although the average error in years per group was generally not higher than two years. Overall error as measured by bias and inaccuracy is low for the method as a whole. However, it should also be noted that there are very few individuals in the sample over the age of 35. Additionally, the only individual given a composite score of 14 was misclassified. Those groups that show a tight cluster around the mean age per group generally have lower overall error, whereas those groups with a greater spread from the mean have higher overall error.

The Suchey-Brooks method has an overall correct classification rate of 97.9 percent, the highest of the three pubic symphysis methods. Figure 11.3 demonstrates this high correct classification rate; only two of 93 individuals were incorrectly classified and both were placed into phase one. Only phase one underages and all other phases overage (Figure 11.4). No individuals were assigned to phase six in the JPAC-CIL identified sample. The highest average error for the Suchey-Brooks method is 7.27 years for phase five. The

FIGURE 11.3
KNOWN AGES OF IDENTIFIED MALES SUPERIMPOSED OVER THE SUCHEY-
BROOKS AGE INTERVALS FOR EACH PHASE. DIAMONDS REPRESENT
THE MEAN AGE FOR EACH PHASE (FROM BROWN 2009:117)

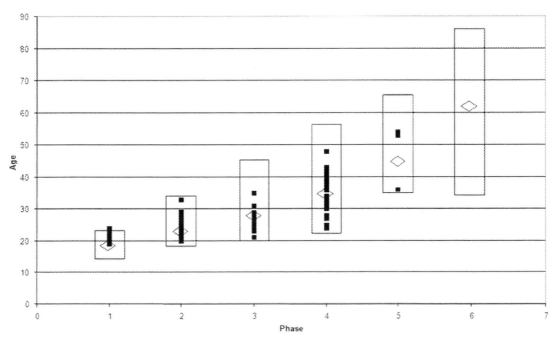

FIGURE 11.4
ERROR VALUES FOR PHASES OF THE SUCHEY-BROOKS METHOD

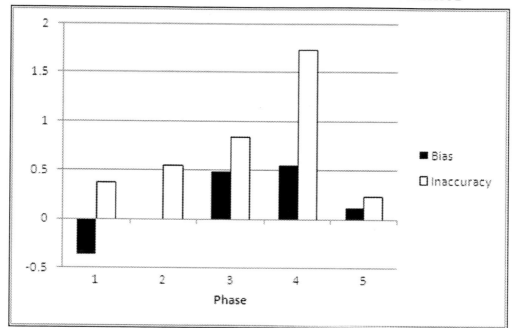

first three phases do not exceed 3.5 years and phase four is just over five years. Bias for phases one through four is generally low and increases primarily in phase five.

Breaking the samples down into five-year age intervals and recalculating bias and inaccuracy values (because both are dependent on sample size) allows for the comparison of the McKern-Stewart and Suchey-Brooks methods for different age classes. Because there were generally a limited number of individuals over the age of 40, a category of 41+ was used. Table 11.5 gives the sample sizes and values for each method and age interval for both bias and inaccuracy. A majority of the individuals aged with both of these methods are between the ages of 21 and 30.

The bias for the youngest age group is very low for McKern-Stewart and higher for Suchey-Brooks. For the next three age interval groups, bias is nearly identical in value but reversed in direction for both methods; where one method overages, the other underages. For the 36–40 age group, both methods underage those individuals analyzed. The Suchey-Brooks method performs better for the 41 and over group, showing a tendency to overage, while the McKern-Stewart method drastically underages individuals 41 and older.

TABLE 11.5
COMPARISON OF BIAS AND INACCURACY; McKERN-STEWART AND SUCHEY-
BROOKS PUBIC SYMPHYSIS METHODS (ADAPTED FROM BROWN, 2009:120)

Known Age	McKern-Stewart			Suchey-Brooks		
	N	Bias	Innaccuracy	N	Bias	Inaccuracy
16–20	7	0.05	0.72	5	-2.30	2.30
21–25	30	0.54	2.17	31	-0.39	2.92
26–30	22	-1.34	2.39	21	1.55	2.57
31–35	9	-3.79	3.79	10	4.00	5.32
36–40	2	-1.41	5.41	11	-0.84	6.00
41+	3	-9.27	9.27	8	3.25	5.60
All Ages	73	-1.07	2.68	86	0.76	3.72

There is a marked decrease in sample size for the last two age groups.

The McKern-Stewart method has a lower average error in years (measured by inaccuracy) than the Suchey-Brooks method for all individuals under the age of 40. However, both methods have low error for individuals under the age of 30 as compared to the error seen in individuals 31 and older. For individuals under the age of 30, the average error is never more than three years for either method, although McKern-Stewart clearly is better for the youngest age range. Inaccuracy values increase for both methods for individuals over the age of 30 and Suchey-Brooks again performs better for individuals 41 and older.

A χ^2 test of significance revealed that the choice of method (McKern-Stewart or Suchey-Brooks) was dependent on associated conflict ($\chi^2 = 34.67$, df $= 2$, p $= 0.000$). Table 11.6 gives the tabulation for each method and each conflict. The data in this table were taken directly from archives and represents use of the method as it was referenced in case reports and before data reconfiguration occurred. Therefore, the sample sizes are not identical to those listed above. McKern and Stewart is used more often for individuals associated with World War II (WWII) and Korea conflicts and Suchey-Brooks is used more frequently for Southeast Asia (SEA) conflict-associated individuals. The ages of six individuals were estimated using both methods. The statistically significant relationship between associated conflict and age estimation method suggests that analysts are using appropriate methods given assumed trends of secular change.

TABLE 11.6
COUNT OF METHODS USED BY CONFLICT

Conflict	Method	
	McKern-Stewart	Suchey-Brooks
WWI	0	0
WWII	49	31
Korea	15	2
SEA	18	58
Other	0	1
Total	82	92

DISCUSSION

It is important to mention that of all the age estimation methods employed at the CIL in the past 36 years, pubic symphyseal methods had the most consistent reporting (Brown, 2009). During data collection and data entry, phases or scores as reported by the analysts required no modifications. Analysts were also careful to report which method they had utilized to estimate age at death. This suggests that the pubic symphysis may be easier to apply than other age estimation methods, such as the auricular surface. The availability of casts for both the McKern-Stewart and Suchey-Brooks methods may also aid in consistent reporting between observers.

The Todd method was used in JPAC-CIL case reports for only three cases after 1986 (the year the Suchey-Brooks casts were first distributed). When it was used, the presence of multiple phase assignments in half of the age estimates produced indicates that the Suchey-Brooks six-phase system is warranted in its consolidation of Todd phases, especially considering that the Todd method only correctly classified seven of ten individuals in the JPAC-CIL identified sample. The Todd method has the lowest error values because of its extremely small age intervals per phase and its small range (approximately half the size of the other two methods). Its small sample size (n = 10) eliminated this method from more detailed comparisons of error.

When comparing the McKern-Stewart and Suchey-Brooks pubic symphysis methods, Suchey-Brooks is more accurate, but McKern-Stewart is more precise. While the Suchey-Brooks method is more successful in correctly assigning an individual to a phase that encompasses the individual's known age at death, it also provides larger intervals per phase. However, the McKern-Stewart method has a lower average error in years than the Suchey-

Brooks method, indicating that using the mean value for a composite score group produces a value closer to the known age at death than Suchey-Brooks. Both methods have similar *r*-values and therefore a similar linear relationship between known and estimated age at death. Again, the Suchey-Brooks method has a higher standard error than the McKern-Stewart method (see Table 11.4). The goal of precision versus accuracy can be related to the desired outcome of an age estimate. For example, greater precision may be desired when attempting to match unknown skeletal remains with descriptions of missing persons, whereas greater accuracy may be desired when generating a biological profile for an individual with a presumptive identification. Ideally, an age estimation method should be both accurate and precise.

Examining the five-year age intervals (Table 11.5), the most striking observation is that both methods perform well (i.e., with low error) for individuals under the age of 30. The McKern-Stewart method performs best for the 16–20 year old group, although the age estimation of individuals in this group is not as critical as groups of older individuals because of the presence of other skeletal age indicators at these ages, such as epiphyseal fusion and dental development. The Suchey-Brooks method performs better than the McKern-Stewart method for individuals over the age of 40.

This difference in performance is likely a result of the samples used to construct the methods themselves. The McKern-Stewart sample only contained six individuals over the age of 40 and the majority of individuals in this sample were between the ages of 18 and 30. The Suchey-Brooks sample is larger and more diverse for both known age at death and ancestry (Brooks and Suchey, 1990), thus it performs better for age groups that are underrepresented in the McKern-Stewart sample. Since the JPAC-CIL identifies mainly young males, the use of the McKern-Stewart system is warranted at this laboratory and with this sample. However, the McKern-Stewart system should be used with caution for males believed to be over the age of 30. Both methods are suitable for young adult males (generally under the age of 40). The lack of older adults and females in the JPAC-CIL identified sample means that these data are inconclusive on the use of these methods for individuals over the age of 40 and for females, respectively.

Finally, the relationship between method used and associated conflict suggests that analysts are using the pubic symphysis age estimation methods in accordance with JPAC-CIL SOPs. The first documented use of the Suchey-Brooks method at the JPAC-CIL is from a 1986 case. Therefore, individuals identified before 1986 would have age estimates based only on the Todd or McKern-Stewart methods. This would only affect data for individuals associated with the SEA conflict since all other individuals (e.g., WWII, Korea) would have died prior to 1960, stipulating the use of the McKern-Stewart method. There are more uses of the Suchey-Brooks method for individuals associated with WWII than is to be expected given SOP 3.4, but this SOP may not have been in effect at the time of identification of several of these cases. Because the individuals identified at the JPAC-CIL are generally young and the data above support the use of either method for young adults, the choice of one method over another likely introduces little error to the final age estimate.

SUMMARY

The pubic symphysis is used to estimate the age at death of unknown individuals at the JPAC-CIL with generally low error. Comparing the McKern-Stewart and Suchey-Brooks methods, the analyst is confronted with a decision between accuracy and precision. Better accuracy, such as that achieved with the Suchey-Brooks method, comes with decreased precision. Conversely, better precision, as seen with the McKern-Stewart method, leads to a decrease in accuracy. Further research will be conducted comparing age estimation methods and their performance for older individuals as well as females.

ACKNOWLEDGMENTS

First, I would like to thank Drs. Krista Latham and Mike Finnegan for organizing and editing this volume. The data discussed in this chapter are drawn from my thesis work at California State University, Chico and the JPAC-CIL. Thank you to my thesis committee: Drs. Eric Bartelink, Beth Shook, and John Byrd, whose tireless efforts made my research and writing such a success. Thank you also to all of the faculty and staff at CSU Chico, the entire scientific staff at the JPAC-CIL, as well as my family and friends for their continued support. This work was supported in part by an appointment to the Student Research Participation Program at the JPAC-CIL administered by the Oak Ridge Institute for Science and Education (ORISE) through an interagency agreement between the U.S. Department of Energy and JPAC-CIL.

Appendix A

TABLE A.1
TODD (1920) PUBIC SYMPHYSIS METHOD
SAMPLE (N = 10) (FROM BROWN 2009:110).

Age	Phase	Range	Midpoint	Bias (Σ)	Inaccuracy (Σ)
24	3	22–24	23	=-.1	0.1
24	3	22–24	23	-0.1	0.1
27*	3–4	22–26	24	-0.3	0.3
25*	5	27–30	28.5	0.35	0.35
26*	5	27–30	28.5	0.25	0.25
35	6–7	30–39	34.5	-0.05	0.05
35	6–7	30–39	34.5	-0.05	0.05
36	6–7	30–39	-0.15	0.15	
38	7	35–39	37	-0.1	
41	8–9	39–50	44.5	0.35	0.35
ALL	-	-	-	0.10	1.80

*incorrect classification

REFERENCES

Aykroyd, R. G., Lucy, D., Pollard, A. M., & Roberts, C. A. (1999). Nasty, brutish, but not necessarily short: A reconsideration of the statistical methods used to calculate age at death from adult human skeletal and dental age indicators. *American Antiquity 64*(1):55–70.

Bass, W. M. (2005). Human osteology: A laboratory and field manual (5th ed.). Colombia, MO: Missouri Archaeological Society, Special Publication No. 2. 365 pp.

Brooks, S. T. (1955). Skeletal age at death: The reliability of cranial and pubic age indicators. *American Journal of Physical Anthropology 13*:567–597.

Brooks S., & Suchey, J. M. (1990). Skeletal age determination based on the Os Pubis: A comparison of the Acsádi-Nemeskéri and Suchey-Brooks methods. *Human Evolution 5*(3):227–238.

Brown, C. A. (2009). Uncertainty in skeletal aging: A retrospective study and test of skeletal aging methods at the Joint POW/MIA Accounting Command Central Identification Laboratory. Unpublished Master's Thesis, Department of Anthropology, California State University, Chico. 231 p.

Dirkmaat, D. C., Cabo, L. L., Ousley, S. D., & Symes, S. A. (2008). New perspectives in forensic anthropology. *Yearbook of Physical Anthropology 51*:33–52.

Gilbert, B. M., & McKern, T. W. (1973). A method for aging the female Os Pubis. *American Journal of Physical Anthropology 38*:31–38.

JPAC-CIL. (2008). JPAC Laboratory Manual. Part IV, SOP 3.4. Last revised 02 April 2008.

Katz, D., & Suchey, J. M. (1986). Age determination of the male Os Pubis. *American Journal of Physical Anthropology 69*(4):427–435.

McKern, T. W., & Stewart, T. D. (1957). Skeletal age changes in young American males.

Technical Report EP-45. Natick (MA): Quartermaster Research and Development Command. 179 p.

Meindl, R. S., & Lovejoy, C. O. (1989). Age changes in the pelvis: Implications for paleodemography. In M. Y. İscan MY (Ed.), *Age markers in the human skeleton,* pp. 137–168. Springfield, IL: Charles C Thomas.

Meindl, R. S., Lovejoy, C. O., Mensforth, R. P., & Walker, R. A. (1985). A revised method of age determination using the Os Pubis, with a review and tests of accuracy of other current methods of pubic symphyseal aging. *American Journal of Physical Anthropology 68*:29–45.

Saunders, S. R., Fitzgerald, C., Rogers, T., Dudar, C., & McKillop, H. (1992). A test of several methods of skeletal age estimation using a documented archaeological sample. *Canadian Society of Forensic Science Journal 25*(2):97–118.

Saunders, S., DeVito, C., Herring, A., Southern, R., & Hoppa, R. (1993). Accuracy tests of tooth formation age estimations for human skeletal remains. *American Journal of Physical Anthropology 92*:173–188.

Suchey, J. M. (1979). Problems in the aging of females using the Os Pubis. *American Journal of Physical Anthropology 51*:467–470.

Todd, T. W. (1920). Age changes in the pubic bone. I: The male white pubis. *American Journal of Physical Anthropology 3*(3):285–334.

Todd, T. W. (1921). Age changes in the pubic bone. II: The pubis of the male negro-white hybrid. III: The Pubis of the White Female. IV: The Pubis of the Female Negro-White Hybrid. *American Journal of Physical Anthropology 4*(1):1–70.

Chapter 12

RECENT ADVANCES IN THE ESTIMATION OF AGE AT DEATH FROM THE ASSESSMENT OF IMMATURE BONE

Douglas H. Ubelaker

Accurate assessment of age at death of immature remains represents a key element in the methodology of forensic anthropology (Ubelaker, 2005). Such assessments are best made from dental development, since considerable research indicates that the rate of dental formation has the greatest correlation with chronological age at death (Ubelaker, 1999). However, when teeth are not available or damaged to the point that assessment is compromised, the non-dental skeleton offers considerable information as well (Lewis and Flavel, 2006). Although age assessment of immature remains is usually directed toward skeletal cases, problems relating to immigration age or other age-related issues involving the living (Cunha and Cattaneo, 2006) emerge as well.

The process of age estimation in general recognizes a potential difference between chronological age and biological or physiological age (Introna and Campobasso, 2006). To estimate chronological age at death, information must be gathered from the different physiological aging systems. Once assembled, these data must be assessed in consideration of the myriad of influencing factors to arrive at the estimate of chronological age.

Information on age at death from the immature human skeleton is available from three primary sources: (1) the extent and nature of early bone maturation; (2) bone size, especially long bone lengths; and (3) the state of epiphyseal union. Information on early bone maturation consists of such observations as bone density, cortical thickness, the appearance and extent of development of ossification centers and fusion of skeletal elements during development. Bone size assessment involves evaluation of the growth in length and breadth of the major bones of the skeleton. Data on epiphyseal union are most useful for the adolescent years and involve observations on the formation and progression of fusion of epiphyses. All of these factors must be assessed in recognition of population variation, sex differences, evidence of morbidity and nutrition, and taphonomic effects (Bass, 2005; Krogman and Îscan, 1986; Lewis, 2007; Lewis and Flavel, 2006; Scheuer and Black, 2000; Steele and Bramblett, 1988; Stewart 1979; Sundick, 1977; Ubelaker, 1987, 1989; White, 1991). This chapter provides a general survey of the methodology involved, with special emphasis on recent research developments.

EARLY BONE MATURATION

The processes of bone formation are well known and generally relate to the early formation of ossification centers, bone proliferation and growth and union of skeletal segments (Beals and Skyhar, 1984; Burkus and Ogden, 1982; Felts, 1954; Gardner and Gray, 1970; Hall, 1988; Moss et al., 1955). Endochondral ossification involves bone formation on a pre-existing cartilage matrix and represents very early bone formation as well as the rapid growth in length of long bones. Endochondral ossification also is involved in growth at the basilar synchondrosis producing strong growth factors in the cranial base. Growth in the width of long bones is accomplished through intramembraneous ossification with bone being generated directly by the periosteum. Following initial formation, bone mineralization progresses and the remodeling process begins. Through remodeling, osteoclasts cut channels into the pre-existing bone creating resorption spaces which are subsequently filled in to produce secondary osteons. With advancing age, the bone produced by these processes changes, undergoing not only an increase in size but also changes in density and texture as well.

APPEARANCE OF OSSIFICATION CENTERS

Considerable literature exists on the timing of the formation of ossification centers throughout the skeleton (Acheson, 1957; Adair and Scammon, 1921; Bagnall et al., 1982; Camp and Cilley, 1931; Christie, 1949; Ellis and Joseph,

1954; Francis, 1940; Francis and Werle, 1939; Gardner et al., 1959; Girdany and Golden, 1952; Hansman, 1962; Harding, 1952a, 1952b; Hill, 1939; Kelly and Reynolds, 1947; Kjar, 1974; Kraus, 1961; Mall, 1906; Meyer and O'Rahilly, 1958, 1976; Noback and Robertson, 1951; O'Rahilly, 1973; O'Rahilly and Gardner, 1972; O'Rahilly and Meyer, 1956; O'Rahilly et al., 1960; Pryor, 1927-1928, 1933; Pyle and Sontag, 1943; Roche, 1964; Sawtell, 1929; Selby, 1961; Sontag et al., 1939; Walmsley, 1940). In the early stages of formation, ossification centers are difficult to recover and troublesome to identify if recovered. In the forensic context, data from newly forming ossification centers are most useful in contexts in which soft tissue is also present allowing recognition of the anatomical part present. It is important to remember that the timing and sequence of ossification center formation varies throughout the body (Kraus, 1961; Noback and Robertson, 1951; O'Rahilly and Gardner, 1972).

Knowledge of the details of this process enables the forensic anthropologist to make assessments of general age at death even from fragmentary evidence. For example, careful examination of bone fragments thought to represent a newborn infant might reveal large fragments of compact bone showing considerable bone density; evidence of an older individual and commingling. Another case thought to represent a femur of an adolescent might reveal morphological details of a femur but evidence of the recent bone formation of a young infant. In short, details of the nature and extent of the growth process can not only define age at death but assist in the evaluation of commingling; the determination of the minimum number of individuals represented and related issues.

Recent advances in this area of immature age assessment have largely originated from the increasingly diverse nature of cases involving anthropological analysis. Such issues arise in analyses related to disputes involving cremations in which questions abound regarding who is presented by the cremated fragments and if commingling has occurred. Cases involving terrorism and mass disasters also call for such analysis when incomplete evidence challenges bone fragment recognition and victim identification.

ASSESSMENT OF BONE SIZE

Increases in bone size, particularly diaphyseal length, during the growth process present primary information useful in assessing age at death in immature remains. For assessing fetal remains, formulae are available in (Fazekas and Kósa, 1978), and (Scheuer et al., 1980) which allow body length and fetal age to be estimated from individual bone measurements. Publications also are available to assist in the determination of fetal age from radiographic evidence and bones covered with soft tissue (Adalian et al., 2001; Huxley, 1998; Huxley and Kósa, 1999; Piercecchi-Marti et al., 2002). Details regarding approaches to fetal remains are provided in a separate chapter of this volume.

For non-fetal material (newborns and older immature individuals), bone measurements, especially those of diaphyseal length also are useful to estimate age at death. Comparative data are available from radiographic studies of immature individuals of known sex and age at death (Anderson and Green, 1948; Anderson et al., 1963, 1964; Francis, 1939; Ghantus, 1951; Gindhart, 1973; Hoffman, 1979; Maresh, 1943, 1955; Maresh and Deming, 1939). Additional data are available from research on remains of archeological origin (Hoppa, 1992; Hoppa and Gruspier, 1996; Johnston, 1962; Merchant and Ubelaker, 1977; Miles and Bulman, 1994; Stewart, 1968; Steyn and Henneberg, 1996; Sundick, 1972, 1979; Walker, 1969). In the studies of archeological specimens, age at death is usually estimated from dental evidence and then correlated with bone measurements. Although the ages at death are estimated in studies of archeological material and thus lack the precision of radiographic studies of living individuals, they offer valuable comparative data on past populations and contribute to an understanding of human variation in the processes involved.

Generally, the literature on long bone growth indicates that the range of variation (and thus the potential error of individual estimates) increases with advancing age. Sex differences and population of origin also contribute to this range of variation. Information provided about the sex and/or population origin of the individual in question thus reduce the potential error involved in the estimated age. Investigators should also be aware that the extent of sexual dimorphism in bone maturation varies within different areas of the skeleton (Humphrey, 1998).

Norris (2002) and Franklin and Cardini (2007) have called attention to the potential value of mandibular morphology, especially the measurement of ramus height, to estimate age at death. In their study of 79 immature skeletons of South African Bantu and African American individuals, Franklin and Cardini (2007) found a standard error of age estimation of 2.4 years for the entire sample and only 1.1 years if adolescents were excluded.

EPIPHYSEAL UNION

Once epiphyses are fully formed, the timing of their union offers key age information, especially during the adolescent and early adult years (Colwell, 1927; Cundy et al., 1988; Hoerr et al., 1962; Krogman, 1962; Lewis and Garn, 1960; McKern and Stewart, 1957; Posener et al., 1939; Pyle and Hoerr, 1955). In making age assessments using epiphyseal union information it is important to be aware of (1) sex differences, (2) population differences, (3) variation in timing within different areas of the skeleton (4) the time lapse between beginning and final fusion, and (5) differences in the literature between measures of union in dry bone and those determined radiographically from living individuals.

In general, females mature earlier than males (Krogman, 1962; Lewis and Garn, 1960). The impact of sexual dimorphism on epiphyseal union varies among populations, individuals and at each epiphyseal site. However, since the magnitude of sex differences in epiphyseal union can be as much as two years, it is advisable to consider sex in assessing age at death with this type of data. If sex is known, sex-specific data should be consulted to determine age. If sex is unknown, the usual situation in examining unidentified skeletal remains, then the range of variation in the timing of epiphyseal union in both sexes should be considered.

Similarly, if the population origin is generally known, data from that population should be considered. For example, in their comparison of the timing of epiphyseal union in North American and Bosnian individuals, Schaefer and Black (2005) found that the Bosnian individuals fused about two years earlier than their North American counterparts.

Crowder and Austin (2005) examined the age ranges of epiphyseal fusion in the distal tibia and fibula of contemporary males and females. Their radiographic study of 270 females between the ages of 9 and 17 years and 300 individuals between the ages of 11 and 20 years revealed significant population differences. Epiphyseal fusion occurred earlier in their samples with African and Mexican ancestry than in individuals of European ancestry.

Research on the timing of epiphyseal union also has elucidated the variation that needs to be considered in assessing the probabilities involved with individual estimates. Kahana et al. (2003) offer such information regarding fusion of the basilar synchondrosis. Although the basilar synchondrosis is usually not considered to be an "epiphysis" it involves similar growth processes of endochondral ossification. Kahana et al. (2003) found considerable variation in their study of cadavers between the ages of 8 and 26 years. Using an "open" or "closed" classification system, they found that some males remained open throughout the entire age range examined whereas all females were closed by age 16. The earliest "closed" example was age 11 in males and age 13 in females.

Knowledge of the sequence of epiphyseal union can be useful not only to assess age at death in individual skeletons, but also to evaluate the possibility of commingling in samples where that is an issue. Schaefer and Black (2007) examined the sequence of epiphyseal union in 258 male Bosnia individuals between the ages of 14 and 30 years. They noted beginning and complete union for 21 epiphyses throughout the skeleton documenting patterns and variation of the sequence and process of union. A key finding was that differences exist between the sequence of initial union and that of final union.

OTHER APPROACHES

Although the traditional approaches to the estimation of age at death of immature bone are those outlined above, research has revealed other lines of investigation. Of particular interest is racemization of aspartic acid. The technique examines the extent of change of the normal form (L) of amino acids to an alternative form (D). Although considerable data exist on this age change in teeth (Ohtani et al., 2005), similar research has been conducted on bone. Studies have focused on total amino acid content in bone and rib cartilage (Ohtani et al., 2002), aspartic acid, glutamic acid and alanine in the femur (Ohtani et al., 2004) and the proteins osteocalcin and elastin (Ohtani and Yamamoto, 2005).

MORBIDITY AND NUTRITION ISSUES

Processes of human bone growth and development are influenced by genetics, nutrition, morbidity and a variety of environmental factors. The vast literature on these issues documents both the multitude of factors involved and the complexity of their interpretation. These factors include not only the obvious ones of nutrition and childhood disease but also socioeconomic status, altitude of living environment, the extent of physical activity, urban living versus country living, noise pollution and smoking (Lewis and Flavel, 2006) among others. Lewis (2007) provides a recent, thorough discussion of the relevant literature and notes the complexity of factors involved in human growth. This literature generally suggests that while many conditions can affect bone growth, it is usually difficult in an individual case to determine with precision, the nature of the specific influences. Fractures, chronic infection and some specific disorders can be diagnosed from skeletal remains, but most others only have general effects on growth and skeletal development.

TAPHONOMIC EFFECTS

Taphonomic forces operate to limit the nature of the evidence examined for age determination and thus play a pivotal role in any forensic investigation (Haglund and Sorg, 1997, 2002). The selection of methodology to estimate age at death in a forensic case is driven by the general age of the individual but also usually by the condition and completeness of the remains. Loss of the ends of the long bones due to animal chewing may eliminate evidence on epiphyseal union. An incomplete skeleton created by construction activity or surface erosion and bone scattering affects the bones available for examination and thus the techniques employed. Extreme fragmentation due to cremation processing or events involving explosives redirects analysis toward those relevant approaches. The condition and completeness of the remains also affects the accuracy of the estimate, usually calling for an estimate range, which expands with the extent of taphonomic influence. Taphonomic alteration also can present confusing and difficult to interpret morphology leading the inexperienced investigator toward error. The taphonomic impact is especially prevalent with immature remains, which generally are more fragile and vulnerable than those of older individuals.

SUMMARY

The estimation of age at death, especially in the absence of the dentition, can be challenging even for experienced anthropologists. Fortunately, research and case experience have strengthened the methodological approaches available. At the same time, this activity has generated increased appreciation for the variability involved and the multitude of factors that must be considered. Unfortunately, the skeletons of the immature continue to enter our laboratories in need of age estimation and identification. Through research, our collective ability to meet this need is strengthened.

REFERENCES

Acheson, R. M. (1957). The Oxford Method of Assessing Skeletal Maturity. *Clinical Orthopedics 10:*19–39.

Adair, F. L., & Scammon, R. E. (1921). A study of the ossification centers of the wrist, knee and ankle at birth, with particular reference to the physical development and maturity of the newborn. *American Journal of Obstetrics and Gynecology 2:*35–60.

Adalian, P., Piercecchi-Marti, M. D., Boorliere-Najean, B., Panuel, M., Fredouille, C., Dutour, O., & Leonetti, G. (2001). Postmortem assessment of fetal diaphyseal femoral length: Validation of a radiographic methodology. *Journal of Forensic Sciences 46*(2):215–219.

Anderson, M., & Green, W. T. (1948). Lengths of the femur and tibia: Norms derived from orthoentgenograms of children from five years of age until epiphysial closure. *American Journal of Disabled Children 75:*279–290.

Anderson, M., Green, W. T., & Messner, M. B. (1963). Growth and predictions of growth in the lower extremities. *Journal of Bone and Joint Surgery 45*(1):1–14.

Anderson, M., Messner, M. B., & Green, W. T. (1964). Distribution of lengths of the normal femur and tibia in children from one to eighteen years of age. *Journal of Bone and Joint Surgery 46*(6):1197–1202.

Bagnall, K. M., Harris, P. F., & Jones, P. R. M. (1982). A radiographic study of the longitudinal growth of primary ossification centers in limb long bones of the human fetus. *The Anatomical Record 203*(2):293–299.

Bass, W. M. (2005). *Human osteology: A laboratory and field manual* (5th ed.). Columbia, MO: Missouri Archaeological Society, Inc.

Beals, R. K., & Skyhar, M. (1984). Growth and development of the tibia, fibula, and ankle joint. *Clinical Orthopaedics and Related Research 182:*289–292.

Burkus, J. K., & Ogden, J. A. (1982). Bipartite primary ossification in the developing human femur. *Journal of Pediatric Orthopedics 2*(1):63–65.

Camp, J. D., & Cilley, E. I. L. (1931). Diagrammatic chart whowing time of appearance of the various centers of ossification and period of union. *American Journal of Roentgenology and Radium Therapy 26*(6):905.

Christie, A. (1949). Prevalence and distribution of ossification centers in the newborn infant. *American Journal of Disabled Childred 77:*355–361.

Colwell, H. A. (1927). Case showing abnormal epiphyses of metatarsals and first metacarpals. *Journal of Anatomy 62:*183.

Crowder, C., & Austin, D. (2005). Age ranges of epiphyseal fusion in the distal tibia and fibula of contemporary males and females. *Journal of Forensic Sciences 50*(5):1001–1007.

Cundy, P., Paterson, D., Morris, L., & Foster, B. (1988). Skeletal age estimation in leg length discrepancy. *Journal of Pediatric Orthopedics 8*(5):513–515.

Cunha, E., & Cattaneo, C. (2006). Forensic anthropology and forensic pathology: The state of the art. In A. Schmitt, E. Cunha, & J. Pinheiro (Eds.), *Forensic anthropology and medicine: Complementary sciences from recovery to cause of death,* pp. 39–53. Totowa, NJ: Humana Press.

Ellis, F. G., & Joseph, J. (1954). Time of appearance of the centres of ossification of the fibular epiphyses. *Journal of Anatomy 88:*533–536.

Fazekas, I. G., & Kósa, F. (1978). *Forensic fetal osteology.* Budapest: Akadémiai Kiadó.

Felts, W. J. L. (1954). The prenatal development of the human femur. *American Journal of Anatomy 94*(1):1–44.

Francis, C. C. (1939). Growth of the human tibia. *American Journal of Physical Anthropology 25*(3):323–331.

Francis, C. C. (1940). The appearance of centers of ossification from 6 to 15 years. *American Journal of Physical Anthropology 27*(1):127–138.

Francis, C. C., & Werle. P. P. (1939). The appearance of centers of ossification from virth to 5 years. *American Journal of Physical Anthropology 24*(3):273–299.

Franklin, D., & Cardini, A. (2007). Mandibular morphology as an indicator of human subadult age: Interlandmark approaches. *Journal of Forensic Sciences 52*(5):1015–1019.

Gardner, E., & Gray, D. J. (1970). The prenatal development of the human femur. *American Journal of Anatomy 129*(2):121–140.

Gardner, E., Gray, D. J., & O'Rahilly, R. (1959). The prenatal development of the skeleton and joints of the human foot. *Journal of Bone and Joint Surgery 41*(5):847–876.

Ghantus, M. K. (1951). Growth of the shaft of the human radius and ulna during the first two years of life. *American Journal of Roentgenology 65*(5):784–786.

Gindhart, P. S. (1973). Growth standards for the tibia and radius in children aged one month through eighteen years. *American Journal of Physical Anthropology 39*(1):41–48.

Girdany, B. R., & Golden, R. (1952). Centers of ossification of the skeleton. *American Journal of Roentgenology, Radium Therapy and Nuclear Medicine 68*(6):922–924.

Haglund, W. D., & Sorg, M. H. (1997). *Forensic taphonomy: The postmortem fate of human remains.* Boca Raton, FL: CRC Press.

Haglund, W. D., & Sorg, M. H. (2002). *Advances in forensic taphonomy: Method, theory, and archaeological perspectives.* Boca Raton, FL: CRC Press.

Hall, B. K. (1988). The embryonic development of bone. *American Science 76*(2):174–181.

Hansman, C. F. (1962). Appearance and fusion of ossification centers in the human skeleton. *American Journal of Roentgenology, Radium Therapy and Nuclear Medicine 88*(3):476–482.

Harding, V. S. V. (1952a). A method of evaluating osseous development from birth to 14 years. *Child Development 23*(4):247–271.

Harding, V. V. (1952b). Time schedule for the appearance and fusion of a second accessory center of ossification of the calcaneus. *Child Development 23*(3):181–184.

Hill, A. H. (1939). Fetal age assessment by centers of ossification. *American Journal of Physical Anthropology 24*(3):251–272.

Hoerr, N. L., Pyle, S. I., & Francis, C. C. (1962). *Radiographic atlas of skeletal development of the foot and ankle: A standard of reference.* Springfield, IL: Charles C Thomas.

Hoffman, J. M. (1979). Age estimations from diaphyseal lengths: Two months to twelve years. *Journal of Forensic Sciences 24*(2):461–469.

Hoppa, R. D. (1992). Evaluating human skeletal growth: An Anglo-Saxon example. *International Journal of Osteoarchaeology 2*(4):275–288.

Hoppa, R. D., & Gruspier, K. L. (1996). Estimating diaphyseal length from fragmentary subadult skeletal remains: Implications for paleodemographic reconstructions of a Southern Ontario ossuary. *American Journal of Physical Anthropology 100*(3):341–354.

Humphrey, L. T. (1998). Growth patterns in the modern human skeleton. *American Journal of Physical Anthropology 105*(1):57–72.

Huxley, A. K. (1998). Analysis of shrinkage in human fetal diaphyseal lengths from fresh to dry bone using Petersohn and Köhler's data. *Journal of Forensic Sciences 43*(2):423–426.

Huxley, A. K., & Kósa, F. (1999). Calculation of percent shrinkage in human fetal diaphyseal lengths from fresh bone to carbonized and calcined bone using Petersohn and Köhler's data. *Journal of Forensic Sciences 44*(3):577–583.

Introna, F., & Campobasso, C. P. (2006). Biological vs legal age of living individuals. In A. Schmitt, E. Cunha, & J. Pinheiro (Eds.), *Forensic anthropology and medicine: Complementary sciences from recovery to cause of death,* pp. 57–82. Totowa (NJ): Humana Press.

Johnston, F. E. (1962). Growth of the long bones of infants and young children at Indian Knoll. *American Journal of Physical Anthropology 20*(3):249–254.

Kahana, T., Birkby, W. H., Goldin, L., & Hiss, J. (2003). Estimation of age in adolescents–The basilar synchondrosis. *Journal of Forensic Sciences 48*(3):504–508.

Kelly, H. J., & Reynolds, L. (1947). Appearance and growth of ossification centers and increases in the body dimensions of White and Negro infants. *American Journal of Roentgenology and Radium Therapy 57*(4):477–516.

Kjar, I. (1974). Skeletal maturation of the human fetus assessed radiographically on the basis of ossification sequences in the hand and foot. *American Journal of Physical Anthropology 40*(2):257–275.

Kraus, B. S. (1961). Sequence of appearance of primary centers of ossification in the human foot. *American Journal of Anatomy 109*(2):103–115.

Krogman, W. M. (1962). *The human skeleton in forensic medicine.* Springfield, IL: Charles C Thomas.

Krogman, W. M., & Îscan, M. Y. (1986). *The human skeleton in forensic medicine* (2nd ed.). Springfield, IL: Charles C Thomas.

Lewis, M. E. (2007). *The bioarchaeology of children: Perspectives from biological and forensic anthropology.* Cambridge: Cambridge University Press.

Lewis, M. E., & Flavel, A. (2006). Age assessment of child skeletal remains in forensic contexts. In A. Schmitt, E. Cunha, & J. Pinheiro (Eds.), *Forensic anthropology and medicine: Complementary sciences from recovery to cause of death,* pp. 243–257. Totowa (NJ): Humana Press.

Lewis, A. B., & Garn, S. M. (1960). The relationship between tooth formation and other maturational factors. *Angle Orthodontics 30*:70–77.

Mall, F. P. (1906). On ossification centers in human embryos less than one hundred days old. *American Journal of Anatomy 5*(4):433–458.

Maresh, M. M. (1943). Growth of major long bones in healthy children. *American Journal of Disabled Childred 66*(3):227–257.

Maresh, M. M. (1955). Linear growth of long bones of extremities from infancy through adolescence. *American Journal of Disabled Children 89*:725–742.

Maresh, M. M., & Deming, J. (1939). The growth of long bones in 80 infants. *Child Development 10*(2):91–106.

McKern, T. W, & Stewart, T. D. (1957). Skeletal Age Changes in Young American Males. Natick, MA: Headquarters Quartermaster Research & Development Command, Quartermaster Research & Development Center, Environmental Protection Research Division. Technical Report EP–45.

Merchant, V. L., & Ubelaker, D. H. (1977). Skeletal growth of the protohistoric Arikara. *American Journal of Physical Anthropology 46*(1):61–72.

Meyer, D. B., & O'Rahilly, R. (1958). Multiple techniques in the study of the onset of pre-natal ossification. *The Anatomical Record 132*(2):181–193.

Meyer, D. B., & O'Rahilly, R. (1976). The onset of ossification in the human calcaneus. *Anatomy of Embryology 150*(1):19–33.

Miles, A. E. W., & Bulman, J. S. (1994). Growth curves of immature bones from a Scottish island population of sixteenth to mid-nineteenth century: Limb-bone diaphyses and some bones of the hand and foot. *International Journal of Osteoarchaeology 4*(2):121–136.

Moss, M. L., Noback, C. R., & Robertson, G. G. (1955). Critical developmental horizons in human fetal long bones: Correlated quantitative and histological criteria. *American Journal of Anatomy 97*(1):155–175.

Noback, C. R., & Robertson, G. G. (1951). Sequences of appearance of ossification centers in the human skeleton during the first five prenatal months. *American Journal of Anatomy 89*(1):1–28.

Norris, S. P. (2002). Mandibular ramus height as an indicator of human infant age. *Journal of Forensic Sciences 47*(1):8–11.

Ohtani, S., Abe, I., & Yamamoto, T. (2005). An application of D- and L-aspartic acid mix-tures as standard specimens for the chronological age estimation. *Journal of Forensic Sciences 50*(6):1298–1302.

Ohtani, S., Matsushima, Y., Kobayashi, Y., & Yamamoto, T. (2002). Age estimation by meas-uring the racemization of aspartic acid from total amino acid content of several types of bone and rib cartilage: A preliminary account. *Journal of Forensic Sciences 47*(1):32–36.

Ohtani, S., Yamada, Y., Yamamoto, T., Arany, S., Gonmori, K., & Yoshioka, N. (2004). Comparison of age estimated from degree of racemization of aspartic acid, glutamic acid and alanine in the femur. *Journal of Forensic Sciences 49*(3):441–445.

Ohtani, S., & Yamamoto, T. (2005). Strategy for the estimation of chronological age using the aspartic acid racemization method with special reference to coefficient of correlation between D/L ratios and ages. *Journal of Forensic Sciences 50*(5):1020–1027.

O'Rahilly, R. (1973). The human foot. Part 1: Prenatal development. In N. J. Giannestras (Ed.), *Foot disorders: Medical and surgical management* (2nd ed.), pp. 16–23. Philadelphia (PA): Lea and Febiger.

O'Rahilly, R., & Gardner, E. (1972). The initial appearance of ossification in staged human embryos. *American Journal of Anatomy 134*(3):291–301.

O'Rahilly, R., Gardner, E., & Gray, D. J. (1960). The skeletal development of the foot. *Clinical Orthopaedics and Related Research 16*:7–14.

O'Rahilly, R., & Meyer, D. B. (1956). Roentgenographic investigation of the human skeleton during early fetal life. *American Journal of Roentgenology, Radium Therapy Nuclear Medicine 76*(3):455–468.

Piercecchi-Marti, M. D., Adalian, P., Bourliere-Najean, B., Gouvernet, J., Maczel, M., Dutour, O., & Leonetti, G. (2002). Validation of a radiographic method to establish new fetal growth standards: Radio-anatomical correlation. *Journal of Forensic Sciences 47*(2):328–331.

Posener, K., Walker, E., & Weddell, G. (1939). Radiographic studies of the metacarpal and metatarsal bones in children. *Journal of Anatomy 74*:76–79.

Pryor, J. W. (1927–1928). Difference in the ossification of the male and female skeleton. *Journal of Anatomy 62*:499–506.

Pryor, J. W. (1933). Roentgenographic investigation of the time element in ossification.

American Journal of Roentgenology Radium and Therapy 28:798–804.

Pyle, S. I., & Hoerr, N. L. (1955). *Radiographic atlas of skeletal development of the knee: A standard of reference.* Springfield, IL: Charles C Thomas.

Pyle, I., & Sontag, L. W. (1943). Variability in onset of ossification in epiphyses and short bones of the extremities. *American Journal of Roentgenology and Radium Therapy 49*(6):795–798.

Roche, A. F. (1964). Epiphyseal ossification and shaft elongation in human metatarsal bones. *The Anatomical Record 149*(3):449–451.

Sawtell, R. O. (1929). Ossification and growth of children from one to eight years of age. *American Journal of Disabled Children 37*:61–87.

Schaefer, M. C., & Black, S. M. (2005). Comparison of ages of epiphyseal union in North American and Bosnian skeletal material. *Journal of Forensic Sciences 50*(4):777–784.

Schaefer, M. C., & Black, S. M. (2007). Epiphyseal union sequencing: Aiding in the recognition and sorting of commingled remains. *Journal of Forensic Sciences 52*(2):277–285.

Scheuer, L., & Black, S. (2000). *Developmental juvenile osteology.* San Diego, CA: Academic Press.

Scheuer, J. L., Musgrave, J. H., & Evans, S. P. (1980). The estimation of late fetal and perinatal age from limb bone length by linear and logarithmic regression. *Ann Hum Biol 7*(3):257–265.

Selby, S. (1961). Separate centers of ossification of the tip of the internal malleolus. *American Journal of Roentgenology, Radium Therapy and Nuclear Medicine 86*(3):496–501.

Sontag, L. W., Snell, D., & Anderson, M. (1939). Rate of appearance of ossification centers from birth to the age of five years. *American Journal of Disabled Childred 58*:949–956.

Steele, D. G., & Bramblett, C. A. (1988). *The anatomy and biology of the human skeleton.* College Station, TX: Texas A&M University Press.

Stewart, T. D. (1968). Identification by the skeletal structures. In F. E. Camps (Ed.), *Gradwohl's legal medicine* (2nd ed.), pp. 123–154. Bristol: Wright.

Stewart, T. D. (1979). *Essentials of forensic anthropology: Especially as developed in the United States.* Springfield, IL: Charles C Thomas.

Steyn, M., & Henneberg, M. (1996). Skeletal growth of children from the iron age site of K2 (South Africa). *American Journal of Physical Anthropology 100*(3):389–396.

Sundick, R. I. (1972). Human skeletal growth and dental development as observed in the Indian Knoll population [dissertation]. Toronto: University of Toronto.

Sundick, R. I. (1977). Age and sex determination of subadult skeletons. *Journal of Forensic Sciences 22*(1):141–144.

Sundick, R. I. (1979). Human skeletal growth and age determination. *Homo 29*:228–249.

Ubelaker, D. H. (1987). Estimating age at death from immature human skeletons: An overview. *Journal of Forensic Sciences 32*(5):1254–1263.

Ubelaker, D. H. (1989). The estimation of age at death from immature human bone. In M. Y. İscan (Ed.), *Age markers in the human skeleton,* pp. 55–70. Springfield, IL: Charles C. Thomas.

Ubelaker, D. H. (1999). *Human skeletal remains, excavation, analysis, interpretation* (3rd ed.). Washington, D.C.: Taraxacum.

Ubelaker, D. H. (2005). Estimating age at death. In J. Rich, D. E. Dean, & R. H. Powers (Eds.), *Forensic medicine of the lower extremity: Human identification and trauma analysis of the thigh, leg, and foot,* pp. 99–112. Totowa (NJ): Humana Press.

Walker, P. L. (1969). The linear growth of long bones in late woodland Indian children. *Proceedings of the Indiana Academy of Science 78*:83–87.

Walmsley, R. (1940). The development of the patella. *Journal of Anatomy 74*:360–368.

White, T. D. (1991). *Human osteology.* San Diego, CA: Academic Press, Inc.

Section 3

HISTOLOGICAL AND MULTIFACTORIAL AGING TECHNIQUES

Chapter 13

THE APPLICATION OF CORTICAL BONE HISTOMORPHOMETRY TO ESTIMATE AGE AT DEATH

CHRISTIAN CROWDER AND SUSAN PFEIFFER

INTRODUCTION

Most of the quantitative and qualitative methods for estimating adult age at death are assessments of degenerative changes to gross bone morphology. Criteria for age estimation based on these changes are often subjective and they produce wide age intervals, especially after the fifth decade of life. The gross anatomical locations of interest include skeletal elements such as the pubic symphysis (Brooks and Suchey, 1990), auricular surface (Lovejoy et al., 1985a, 1985b; Buckberry and Chamberlain, 2002), and mid thoracic sternal rib end (Îscan et al. 1984; Îscan 1993). These surfaces are often altered by post-depositional taphonomic factors, leading researchers to resort to less accurate methods such as those that are based on patterns of trabecular involution, cranial suture closure, and the presence or absence of degenerative joint disease as bases for age assessment. It has been argued that quantitative cortical bone histology, or histomorphometry, provides an approach to estimating the age of adult skeletal material that has the potential to bridge the 50+ boundary, and to provide age intervals that are less broad (Thompson, 1979; Stout and Gehlert, 1982; Ubelaker, 1986), yet histological methods are still not widely accepted or applied.

Histological methods for age estimation are based on the assumption that the replacement of primary cortical bone with secondary cortical bone, including steady turnover of secondary osteons, will occur at a predictable

193

rate (Pfeiffer, 1992). As chronological age increases, the cortex becomes crowded with intact and fragmentary secondary osteons (Robling and Stout, 2000). The length of time during which remodeling occurs (chronological age) will be the primary influence on how many secondary osteon creations (intact and fragmentary osteons) accumulate per unit of area. This relationship should be evident in a normal adult until remodeling rates begin to fluctuate after the sixth decade of life, as homeostasis gradually becomes compromised thereafter (Wu et al., 1970).

In 1965, Ellis Kerley developed the first applicable method of histological age estimation. Since the introduction of this method numerous others have followed; however, the reliability of quantitative bone histology for adult age estimation has yet to be fully demonstrated. The reliability of cortical bone histomorphology in estimating age at death is dependent on measuring the amount of non-stochastic cortical bone remodeling between individuals of the same chronological age within and between populations, the strength and predictability of the relationship between bone remodeling and chronological age, and the levels of accuracy and precision produced by the method. Most research has focused on exploring the first two aspects, while the latter has not been as well explored. There is a large body of research exploring the changes in human bone microstructure over chronological age. Among the histological methods that have been proposed, the human skeleton is well represented: femur (Ericksen, 1991; Thompson, 1979; Singh and Gunberg, 1970; Ahlqvist and Damsten, 1969; Kerley, 1965), tibia (Kerley, 1965; Singh and Gunberg, 1970; Thompson and Galvin, 1983), fibula (Kerley, 1965), ulna (Thompson, 1979), clavicle (Stout and Paine, 1992; Stout et al., 1996), 4th rib (Stout et al., 1994; Kim et al., 2007) and 6th rib (Stout, 1986; Stout and Paine, 1992; Cho et al., 2002), cranium (Clarke, 1987; Cool et al., 1995; Curtis, 2004), mandible (Singh and Gunberg, 1970), and humerus (Thompson, 1979; and Yoshino et al., 1994).

The application of quantitative bone histology as a preferred method in anthropological analyses has been hindered by researchers' inability to apply the methods without some degree of training, and, more importantly, by uncertainty regarding the reliability of the methods. While microscopic age changes are considered to be universal, inconsistencies in the reported accuracy of the methods when they are applied to individuals outside of the reference samples suggest that intrinsic and extrinsic factors, such as genetics and a wide range of suggested behaviors, have varying effects on bone microstructure.

The development and application of histological methods requires researchers to learn about factors that do not affect gross anatomical methods. Diagenesis, which refers to the chemical, physical, and biological changes that remains undergo after initial deposition, is a factor in determining suitable samples (Pfeiffer, 2000). The existence of an osteon asymptote may influence the decision to embark on histological assessment, if the skeletal material is presumed to be from an elderly person. The asymptote occurs when the bone has become completely remodeled so that new osteon creations simply replace older ones and the proportion of the cortex that is remodeled does not increase (Frost, 1987a, 1987b).

As noted by Lazenby (1984) biological issues may all be secondary to concerns relating to the design of the methods. Methodological concerns include sample size, sample demography, variable definitions, and measurement techniques. With regard to method accuracy, current algorithms and predictive equations appear to adequately estimate age in the sample populations in which they were developed yet their broad application is often questioned. Confusion occurs when researchers use samples of unknown sex and age to explore the accuracy of methods. Such is often the case in paleodemographic research when histological age estimates are compared against some "gold" standard determined by familiar methods that assess gross skeletal morphology. Bocquet-Appel and Masset (1982, 1996) argue that developing a method of age estimation on a sample will result in the replication of the original sample's mortality profile. Therefore, methods tend to work best for the samples that have a distribution close to the reference or developmental sample. Considering this relationship, methodological bias due to sample demography can have a significant effect on method accuracy; however, the point that Bocquet-Appel and Masset (1982) made is often misunderstood. Reconstructed age distributions will not replicate the actual reference sample age distribution. It is the skewness of the reference sample that will be reflected in the accuracy of the target sample age distribution. Reference samples with positively skewed distributions toward younger ages will produce more accurate age estimates for younger individuals and those with negatively skewed distributions toward older ages will produce more accurate age estimates for older individuals. The magnitude of this error can only be derived through testing methods on large skeletal samples of known age and sex.

The research described here systematically tests a selection of histological methods on a large, documented age skeletal sample to explore their accuracy. Recognizing and quantifying potential biases in histological analyses will support the development and application of the best methods for estimating adult age at death. The research design is comprised of two main components. The first examines the accuracy of current histological methods of age estimation that utilize rib cross-sections (Stout, 1986; Stout and Paine, 1992; Cho et al., 2002) and femoral anterior wedges (Singh and Gunberg, 1970; Thompson, 1979; Ericksen, 1991). The evaluation involves calculating the accuracy of each method to predict the known age, and the agreement between the rib and femur methods independent from one another. The second component evaluates a subsample in which both rib and femoral histological sections are available from the same individuals, thus providing a unique opportunity to evaluate histological age estimates from two different biomechanical loading environments. This analysis examines if accuracy is increased when multiple histological methods are used to develop a multiregional age estimate. In addition, the accuracy and bias of selected histological methods are compared to those of commonly used gross anatomical methods.

MATERIALS AND METHODS

The sample from Christ Church in Spitalfields, London, is derived from remains that were interred in the church crypt between 1729 and 1857 AD (Molleson and Cox, 1993). The sample contains 383 individuals of documented age and sex. Prior to this research, tissue samples from the mid-thoracic ribs and anterior femora were removed and non-decalcified thin sections were prepared following standard methods (Aiello and Molleson, 1993; Dupras and Pfeiffer, 1996). The thin sections were divided into three subsets for this research (Table 13.1). Subset one (S1) consists of rib samples from 215 individuals. Subset two (S2) consists of femur samples from 187 individuals. Subset three (S3) draws from the previous subsets and consists of both rib and femur samples from 149 individuals.

Histomorphometric variables were collected using an Olympus BX-41 transmitted light microscope equipped with 10× widefield oculars (Olympus America, Center Valley, PA), 10× and 20× UPLanFL objectives (Olympus America, Center Valley, PA), and an Evolution LC (PL-A641) color firewire digital camera (Media Cybernetics, Inc., Bethesda, MD) Evaluation techniques were dependent on the individual methods and, therefore, established method protocols were followed as closely as possible.

TABLE 13.1
DESCRIPTIVE STATISTICS FOR THE KNOWN SPITALFIELDS HISTOLOGICAL SAMPLE

Study Sample Rib Subset (S1)

Sex	N	Age Range in Years	Mean Age in Years	Std. Deviation	Skew
Males	107	13–92	54.68	19.89	-0.83
Females	108	13–89	55.72	20.62	-0.61
Total	215	13–92	55.20	20.22	-0.71

Study Sample Femur Subset (S2)

Sex	N	Age Range in Years	Mean Age in Years	Std. Deviation	Skew
Males	96	16–92	55.99	16.97	-0.45
Females	91	16–89	55.66	19.37	-0.31
Total	187	16–92	55.83	18.13	-0.37

Individuals with Both Rib and Femur Sampled (S3)

Sex	N	Age Range in Years	Mean Age in Years	Std. Deviation	Skew
Males	77	16–92	56.08	17.69	-0.48
Females	72	17–89	58.19	18.58	-0.38
Total	149	16–92	57.10	18.09	-0.41

Rib Analysis

Three methods are available for the estimation of age using the middle third of the 6th rib, each having been built on the study sample used to develop the previous method. These methods, developed by Stout (1986), Stout and Paine (1992), and Cho and colleagues (2002) use a Merz counting reticule to evaluate the cross-section and collect area measurements. This study employed a gridded reticle, which superimposes a 100-square grid containing 100 intersections over the field of view. Histological structures are included if more than one-half of their area is located within the perimeter of the grid. The researcher can evaluate the entire bone cross-section or half of the cross-section in a checkerboard configuration. The earliest of these methods (Stout, 1986) does not provide the information needed to construct an error term. See Appendices 1 and 2 for methodological details.

Femur Analysis

This research explored the evaluation of the anterior femur using the methods of Singh and Gunberg (1970), Thompson (1979), and Ericksen (1991). Unlike methods developed for the rib, the age estimation methods using the anterior femur were developed independently, so there is a wide range of variable definitions and evaluation techniques. The Singh and Gunberg method employs two circular microscopic fields at unspecified locations along the periosteal border. The Thompson method evaluates four consecutive 0.99 mm² fields along the anterior periosteal border and the Ericksen method evaluates five consecutive 0.886 mm² fields along the anterior periosteal border. See Appendices 1 and 2 for methodological details.

There were difficulties in replicating the Singh and Gunberg (1970) and Ericksen (1991) microscopic fields, requiring correction factors calculated as described by Kerley and Ubelaker (1978).

Method Agreement

In order to assess the agreement between each histological method and known age of death, the approach described by Bland and Altman (1986, 1995) was employed. The differences between the age estimates for each method are plotted against the known age. Age estimates are plotted against the line of equality, which is the line where all values would lie if there were complete agreement between estimated and known age. Next, the differences between estimated and known ages are plotted against the known ages. The limits of agreement, provide a range for which 95 percent of the variability between estimated and known ages will fall, are then calculated. The upper and lower limits of agreement are calculated by taking the mean difference bracketed by two standard deviations. The themes of analysis are accuracy, namely the ability of a method to determine the chronologic age, and the direction of inaccuracy, referred to here as bias.

RESULTS

Rib Methods: Accuracy and Bias

Tests of inaccuracy and bias were performed on the sample overall, the sample divided into age cohorts, and the sample separated by sex. ANCO-VA and Chow test results show that there are no significant sex and age inter-

TABLE 13.2
BIAS AND INACCURACY VALUES FOR THE
RIB HISTOLOGICAL AGE ESTIMATES (IN YEARS)

| | **Pooled Sample** | | | | | | |
| | *Stout (1986)* | | *Stout & Paine (1992)* | | *Cho et al. (2002)* | | |
Age Group	Bias	Inaccuracy	Bias	Inaccuracy	Bias	Inaccuracy	N
13–19	-2.2	9.5	0.7	2.5	10.0	11.2	8
20–29	-1.4	5.6	-6.0	6.2	3.9	6.6	14
30–39	1.1	10.5	-10.2	10.8	5.0	9.6	20
40–49	-4.4	10.9	-18.1	18.2	-3.3	9.2	22
50–59	-3.9	12.9	-21.2	22.2	-4.8	10.4	41
60–69	-6.4	11.7	-26.5	27.7	-7.6	9.2	50
70–79	-15.1	18.4	-36.0	36.6	-16.2	17.2	42
80+	-17.8	17.8	-41.9	41.9	-19.6	19.6	18
All Ages	-7.2	13.1	-23.9	24.7	-6.7	11.8	215
Normalized	-6.3	12.2	-19.9	20.8	-4.1	11.6	

actions within the methods. The slopes and intercepts are equal between the sexes within each method; therefore, the analysis of the pooled sample is presented (Table 13.2).

Of the three methods assessed, the Stout and Paine (1992) equation demonstrates the most bias and inaccuracy, in a manner consistent with reports in the literature (Dudar et al., 1993; Stout et al., 1996; Pratte and Pfeiffer, 1999). The magnitude of this error indicates that the equation consistently and progressively underestimates age. Overall and normalized, the Stout (1986) and the Cho et al. (2002) equations perform similarly (Figures 13.1 and 13.2). Both methods demonstrate trends toward increasing bias and inaccuracy with older chronological ages. Bias values steadily increase after 50 years of age, jumping twofold after the 60-69 year age cohort. This is not surprising, given that the predicted asymptote associated with the rib is near this age interval (Wu et al., 1970). Reasoning that a remodeling asymptote occurs sometime around 60 years of age, the data set was truncated at 60, thus removing 110 individuals. Paired t-tests comparing estimated and known age within the truncated sample (N = 105) show that the Stout (1986) age estimations are still significantly different from the known ages (t = 1.998, df = 104, p = 0.048), whereas the Cho et al. (2002) age estimates are not significantly different from the known ages (t = 0.256, df = 104, p = 0.799).

Mean differences, upper and lower limits of agreement, and bias values for both the complete and truncated data sets indicate the overall propensity of

Age Estimation of the Human Skeleton

FIGURE 13.1
DIFFERENCES IN STOUT (1986) ESTIMATED AGES FROM KNOWN AGES
AGAINST KNOWN AGES (IN YEARS) FOR THE TRUNCATED SAMPLE, WITH 95%
LIMITS OF AGREEMENT (+23.9, -29.1; BIAS -2.6) AND BEST-FIT LINE (N = 105)

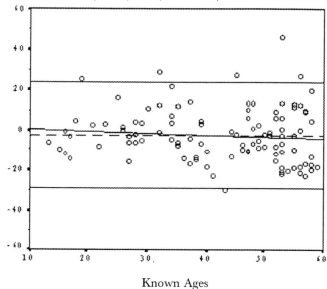

Known Ages

FIGURE 13.2
DIFFERENCES IN CHO et al. (2002) ESTIMATED AGES FROM KNOWN AGES
AGAINST KNOWN AGES (IN YEARS) FOR THE TRUNCATED SAMPLE, WITH 95%
LIMITS OF AGREEMENT (+25.3, -24.6; BIAS -0.3) AND BEST-FIT LINE (N = 105)

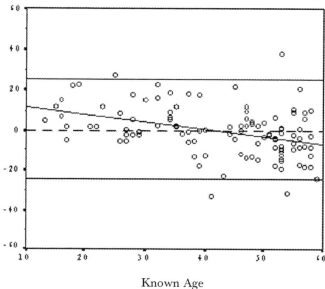

Known Age

the methods to overestimate the ages of younger individuals and underestimate the ages of older individuals. Both methods demonstrate similarly wide ranges for their limits of agreement and the mean differences are significantly different from zero. Mean difference values and the lower limits of agreement are noticeably improved through use of the truncated data set. Both methods still demonstrate similarly wide ranges for their limits of agreement; however, the Cho et al. (2002) method produces fewer values beyond the 95 percent limit.

The limits of agreement establish a range within which 95 percent of the variability between estimated and known ages will fall. Best-fit lines show the degree of overestimation at younger ages and underestimation at older ages of the methods. This trend is more prevalent in the Cho et al. (2002) method, but the mean difference in age estimates is not significantly different from zero. In summary, the Cho et al. (2002) method appears to be the more appropriate method for the estimation of adult age at death from rib cortical bone for the following reasons: (1) narrower limits of agreement containing 95 percent of the values, (2) non-significant mean differences, and (3) the descriptive statistics are available for the method to calculate confidence intervals for the age estimate.

Femur Methods: Accuracy and Bias

The Thompson (1979) and Ericksen (1991) methods provide both general and sex-specific equations; however, analysis of the sex-specific equations did not produce significant differences to warrant further analyses. ANCOVA and Chow test results show that there are no significant sex and age interactions within any of the methods, indicating that slopes and intercepts are equal between the sexes. These tests, combined with the overall pattern of bias and inaccuracy between the sexes, indicate only some subtle differences, thus permitting the remainder of the analyses to be performed on the general (non-sex specific) equations. Results of inaccuracy and bias for the pooled sample are presented in Table 13.3.

Overall and normalized, the Thompson (1979) method exhibits less bias, but similar levels of inaccuracy when compared to that of the Ericksen (1991) method (Figures 13.3 and 13.4). The Singh and Gunberg (1970) method demonstrates the most bias and inaccuracy (29 and 33 years, respectively), indicating a tendency to severely overestimate age in almost every age cohort. It was therefore removed from subsequent analysis. Estimated and known age paired t-tests considering the pooled sample and general equa-

TABLE 13.3
BIAS AND INACCURACY VALUES FOR THE FEMUR
HISTOLOGICAL AGE ESTIMATES (IN YEARS)

	Thompson (1979)			Singh & Gunberg (1970)			Ericksen (1992)		
Age Group	Bias	Inaccuracy	N	Bias	Inaccuracy	N	Bias	Inaccuracy	N
16–19	0.2	6.9	6	20.6	20.8	7	10.4	10.4	4
20–29	0.5	10.3	15	22.5	23.7	15	4.0	10.5	11
30–39	10.4	15.9	19	35.5	36.4	19	7.7	14.4	13
40–49	4.8	13.9	23	30.4	32.5	23	3.7	9.9	19
50–59	6.8	10.6	33	33.2	33.9	32	1.4	5.1	24
60–69	1.0	6.6	38	35.4	39.7	38	-3.7	4.9	27
70–79	-6.5	6.7	37	31.8	34.7	38	-10.2	10.5	34
80+	-15.5	15.5	13	-8.6	13.8	12	-18.8	18.8	10
All Ages	0.7	10.1	184	29.2	32.7	184	-2.4	9.4	142
Normalized	0.2	10.8		25.1	29.4		-0.7	10.6	

Pooled Sample

tions indicate that the Thompson (1979) method produces age estimates that are not significantly different from the known ages (t = -0.78, df = 183, p = 0.43), while the Ericksen (1991) method does produce significantly different mean ages (t = 2.474, df = 141, p < 0.05).

The Thompson (1979) and Ericksen (1991) methods demonstrate an overall propensity to overestimate ages of younger individuals and underestimate ages of older individuals. Both methods demonstrate wide ranges for their limits of agreement, with the Ericksen limits being slightly narrower. The Thompson mean age difference is not significantly different from zero, but only 94 percent of the values are within the limits of agreement. The Ericksen mean age difference is significantly different from zero, but this method provides tighter limits and 95 percent of the differences are within these limits. Best-fit lines show that the degree of overestimation at younger ages and underestimation at older ages is more pronounced in the Ericksen method.

The two methods perform similarly, but the Thompson sample allows inclusion of specimens with levels of diagenesis that preclude their evaluation using the Ericksen (1991) method. This may introduce additional bias to the comparison of the two methods. In order to explore this, the 42 individuals that were not included in the Ericksen method were removed from the Thompson data set. Despite the removal of the diagenetically altered samples, value distributions and limits do not change significantly. The Ericksen (1991) method has a directional bias in age differences, consistently underes-

FIGURE 13.3
DIFFERENCES IN ESTIMATED AGES FROM KNOWN AGES (IN YEARS)
USING THOMPSON'S GENERAL EQUATION, WITH 95% LIMITS OF
AGREEMENTS (+26.5, -25; BIAS -0.7) AND BEST-FIT LINE (N = 184)

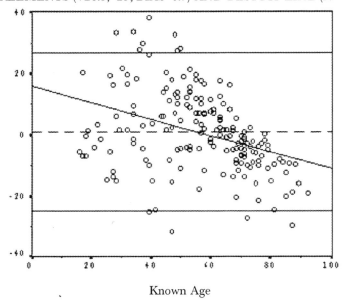

Known Age

FIGURE 13.4
DIFFERENCES IN ESTIMATED AGES FROM KNOWN AGES (IN YEARS)
USING ERICKSEN'S GENERAL EQUATION, WITH 95% LIMITS OF
AGREEMENTS (+20.8, -25.6; BIAS -2.4) AND BEST-FIT LINE (N = 142)

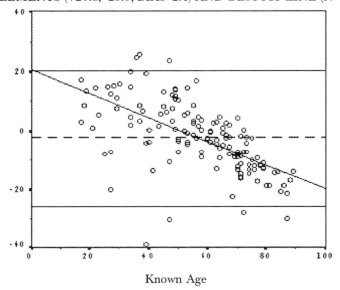

Known Age

timating age, but it provides tighter limits of agreement within which 95 percent of the values fall. The Thompson method presents no overall bias in mean age differences, but it has slightly larger limits of agreement and more than 5 percent of the values fall outside these limits. The Thompson method demonstrates less bias and can be used on diagenetically altered samples, making this method more broadly applicable. In related research (Crowder, 2005), it was found that the Ericksen (1991) method performed less well with respect to repeatability. For these reasons, the Thompson (1979) method is preferred over the Ericksen (1991) method.

Within-Individual Patterns, Rib and Femur

The typical approach to skeletal age estimation is to assess as many components as are available and to then construct a summary age estimate. To develop a summary histological age estimate, assessments of the rib and femur from the same individual could be combined. Will those values produce similar age estimates? Research with the Spitalfields samples allows exploration of which skeletal element(s) should be used when both sample locations are available.

The age estimates derived from Cho et al. (2002) and Thompson (1979) methods were compared. In this comparison of skeletal elements, inaccuracy results are similar to those seen for the pooled and sex divided samples (Table 13.4). The femur age estimates demonstrate very little bias, while the rib age estimates show a consistent negative bias. Once again, bias values for the ribs steadily increase after 50 years of age. This trend appears to occur later in the femur, beginning at 70 years of age. Comparing the two sampling locations, the rib age estimates are more accurate for individuals under 50-60 years of age, while the femur age estimates are more accurate for individuals over 50-60 years of age. Estimated and known age paired t-tests indicate that the Thompson (1979) method does not produce a significantly different mean age compared to the known sample (t = -0.89, df = 148, p = 0.38), while the Cho et al. (2002) method produces significantly different mean ages (t = 6.120, df = 148, p < 0.05). These results mirror those previously described from the analysis of the larger sample. Paired t-tests of the Thompson (1979) age estimates and Cho et al. (2002) age estimates indicate that the two methods produce significantly different mean age estimates (t = -6.29, df = 148, p < 0.05).

When the mean difference, upper and lower limits of agreement and bias values for the rib and femur estimates are compared (Figure 13.5), it can be said that the methods partially counteract each other. The rib method pro-

TABLE 13.4
BIAS AND INACCURACY VALUES FOR THE RIB AND FEMUR SAMPLES
FROM THE SAME INDIVIDUAL (IN YEARS)

| | **Pooled Sample** | | | | |
| | *Cho et al. (2002)* | | *Thompson (1979)* | | |
Age Group	Bias	Inaccuracy	Bias	Inaccuracy	N
16–19	6.5	8.9	0.2	10.0	4
20–29	2.2	5.3	0.7	11.7	12
30–39	5.8	11.0	12.5	15.9	15
40–49	-4.3	10.8	6.1	15.0	16
50–59	-2.8	9.9	8.1	11.7	24
60–69	-6.7	8.4	1.2	6.3	34
70–79	-16.1	16.8	-6.0	6.2	32
80+	-20.3	20.3	-16.0	16.0	12
All Ages	-6.6	11.7	1.0	13.1	149
Normalized	-4.5	11.4	0.9	11.6	

duces older estimates than the femur method for younger ages and younger estimates than the femur method for the older ages. The greatest discrepancy between methods occurs among individuals 50 years and younger. Plotting the age estimates for each method against the known ages with the line of equality demonstrates patterns of accuracy that are consistent with the analyses of the larger samples. Both methods demonstrate moderate r-squared values (Cho et al., 2002 [$r^2 = 0.49$], Thompson, 1979 [$r^2 = 0.53$]). The line of equality illustrates the inaccuracy of the Cho et al. (2002) method when it is used to estimate age at death for individuals over 60 years. The Thompson (1979) method demonstrates this problem closer to 80 years of age.

Averaging the point age estimates for the two methods per individual improves average accuracy ($r^2 = 0.64$), but this is because the Cho et al. (2002) method is more accurate for younger individuals and less accurate for older individuals. When averaged, the two methods compensate for each other to a certain degree, producing age estimates closer to the line of equality. Plotting the mean differences of the averaged age estimates for both methods against the known ages illustrates that the over and underestimation of age at death is still prevalent (Figure 13.6). Averaging the age estimates produces ten values outside of the 95 percent limit demonstrating that agreement was not achieved, which indicates that averaging the methods does not fully eliminate the inherent bias.

FIGURE 13.5
DIFFERENCES IN THOMPSON (1979) AND CHO et al. (2002) ESTIMATED AGES
FROM FEMORA AND RIBS OF THE SAME INDIVIDUALS, WITH 95% LIMITS
OF AGREEMENTS (+36.9, -21.8, BIAS 7.6) AND BEST-FIT LINE. THE VERTICAL
LINES SEPARATE THE AGE COHORTS BY DECADE (N = 149)

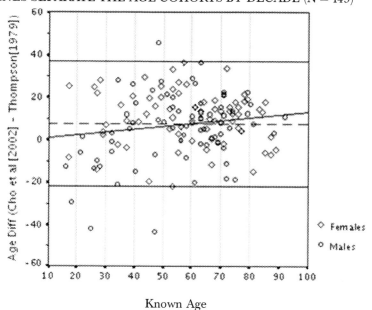

FIGURE 13.6
DIFFERENCES IN THE THOMPSON (1979) AND CHO et al. (2002) MEAN
ESTIMATED AGES FROM THE KNOWN AGES (IN YEARS), WITH 95% LIMITS
OF AGREEMENTS (+19, -24.7, BIAS -2.8) AND BEST-FIT LINE (N = 149)

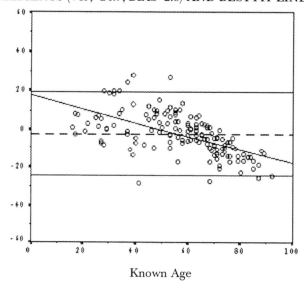

TABLE 13.5
OVERALL ACCURACY OF THE SPITALFIELDS HISTOLOGICAL AGE
ESTIMATES EXPRESSED AS YEARS DEVIATING FROM KNOWN AGE.
THE RIB SAMPLE INCLUDES THE TRUNCATED DATA SET AND
THE FEMUR SAMPLE INCLUDES THE COMPLETE DATA SET

# of individuals for Cho et al. (2002)	Cumulative sample	Years deviating from known age	% of total sample
38	38	±5	36.20%
27	65	±10	61.90%
16	81	±15	77.10%
13	94	±20	89.50%
8	102	±30	97.10%
3	105	±40	100.00%
# of individuals for Thompson (1978)	Cumulative sample	Years deviating from known age	% of total sample
60	60	±5	32.60%
51	111	±10	60.30%
28	139	±15	75.50%
25	164	±20	89.10%
16	180	±30	97.80%
4	184	±40	100.00%

DISCUSSION AND CONCLUSIONS

The methods proposed by Cho and colleagues (2002) for the sixth rib and Thompson (1979) for the anterior femur midshaft can be applied with reasonable accuracy once the methods' limitations are recognized. Table 13.5 provides the accuracy of the estimated ages from the truncated Spitalfields sample using the Cho and colleagues' equation and the complete sample for the Thompson method expressed in years deviating above and below the known age.

The rib method becomes too inaccurate beyond 50 to 60 years of age to be used independently from other methods of age estimation. The Thompson (1979) method is more versatile and thus more applicable than the other femur assessment methods. The absence of younger individuals in the original reference sample for the Thompson (1979) method may explain the higher levels of inaccuracy in the younger age cohorts (40 years and below). Because of remodeling rate differences in the femur compared to that of the rib, a larger percentage of the periosteal cortical bone remains unremodeled as an individual ages. Owing to these differences, it is believed that the asymptote is reached at a later age in the femur. A large portion of individuals from the Spitalfields sample who were younger than 40 years of age demonstrate significant amounts of unremodeled periosteal bone. Sampling procedures that evaluate the entire cortical envelope from the periosteal to endosteal surfaces may increase the predictive relationship of microstructures to chronological age.

Not presented in this research, but equally important, is the relationship of method reliability to the histological evaluation technique as a factor in the amount of observer error that is expected or introduced. Crowder (2005) describes the amount of observer error introduced with the aforementioned histological methods and recommends ways to limit this error in future research.

As with all methods of age estimation, there are limitations in their application. One of the challenges for anthropologists is to determine which methods will be most appropriate for the analysis of unknown remains. The age and sex distributions of the reference sample partially determine the accuracy of the method. Regarding histological methods, this may be illustrated by the fact that some practitioners report favorable results from the Stout and Paine (1992) equation. A closer look at these results typically reveals sample demographics similar to that of the 1992 method. To properly evaluate potential reference-target sample issues, explicit descriptions of the samples are needed to allow investigators to recognize potential difficulties in applying methods of age estimation. In addition to the age and sex distribution issue, age indicators that poorly correlate with chronological age or specific age cohorts will amplify the inherent bias introduced by sample demography. Such may be the case with older individuals that have reached the osteon asymptote.

The statistical model used to develop a predictive equation should also be scrutinized. Least squares linear regression has been the most common approach applied. Inverse calibration is a common procedure used to develop a regression line, which produces a regression of the mean effect (Kroll and Saxtrup, 2000). This causes a systematic bias in age estimates, resulting in the overestimation of age in younger individuals and the underestimation of age in older individuals. All the histological methods evaluated in this research demonstrate this bias, as do most gross morphological methods of adult age estimation. It is for this reason that Bayesian models of analysis are currently being used to re-evaluate established methods of age estimation.

Coupling the rib and femur histological methods in the form of a point age average does not greatly improve the accuracy of age estimates. Developing a statistical model that incorporates the two regions may provide for a more accurate model. However, results suggest that in order to select the skeletal element that will produce the most accurate histological age estimate when analyzing unknown human remains, a general evaluation of age using gross morphological methods may be warranted. If a gross evaluation is not possible, both skeletal locations should be evaluated histologically to reveal patterns that can be interpreted in order to guide the analyst in determining which analysis warrants more weight.

There are two ways in which the results of this analysis might be interpreted. One possible conclusion is that because the remodeling capacity of rib and femur are different, the age estimates will not be equally reliable for all age cohorts and, therefore, one should try to choose the approach that seems most expedient, based on gross morphological indicators if they are available. From another perspective, because the methods use different approaches to derive age estimates, the predictive variables and sampling techniques may exaggerate the disparity between age estimates from the rib and femur. The rib method evaluates the entire cortex and calculates the osteon population density, while the femur method evaluates four periosteal fields and calculates the percentage of area of fields a structure occupies. More investigation is warranted, using approaches that apply similar variables and sampling strategies to different anatomical locations.

In comparisons with the performance of the commonly used methods of age estimation that are based on gross morphology, histological methods appear to have been overly criticized in the literature. The results of this study indicate that quantitative assessment of bone histology is a useful method for estimating adult age at death, producing accuracy values that are comparable to conventional gross morphological methods (Crowder, 2009). Histological methods utilizing the femur appear to be more promising than gross morphological methods, especially if the goal is to increase the accuracy of age estimates for individuals over 50 years of age. A final consideration to improve the construction of age estimates is to use both gross morphological and microscopic methods. Both gross and histological changes reflect tissue remodeling, thus evaluation of both may provide insight into age-related changes and may provide a stronger interpretation of age at death.

ACKNOWLEDGMENTS

This research would not have been possible without the support of the Natural History Museum in London, England, notably Louise Humphrey and Theya Molleson, who provided access to the Spitalfields skeletal material. We also thank Drs. Sam Stout, Robert Paine, and Helen Cho for discussing in detail the methods they developed for evaluating the rib.

Appendix A

THE VARIABLES COLLECTED FOR THE METHODS USED IN THIS STUDY

RIB METHODS

1. *Total Area (Tt.Ar).* The total cross-sectional area of bone within the periosteal envelope.
2. *Cortical Area (Ct.Ar).* The area of cortical bone contained within the periosteum and endsoteum.
3. *Relative Cortical Area (Ct.Ar/Tt.Ar).* The area of bone between the periosteum and endosteum divided by the total area of the cross-section.
4. *Cortical Area Evaluated (Sa.Ar)*: the actual area of bone evaluated for microstructures per section.
5. *Intact Osteon Density ($_I$OPD).* The number of secondary osteons per grid unit area that have 90% of their Haversian canal perimeters intact or unremodeled, divided by the Sa.Ar.
6. *Fragmentary Osteon Density ($_F$OPD).* The number of secondary osteons per grid unit area, in which 10% or more of the perimeters of their Haversian canals, if present, has been remodeled by subsequent generations of secondary osteons. The total fragmentary osteon counts are divided by the Sa.Ar.
7. *Osteon Population Density (OPD).* Sum of $_I$OPD and $_F$OPD.
8. *Mean Osteonal Cross-Sectional Area (On.Ar).* The average area of bone contained within the cement lines of structurally complete secondary osteons (reversal lines are intact). Mean osteonal area is calculated as the average cross-sectional area of a minimum of 25 complete osteons per cross-section.

THOMPSON (1979) METHOD

1. *Aggregate Osteon Lamellae Area (OSTA).* Percentage of area of fields containing osteon lamellae
2. *Aggregate Haversian Canal Area (HCA).* Percentage of area of fields containing canals
3. *Osteon Area (OSTHC).* Aggregate osteon lamellae plus Haversian canal area

SINGH AND GUNBERG (1970) METHOD

Secondary Osteons (X^1), number of intact osteons (complete Haversian systems) counted in two fields (not an average). Histologically, each osteon is clearly demarcated from the neighboring ones as well as from the interstitial systems by prominent cement lines. Osteons that were partially obscured by the periphery of the field, or were cut obliquely or only seen as fragments, were included if the complete Haversian canal was seen.

ERICKSEN (1991) METHOD

Secondary Osteons (X_1) are surrounded by a cement (reversal) line. The main criterion of an osteon is that its Haversian canal is intact and not breached by a resorption space or impinged upon by the walls of a later osteon. Osteons whose Haversian canals lie entirely outside of the photographic field are not counted but are marked with a cross for future reference.

Type II Osteons (X_2) appear to be the result of an episode of resorption along a limited stretch of the Haversian canal of a mature osteon (Richman et al., 1979). The new resorption space is relatively small and is eventually provided with a cement line and filled in with new lamellae, forming an osteon-within-an-osteon structure (Ortner, 1975).

Fragments (X_3) are remnants of former osteons, and they range from tiny slivers to full-sized "dead" osteons whose Haversian canals show Howship's lacunae, indicating that resorption has been initiated by their own blood vessels. All fragments are counted, including those partly within the field.

Resorption Spaces (X_4) represent the first step in the formation of an osteon; they destroy older bone to make space for the laying down of new bone. They are distinguished by their scalloped edges formed by Howship's lacunae and range from the first tiny breakthrough of its walls by a vessel in unremodeled lamellar bone or within the Haversian canal of an osteon to the grossly visible resorption cavities in the bones of older individuals.

Non-Haversian Canals (X_5) (pseudo-Haversian canals, primary vascular canals, "primary osteons," of certain authors, e.g., Kerley, 1965; Thompson, 1978; 1979) are the vascular canals incorporated during the deposition of periosteal circumferential lamellae and thus are characteristic of unremodeled bone. Very large non-Haversian canals may be lined by a layer or two of concentric lamellae, but the resulting structures can be distinguished from true osteons by the lack of a cement line and the fact that the unremodeled circumferential lamellae are not interrupted but flow smoothly around the non-Haversian canal.

- Unremodeled Circumferential Bone (X_6)
- Osteonal Bone (X_7), including regular osteons and Volkmann's canals, type II osteons, and the peripheral osteons marked with a cross in the earlier count.
- Fragmental Bone (X_8)

Appendix B

METHOD FIELD LOCATIONS AND PREDICTIVE EQUATIONS FOR THIS RESEARCH

Method	Field Location	Age Prediction Equation(s)
Stout (1986)		$Y = (-12.239\ 00) + (2.873\ 51 * OPD)$
Stout & Paine (1992)		$LnY = 2.343 + (0.050877 * OPD)$
Cho et al. (2002)*		1) $Y = 38.029 + 1.603\ (OPD) - 882.210\ (On.Ar. * 0) - 51.228\ (Ct.Ar./Tt.Ar.) + 57.441\ (Ct.Ar./Tt.Ar. * 0)$
		2) $Y = 38.209 + 1.375 * (OPD) - 699.581 * (On.Ar.)$

Method	Total Area	Fields	Age Prediction Equation(s)	
Singh and Gunberg (1970)	6.28mm2			$Y = 16.10 + 1.38*(X^1)$
Thompson (1979)	3.96mm2		M	$Y = 8.387 + 100.133*(OSTHC)$
			F	$Y = 4.097 + 104.755*(OSTHC)$
			All	$Y = 6.677 + 101.936*(OSTHC)$
Ericksen (1991)	4.45mm2		M	$Y = 59.23 + 1.38(X_1) + 1.88(X_2) + 0.30(X_3) - 0.18(X_4) - 1.61(X_5) - 0.18(X_6) - 0.35(X_7) + 0.01(X_8)$
			F	$Y = 102.45 + 0.53(X_1) + 3.00(X_2) + 0.27(X_3) + 0.93(X_4) - 1.44(X_5) - 0.72(X_6) - 0.60(X_7) - 0.51(X_8)$
			All	$Y = 92.42 + 1.07(X_1) + 2.50(X_2) + 0.25(X_3) - 0.30(X_4) - 1.52(X_5) - 0.57(X_6) - 0.61(X_7) - 0.35(X_8)$

REFERENCES

Aiello, L. C., & Molleson, T. (1993). Are microscopic ageing techniques more accurate than macroscopic ageing techniques? *Journal of Archeological Science 20*:689–704.

Ahlqvist, J., & Damsten, O. (1969). A modification of Kerley's method for microscopic determination of age in human bone. *Journal of Forensic Sciences 14*:205–212.

Bland, J. M., & Altman, D. G. (1986). Statistical methods for assessing agreement between two methods of clinical measurement. *Lancet 8476*:307–310.

Bland, J., M., & Altman, D. G. (1995). Comparing methods of measurement: Why plotting difference against standard method is misleading. *Lancet 346*(8982):1085–1089.

Bocquet-Appel, J. P., & Masset, C. (1982). Farewell to paleodemography. *Journal of Human Evolution 11*:321–333.

Bocquet-Appel, J. P., & Masset, C. (1996). Paleodemography: Expectancy and false hope. *American Journal of Physical Anthropology 99*:571–583.

Brooks, S. T., & Suchey, J. M. (1990). Skeletal age determination based on the os pubis: A comparison of the Ascadi-Nemeskeri and Suchey-Brooks methods. *Human Evolution 5*:227–238.

Buckberry, J. L., & Chamberlain, A. T. (2002). Age estimation from the auricular surface of the ilium: A revised method. *American Journal of Physical Anthropology 119*:231–239.

Cho, H., Stout, S. D., Madsen, R. W., & Streeter, M. A. (2002). Population-specific histological age-estimating method: A model for known African-American and European-American skeletal remains. *Journal of Forensic Sciences 47*(1):12–18.

Clarke, D. F. (1987). Histological and radiographic variation in the parietal bone in a cadaveric population. Thesis, Anatomy Department, The University of Queensland.

Cool, S. M., Hendrikz, J. K., & Wood, W. B. (1995). Microscopic age changes in the human occipital bone. *Journal of Forensic Sciences 40*(5):789–796.

Crowder, C. (2005). Evaluating the use of quantitative bone histology to estimate adult age at death. Doctoral Dissertation, University of Toronto, Ontario.

Crowder, C. (2009). Establishing a biological profile: Histological age estimation. In S. Blau & D. H. Ubelaker (Eds.), *Handbook of forensic anthropology and archaeology,* pp. 222–235. Walnut Creek, CA: Left Coast Press.

Curtis, J. (2004). Estimation of age at death from the microscopic appearance of the frontal bone. Masters Thesis, University of Indianapolis, Indiana.

Dudar, J. C., Pfeiffer, S., & Saunders, S. R. (1993). Evaluation of morphological and histological adult skeletal age-at-death estimation techniques using ribs. *Journal of Forensic Science 38*(3):677–685.

Dupras, T. L., & Pfeiffer, S. K. (1996). Determination of sex from adult human ribs. *Canadian Society of Forensic Science 29*(4):221–231.

Ericksen, M. F. (1991). Histological estimation of age at death using the anterior cortex of the femur. *American Journal of Physical Anthropology 84*:171–179.

Frost, H. M. (1987a). Secondary osteon populations: an algorithm for determining mean bone tissue age. *Yearbook of Physical Anthropology 30*:221–238.

Frost, H. M. (1987b). Secondary osteon population densities: an algorithm for estimating missing osteons. *Yearbook of Physical Anthropology 30*:239–254.

Îscan, M. Y. (1993). *Casts of age phases from the sternal end of the rib for white males and females.*

Fort Collins, CO: France Casting.

Îscan, M. Y., Loth, S. R., & Wright, R. K. (1984). Age estimation from the rib by phase analysis: White males. *Journal of Forensic Sciences 29*(4):1094–104.

Kerley, E. R. (1965). The microscopic determination of age in human bone. *American Journal of Physical Anthropology 23*:149–164.

Kerley, E. R., & Ubelaker, D. H. (1978). Revisions in the microscopic method of estimating age at death in human cortical bone. *American Journal of Physical Anthropology 46*:545–546.

Kim, Y., Kim, D., Park, D., Lee, J., Chung, N., Lee, W., & Han, S. (2007). Assessment of histomorphological features of the sternal end of the fourth rib for age estimation in Koreans. *Journal of Forensic Sciences 52*(6):1237–1241.

Krøll, J., & Saxtrup, O. (2000). On the use of regression for the estimation of human biological age. *Biogerontology 1*:363–368.

Lazenby, R. A. (1984). Inherent deficiencies in cortical bone microstructural age estimation techniques. *OSSA 9-11*:95–103.

Lovejoy, C. O., Meindl, R. S., Pryzbeck, T. R., & Mensforth, R. P. (1985a). Chronological metamorphosis of the auricular surface of the ilium: A new method for the determination of age at death. *American Journal of Physical Anthropology 68*:15–28.

Lovejoy, C. O., Meindl, R. S., Mensforth, R. P., & Barton, T. J. (1985b). Multifactorial determination of skeletal age at death: a method and blind tests of its accuracy. *American Journal of Physical Anthropology 68*:1–14.

Molleson, T., & Cox, M. (1993). The Middling Sort. The Spitalfields Project. Vol. 2. The Anthropology. CBA Research Report 86. York Council for British Archaeology.

Pfeiffer, S. (1992). Cortical bone age estimates from historically known adults. *Zeitschrift fur Morphologie and Anthropologie 79*(1):1–10.

Pfeiffer, S. (2000). Palaeohistology: Health and disease. In M. A. Katzenberg & S. R. Saunders (Eds), *Biological anthropology of the human skeleton,* pp. 287–302. New York: Wiley-Liss, Inc.

Pratte, D. G., & Pfeiffer, S. (1999). Histological age estimation of a cadaveral sample of diverse origins. *Canadian Society of Forensic Science Journal 32*(4):155–167.

Robling, A. G., & Stout, S. D. (2000). Histomorphometry of human cortical bone: Applications to age estimation. In M. A. Katzenberg & S. Saunders (Eds.), *Biological anthropology of the human skeleton.* New York: Wiley-Liss.

Singh, I. J., & Gunberg, D. L. (1970). Estimation of age at death in human males from quantitative histology of bone fragments. *American Journal of Physical Anthropology 33*:373–382.

Stout, S. D., & Gehlert, S. J. (1982). Effects of field size when using Kerley's histological method for determination of age at death. *American Journal of Physical Anthropology 58*:123–125.

Stout, S. D. (1986). The use of bone histomorphometry in skeletal identification: the case of Francisco Pizarro. *Journal of Forensic Sciences 31*(1):296–300.

Stout, S. D., & Paine, R. R. (1992). Brief communication: Histological age estimation using rib and clavicle. *American Journal of Physical Anthropology 87*:111–115.

Stout, S. D., Dietz, W. H., Îscan, M. Y., & Loth, S. R. (1994). Estimation of age at death using cortical histomorphometry of the sternal end of the fourth rib. *Journal of Forensic Sciences 39*(3):778–784.

Stout, S. D., Marcello, A. P., & Perotti, B. (1996). Brief communication: A test and correction of the clavicle method of Stout and Paine for histological age estimation of skeletal remains. *American Journal of Physical Anthropology 100:*139–142.

Thompson, D. D. (1979). The core technique in the determination of age at death in skeletons. *Journal of Forensic Sciences 24*(4):902–915.

Thompson, D. D., & Galvin, C. A. (1983). Estimation of age at death by tibial osteon remodeling in an autopsy series. *Forensic Sciences International 22:*203–211.

Ubelaker, D. (1986). Estimating age at death from immature human bone. In M. Y. İscan(Ed.), *Age markers in the human skeleton.* Springfield, IL: Charles C Thomas.

Wu, K., Schubeck, H., Frost, M., & Villanueva, A. (1970). Haversian bone formation rates determined by a new method in a mastodon, and in human diabetes mellitus and osteoporosis. *Calc Tissue Res 6:*204–219.

Yoshino, M., Imaizumi, K., Miyasaka, & Sueshige, S. (1994). Histological estimation of age at death using microradiographs of humeral compact bone. *Forensic Sciences International 64:*191–198.

Chapter 14

SKELETAL AGING USING FRONTAL BONE HISTOMORPHOMETRICS

Janene M. Curtis and Stephen P. Nawrocki

INTRODUCTION

Microscopic examination of bone tissue is a useful method for determining the age at death of an individual. This process is known as quantitative histology or histomorphometrics. Histomorphometrics quantifies the variation in the microscopic appearance of bone tissue that is attributed to various influences such as the ancestry, age, and sex of the individual, as well as disease, biomechanical loading, environmental factors, and genetics.

Systematic variability in microscopic appearance associated with age was first reported by Kerley (1965). He examined four areas of the midshaft of the tibia, fibula, and femur in cross-section, observing age-related trends in the microstructure of the cortical bone. With age, the number of secondary and fragmentary osteons increased while the percentage of lamellar bone in circumferential lamellae decreased. With a few alterations that correct for the original size of the field of view (Kerley and Ubelaker, 1978), this method is used today and is considered effective in aging long bones (Scheuer and Black, 2000). Since then, other bones have also been examined as potential sources for providing age estimates, including the rib (Stout and Paine, 1992; Stout et al., 1996; Cho et al., 2002), clavicle (Stout et al., 1996), and second metacarpal (Kimura, 1992). Robling and Stout (2000) provide an extensive review of the literature.

Only two studies have examined the possibility of using cranial bones as potential anatomical sites for age estimations via histomorphometrics. Clarke

(1987) and Cool et al. (1995) examined the microstructure of the ectocranial and endocranial layers of the parietal bone and the occipital bone, respectively. Clarke (1987) measured the fractional volume or percent of secondary osteons, secondary osteon fragments, and unremodeled lamellar bone within the bone tissue. Cool and colleagues (1995) used the same methods and measurements as Clarke (1987) in addition to measuring the fractional volumes or percent of primary osteons. Both studies showed that cranial bone is not useful for age estimation due to the low correlation of the variables. However, these studies employed small sample sizes (36 and 17 individuals, respectively), with unbalanced age distributions (primarily very old individuals), which may have contributed to the poor results.

The choice of variables may have affected the results as well. Cool et al. (1995) measured variables as fractional volumes or percentages. Since the percentage of lamellar bone decreases and the percentage of osteon fragments increases with age while the percentage of secondary osteons remains constant, the *size* of the osteon may decrease with age (Clarke, 1987; Cool et al., 1995). However, neither measured nor controlled for osteon size. Other variables, such as the average secondary osteon area and perimeter or osteon population density (OPD), may provide better correlations with age. Therefore, it is worthwhile to revisit the possibility of using cranial bone as a potential age estimator. To date, the frontal bone has not been examined histologically.

MATERIAL AND METHODS

This study is based on bone core samples extracted from 92 modern EuroAmerican cadavers of known age, sex, and cause of death (Curtis, 2003). Cores were collected from 57 individuals from Indiana sources, including the University of Indianapolis, the Indiana University School of Medicine, the Indiana University School of Dentistry, and Indiana University at Bloomington. A total of eight individuals were sampled from the University of Cincinnati and an additional 27 from the SUNY Health Science Center in Syracuse, NY. All had died between 1991 and 2003. Ten individuals were chosen per decade per sex for each decade beyond 60 years of age. Because the numbers of young individuals in anatomical cadaver populations are very low, this study includes few individuals below 60 years of age. The total age range runs from 29 to 99 years, with males ranging from 39 to 97 and females ranging from 29 to 99 (Table 14.1). The mean age of the entire sample is 75.4 years (s = 15.25, n = 92).

TABLE 14.1
AGE DISTRIBUTION OF THE STUDY SAMPLE

Age Range (years)	Males (n)	Males (mean)	Males (s)	Females (n)	Females (mean)	Females (s)	Total (n)
<50	2	42.5	4.95	4	40.8	8.26	6
50–59	3	56.3	3.06	3	58.0	1.00	6
60–69	10	64.5	3.10	10	63.6	2.63	20
70–79	10	74.5	3.03	10	74.4	3.17	20
80–89	10	84.5	3.03	10	84.5	3.03	20
90–99	10	93.9	2.60	10	94.5	3.03	20
Totals	**45**	**76.2**	**14.33**	**47**	**74.6**	**16.21**	**92**

Before the cores were taken, each calotte was examined for the presence and extent of hyperostosis frontalis interna, or HFI (Aufderheide and Rodriguez-Martin, 1998), expressed as the formation of plaque or nodules on the endocranial surface of the frontal and parietal bones. HFI tends to be more common in post-menopausal females (Hershkovitz et al., 1999) and must be considered when one studies the effects of age on the microstructure of the frontal bone. The degree of HFI was rated on a scale from 0 to 3 (Judd, 2002), with 0 indicating no HFI and 3 indicating significant nodulation extending past the coronal suture. As expected, in the current study sample HFI was uncommon in males (9/45) but more common in females (26/47).

A bone core was taken either from the center of the left (n = 69) or right (n = 23) frontal eminence of each individual using a 3/8 inch plug-cutting bit and a standard electric hand drill. All cores were cleaned and dehydrated with xylenes and then embedded in methyl methacrylate (MMA). Each block was sectioned with a diamond wire saw (Histosaw, Delaware Diamond Knives, Wilmington, DE) at a thickness ranging from 70–90 microns (μm) that produced sections that contained the three layers of the frontal bone. The sections were stained with Toluidine Blue (Osborne and Curtis, 2005), cleared in xylenes, mounted with Eukitt's adhesive onto individual glass slides, and coverslipped.

The sections were viewed at 20X and 100X using a Zeiss Universal Research microscope (Thornwood, NY) and analyzed with an IBM-PC XT microcomputer (Armonk, NY) and BIOQUANT image analysis software (BIOQUANT Image Analysis Corporation, Nashville, TN). Calibration of

TABLE 14.2
VARIABLES REFLECTING THE MICROSCOPIC APPEARANCE OF THE FRONTAL BONE

Variable	Abbreviation	Description
Mean Area of Osteon (μm^2)	AOn	Average area measured within the cement line of each "good" secondary osteon in the entire external table area.
Mean Area of Haversian Canal (μm^2)	AHCa	Average area measured within the Haversian canal of each "good" secondary osteon in the entire external table area.
Mean Perimeter of Osteon (μm)	POn	Average perimeter of cement line encompassing each "good" secondary osteon in the entire external table area.
Mean Perimeter of Haversian Canal (μm)	PHCa	Average perimeter of Haversian canal encompassing each "good" secondary osteon in the entire external table area.
Mean Minimum Osteon Diameter (μm)	Min DmOn	Average minimum diameter measured within the cement line of each "good" secondary osteon in the entire external table area.
Mean Maximum Osteon Diameter (μm)	Max DmOn	Average maximum diameter measured within the cement line of each "good" secondary osteon in the entire external table area.
Mean Minimum Haversian Canal Diameter (μm)	Min DmHCa	Average minimum diameter measured within the Haversian canal of each "good" secondary osteon in the entire external table area.
Mean Maximum Haversian Canal Diameter (μm)	Max DmHCa	Average maximum diameter measured within the Haversian canal of each "good" secondary osteon in the entire external table area.
Osteon Count (#)	On Count	Number of secondary osteons and partial osteons counted within the entire area of the external table of the frontal bone. All secondary and partial osteons were counted regardless direction.
"Good" Osteon Count (#)	GOn Count	Number of "good" secondary osteons. "Good" osteons require at least 80% of an intact cement line and a Haversian canal in which its maximum diameter is less than twice its minimum diameter.
Osteon Population Density (#/mm²)	OPD	Number of secondary osteons and partial osteons counted within the entire area of the external table of the frontal bone. All secondary and partial osteons were counted regardless direction. Area was determined for the entire external table.
Percent of "Good" Osteons Density (#mm²)	%GOn	Percentage of the sum of "good" osteons by the measured external table area.
Percent of "Good" Osteon Area (%)	%GAOn	Percentage of the sum of the "good" osteon area by the measured external table area.
Thickness of the External Table (μm)	ExTWi	Average thickness of the external table measured 10 to 15 times across its length.

the software and microscope was checked every two to three slides at the beginning of the analysis. Three types of measurements were taken: counts of the entire cortical table, cortical thickness, and measurements based on selected osteons described as "good." An osteon was considered "good" when the complete Haversian canal was visible and the canal appeared circular. Osteons were not included if the length of the Haversian canal appeared to be more than twice its width. Table 14.2 summarizes the 14 variables that were measured, using acronyms recommended as standards by the American Society for Bone and Mineral Research (Parfitt et al., 1987). Two of these (%GOn and %GAOn) were designed specifically for this study (see Curtis, 2003 for additional details).

The relationships between the 14 dependent variables that reflect the microscopic appearance of the frontal bone and age at death were examined using descriptive statistics, Pearson's correlation, and analysis of covariance (ANCOVA). Data were analyzed using SYSTAT 5.2.1 for the Macintosh (Wilkinson, 1992). A separate ANCOVA was run on each of the 14 dependent variables. In each, sex, side, and HFI were categorical independent variables, while age at death was treated as a continuous covariate. The interaction between sex and HFI (sex*HFI) was also included in the model.

RESULTS

Pearson's correlation was used to determine whether a relationship exists between each dependent variable and age at death. Of the fourteen variables tested, five (AOn, POn, Max DmOn, ExTWi, and OPD) are significantly correlated with age at death (Table 14.3). The first four of these five variables have a negative correlation with age, indicating that they decrease as age increases. OPD has a positive correlation with age, indicating that as age increases, osteon density increases as well. None of the correlations are particularly strong, perhaps because the mean age of the cadaver sample is quite high (see Nawrocki, 1998 and this volume).

Each line in Table 14.4 gives the results of a separate ANCOVA, indicating which independent variables significantly influence frontal bone histomorphology. Not surprisingly, the same five variables that are correlated with age at death are also affected by age in the ANCOVAs, in addition to %GOn. Two variables (ExTWi and OPD) are significantly affected by sex and three (AOn, POn, and Max DmOn) by side. Males have thicker external tables and females have greater osteon densities. The right side of the frontal bone tends

TABLE 14.3
PEARSON CORRELATIONS WITH AGE AT DEATH USING ALL MALES AND FEMALES
(N = 92; NS = NOT SIGNIFICANT AT $a \leq 0.05$)

Variable	r-value	Significance
AOn	-0.230	0.027
AHCa	-	ns
POn	-0.217	0.037
PHCa	-	ns
Min DmOn	-	ns
Max DmOn	-0.255	0.014
Min DmHCa	-	ns
Max DmHCa	-	ns
On Count	-	ns
GOn Count	-	ns
OPD	0.332	0.001
%On	-	ns
%AGOn	-	ns
ExTWi	-0.427	0.000

to have osteons with greater areas, perimeters, and maximum diameters than those on the left side. Neither HFI nor the interaction between sex and HFI affect any of the dependent variables.

Because systematic variation was found with age at death, an age prediction equation could be developed using forward stepwise least-squares linear regression. The default alpha value for inclusion or removal of variables from the regression equation was set at p ≤ 0.15. Two variables, ExTWi and OPD, produced the best estimate. Because two of the individuals were considered outliers or had a very large leverage that disproportionately affected the slope of the line, these two were removed from the sample. Based on the subsample of 90 individuals, the resulting equation is:

AGE = 84.827 - 0.018 (ExTWi) + 478.43(OPD) +/- 26.264 years
    (adj. r^2 = 0.26; inaccuracy = 10.73 years; bias = 0.0 years; se = 13.13 years)

The standard error of the estimate should be doubled to produce a 95 per-

TABLE 14.4
SIGNIFICANCE VALUES FOR 14 SEPARATE ANCOVAS
USING ALL MALES AND FEMALES (N = 92)

Dependent Variables	Independent Variables				
	Sex	**HFI**	**Sex *HFI**	**Side**	**Age**
AOn	ns	ns	ns	0.008	0.037
AHCa	ns	ns	ns	ns	ns
POn	ns	ns	ns	0.009	0.045
PHCa	ns	ns	ns	ns	ns
ExTWi	0.022	ns	ns	ns	0.000
Min DmOn	ns	ns	ns	ns	ns
Max DmOn	ns	ns	ns	0.018	0.014
Min DmHCa	ns	ns	ns	ns	ns
Max DmHCa	ns	ns	ns	ns	ns
On Count	ns	ns	ns	ns	ns
GOn Count	ns	ns	ns	ns	ns
OPD	0.016	ns	ns	ns	0.001
%GOn	ns	ns	ns	ns	0.016
%AGOn	ns	ns	ns	ns	ns

cent error interval for the estimate. It is important to note that this error estimate is simplified, presenting only a rough (and probably underestimated) prediction of the true 95 percent prediction interval for the population (see Klepinger and Giles, 1998; Nawrocki, 1998).

Inaccuracy and bias statistics were calculated for this equation to assess its mean error. The minimum error of the age estimate is 0.559 years while the maximum error is 29.754 years. An overall inaccuracy of 10.77 years indicates that the equation was off on average by almost 11 years. The bias of 0.0 years is a forced result of using regression on all 90 individuals.

To determine how the accuracy of the estimate varies across the age span, inaccuracy and bias statistics were calculated for each decade separately (Table 14.5). In the younger decades, age at death is usually overestimated as a standard result of least-squares regression, being underestimated in the older decades. The obtained bias values follow this general pattern, with high

TABLE 14.5
INACCURACY AND BIAS PER DECADE FOR THE SEX-COMBINED EQUATION (N = 90)

Decade	Sample Size (n)	Bias (years)	Inaccuracy (years)
20–29	1	29.754	29.754
30–39	4	24.684	24.684
40–49	5	17.147	17.147
50–59	6	12.902	13.266
60–69	20	8.935	9.440
70–79	19	3.295	5.580
80–89	20	-7.394	8.641
90–99	19	-15.466	15.533

positive values for the younger decades, indicating systematic overestimation of age at death, reverting to high negative values in the later decades, indicating systematic underestimation of age at death. The obtained inaccuracy values are highest in the youngest decades, decrease with increasing age, and then increase again. Since the overall mean of the sample is 75.4 years, the lowest inaccuracy and bias values fall in that approximate decade.

Because both ExTWi and OPD are affected by sex, bias and inaccuracy statistics were calculated for each sex separately from the sex-pooled equation. Males (n = 44) have slightly higher inaccuracy values than females (n = 46), 11.16 years and 10.31 years, respectively. A comparison of bias values indicates that male ages tend to be underestimated by 2.06 years on average while female ages tend to be overestimated by 1.97 years. Additional regression analysis was therefore conducted to generate sex-specific equations. Like the sex-pooled equation, two variables, ExTWi and OPD, produced the best estimate for females. With the removal of one outlier (n = 46), the resulting equation is:

AGE OF FEMALE = 87.702 - 0.025 (ExTWi) + 515.326(OPD) +/- 23.758 years
(adj. r^2 = 0.45; inaccuracy = 9.00 years; bias = 0.0 years; se = 11.88 years)

One variable, %AGOn, produced the best estimate for males. With the removal of two outliers (n = 43), the resulting equation is:

AGE OF MALE = 62.795 + 2.259(%AGOn) +/- 27.510 years
   (adj. $r^2 = 0.10$; inaccuracy = 11.51 years; bias = 0.0 years; se = 13.76 years)

Note that the sex-specific equation for females performs better than the sex-pooled equation. However, the sex-specific equation for males performs worse than the sex-pooled equation or the female equation.

DISCUSSION

The variables that were significantly affected by age at death in this study have also, for the most part, been found to correlate with age in other histomorphometric aging studies. In this study, increasing age was associated with a decrease in osteon area, perimeter, and maximum diameter. In other words, osteons formed at older ages are smaller than those formed at younger ages. As a result, osteon density *increases* with increasing age. Haversian canal size is not affected by age at death. However, while the absolute size of the Haversian canal remains constant, the *relative size* of the canal increases because osteon size decreases, and the canal takes up a greater percentage of the overall area of the osteon. Therefore, the bone tends to become more porous with increasing age.

The effect of age on the size of secondary osteons has never before been assessed in any cranial bone. Both Cool et al. (1995) and Clarke (1987) found that while the percentage of osteon fragments increased with age, the percentage of osteons remained unaffected by age in the occipital and parietal bone, respectively. Both researchers surmised that the size of the osteon decreased with age because the percentage of lamellar bone decreased as well. The results of this study support their hypothesis. Age does significantly affect the size of osteons, as measured by three parameters: mean osteon area (AOn), perimeter (POn), and maximum diameter (Max DmOn). The negative correlation between osteon size and age at death in the frontal bone in this study is consistent with previous studies using postcranial skeletal elements, including the humerus (Iwamoto et al., 1978; Iwamoto and Konishi, 1982; Yoshino et al., 1994), the femur (Evans, 1977; Watanabe et al., 1998; Narasaki, 1990; Iwamoto and Konishi, 1982; Thompson, 1979), and the tibia (Thompson and Galvin, 1983).

Clarke (1987) and Cool et al. (1995) reported a significant increase in the fractional volume of osteon fragments with age within the parietal and occipital bones, respectively. However, the fractional volume of the osteons remained unchanged with age in both bones. In this study, OPD significantly increased with age at death. Because both the osteons and the osteon fragments were counted together, it is unclear if both or just one structure increases with age. However, the percentage of "good" osteons also increased with age at death, suggesting that the number of secondary osteons increases with age as a result of the remodeling process of the frontal bone. The correlation of age at death and OPD observed in the frontal bone in this study supports previous work with other skeletal elements, including the second metacarpal (Kimura, 1992), the femur (Ericksen, 1991; Hauser et al., 1980; Narasaki, 1990; Stout and Stanley, 1991), the rib (Stout and Paine, 1992; Stout et al., 1996; Cho et al., 2002), the humerus (Yoshino et al., 1994), and the clavicle (Stout et al., 1996).

Prior to this study, Haversian canal size had not been assessed for any cranial bone. Haversian canal area, perimeter, and minimum and maximum diameters were not significantly affected by age at death in the frontal bone in this study. These results support some prior studies using postcranial bones. Yoshino et al. (1994) found that the average Haversian canal area of the humerus did not significantly change with age. Similarly, Watanabe et al. (1998), Samson and Branigan (1987), and Currey (1964) reported that various Haversian canal dimensions did not change with age in the femur. In contrast, Iwamoto et al. (1978) and Jowsey (1966) reported that the diameter of the Haversian canal increased significantly with age, and Iwamoto and Konishi (1982) obtained similar results but only in the older age range (above 76 years of age). Pfeiffer (1998) found a similar positive correlation for the femora of a small Spitalfields sample (n = 20). Singh and Gunberg (1970) reported a significant decrease in the Haversian canal diameter in the femur, tibia, and the mandible. The conflicting results of the effects of age on Haversian canal size may be due in part to high individual variation within each bone sample. Pfeiffer (1998) found that the variation in Haversian canal size was much more variable than osteon size.

Few studies have examined the effects of age on the individual layers of the cranial vault. Some studies have found a significant age-related decrease in the thickness of the external table (Dominok, 1959; Angel and Evans, 1971; Clarke, 1987; Judd 2002) or of the overall cranial vault (see Nawrocki 1990 for an extensive review). The results from this study support past observations: thickness of the external table of the frontal bone decreases with increasing age at death. The results of this study also support the observations of past studies of other skeletal elements based on cortical thickness. Kimura (1992), Thompson (1979), Narasaki (1990), and Thompson and Galvin (1983) found significant negative relationships between cortical thickness and age. However, Samson and Branigan (1987) did not find a significant correlation between age and cortical thickness in an archeological sample.

The r-values of the histological variables that were significantly correlated with age at death in this study tend to be lower than those obtained in previous studies. Cool et al. (1995) reported an r-value of 0.66 for the fractional volume of osteon fragments in the external table of the occipital bone. However, this value may have been inflated due to the autocorrelation of multiple samples taken from the same individual. The highest r-value obtained by Clarke (1987), for the fractional volume of osteon fragments in the external table of the parietal bone, was 0.38. By comparison, the highest correlation with age at death for any histological measure in the current study was 0.332, for OPD. Correlations obtained in studies using postcranial bones tend to be higher than those obtained for the cranium. For example, Watanabe et al. (1998) obtained r-values in excess of -0.83 for the femur, and many others report values in the 0.60 to 0.70 range (both positive and negative; see Curtis 2003 for a review). Taken together, it would seem that factors other than age at death influence the microstructural appearance of the frontal bone. Therefore, age predictions made from frontal bone histomorphometry may not be as accurate as predictions made from other skeletal elements.

Comparison of Age Predictive Equations with Other Studies

In order to compare the results of this study with other studies, it is important that the distributions of the samples be similar. Studies based on small sample sizes and narrow age ranges may have less variability and thus produce smaller standard errors of the estimate than studies based on larger samples. For example, Bouvier and Ubelaker (1977) calculated the standard error for Ahlqvist and Damstens's (1969) method (n = 20) on a larger sample (n = 40) and the standard error increased from ± 6.71 years to ± 11.65 years. Therefore, previous studies with small sample sizes (n < 50) or large differences in mean age (over 20 years) were excluded from consideration here. Others were excluded because such information was not provided in the original study. This comparative information is provided in Table 14.6. The standard error of the estimate in this study for the frontal bone is slightly higher than those obtained for the femur, tibia, or metacarpal. This difference suggests that regression equations using the frontal bone will not be as accurate as those using other bones. However, there may be circumstances in which

TABLE 14.6
PERFORMANCE OF REGRESSION EQUATIONS IN VARIOUS STUDIES (SEXES POOLED)

Bone	n	Mean Age (years)	Range	Standard Error	Author
Femur	90	73.20	30–97	7.1–8.6	Thompson, 1979
Tibia	112	73.16	30–97	7.5–8.6	Thompson, 1979
Metacarpal	227	68.24	30–98	11.10	Kimura, 1992
Femur	328	62.80	14–97	10.1–12.2	Ericksen, 1991
Frontal Bone	90	75.12	29–99	13.132	this study
Frontal Bone	43	75.91	39–97	13.755	this study (males)
Frontal Bone	46	74.54	29–99	11.879	this study (females)

the only skeletal element available for age estimation is the cranium. If the cranium is intact, the cranial suture aging method may be most appropriate. Nawrocki (1998) developed a cranial suture method with age-predictive equations that perform slightly better than the age-predictive equations from the present study (standard errors range from 12.1 to 13.5 years for n = 100). Moreover, estimating the age of an unknown individual based on Nawrocki's equations would be less expensive in terms of time, effort, and money than histomorphometry of the frontal bone. Nevertheless, there may be circumstances in which a cranial suture method could not be utilized; in which case the equations presented here may be useful.

Effects of Sex on Frontal Bone Histomorphology

In this study, sex contributed only to the variation of external table thickness and osteon density. Males tend to have a thicker external table and lower osteon density compared to females. Clarke (1987) found no sex differences in the fractional volume of osteons, osteon fragments, or lamellar bone, but his sample size was small (male n = 23, female n = 13).

The results of the current study are consistent with some previous studies of cranial bone thickness. Dominok (1959) found sex differences in cortical table thickness for the frontal and occipital bones. Results obtained by Lippert and Käfer (1974) are less clear-cut. The external table of the medial side of the frontal bone in males as well as the external tables of the parietal and occipital bones were found to be significantly thicker than those of females. However no significant sex differences were found in the lateral side of the frontal bone. In contrast, Judd (2002) and Clarke (1987) reported that the thickness of the external table of the frontal and parietal bones were not significantly affected by sex.

The results of this study are consistent with studies based on other skeletal elements. Bertelsen et al. (1995) and Narasaki (1990) reported that males tend to have thicker femoral cortices than females. With increasing age, there is greater cortical thinning in the femora of females as a result of endosteal resorption. Similarly, Kimura (1992) reported that the cortical thickness of the metacarpal was significantly greater in males compared to females. Moreover, osteon density was lower in males compared to females. Ericksen (1991) reported sex differences in the total osteon count and total fragment count in a sample of femora. With increasing age the osteon count increased in males, while the osteon fragment count was greater in females. When combining both counts to determine osteon density, females displayed higher values. The increased osteon density in females reflects an increase in the remodeling rate that in turn reflects sex differences in porosity and in the rate of bone resorption.

Kimura (1992) developed sex-specific age estimation equations, reporting lower standard errors for females (12.06 years for a sex-combined equation, 9.99 years for females alone, and 11.10 years for males alone). Ericksen (1991) also reported slightly better results for females (a standard error of 10.07 years for a sex-combined equation, 9.96 years for females alone, and 10.05 years for males alone). The results of these and the current study suggest that age estimates for females may be more accurate than those for males.

The differential performance of sex-specific equations implies that the remodeling rate in females is more tightly correlated with age. This implication is counterintuitive, as one would think remodeling rates in males would tend to have a closer correlation with age because of a more stable hormone level. In contrast, it would seem that hormonal levels in females are less stable and change dramatically with reproduction and menopause. Further studies are warranted to elucidate sex differences at all ages.

CONCLUSION

This study illustrates that variation in the microscopic appearance of the frontal bone is systematically affected by age. Like other skeletal elements, the size of the osteons decreases with age while the osteon density increases with age. However, the degree to which the frontal bone is affected by age is much less systematic than for other skeletal elements. As a result, the predictive ability of regression equations using the external table of the frontal bone is not as good compared to other skeletal elements. Therefore, this method provides an additional tool for forensic scientists and bioarcheologists in certain situations. Since human remains are often found fragmented or incomplete, the frontal bone provides an alternative to traditional aging methods in circumstances where previously an aging method could not be applied.

Examination of the effects of sex on the variation in the microstructural appearance of the frontal bone suggests that bone remodeling in females occurs differently than bone remodeling in males. This study illustrates the importance of controlling for the effects of sex when developing age-estimation equations. For the frontal bone, age-predictive equations work better for females.

ACKNOWLEDGMENTS

We would like to thank Dr. David Burr, Dr. Anton Neff, and Dr. Richard Drake, who permitted access to the cadaver samples from the schools of IU-Medicine and Dentistry, IU-Bloomington, and from the University of Cincinnati, respectively.

All bone histomorphometry was permitted by the generosity of Dr. Burr, who provided access to the Musculoskeletal Research Laboratory in the Department of Anatomy and Cell Biology, Indiana University School of Medicine. We are grateful for the technical and instructional support provided by Dr. Burr, Dr. Alex Robling, Dr. Keith Condon, Dr. John Langdon, Mary Hooser, Dr. Jiliang Li, Dr. Stuart Warden, Erin Hatt, and Marge Wilson. This study was funded in part by the Indiana Academy of Science.

REFERENCES

Ahlqvist, J., & Damsten, O. (1969). A modification of Kerley's method for the microscopic determination of age in human bone. *Journal of Forensic Sciences 14*:205–212.

Angel, J. L., & Evans, M. (1971). Thickness of the adult skull vault change slightly with age, sex, and race. Unpublished manuscript in the National Anthropology Archives, Smithsonian Institute, National Museum of Natural History, Washington, D.C.

Aufderheide, A., & Rodriguez-Martin, C. (1998). *The Cambridge encyclopedia of human paleopathology*. London: Cambridge Press.

Bertelsen, P. K., Clement, J. G., & Thomas, C. D. L. (1995). A morphometric study of the cortex of the human femur from early childhood to advanced old age. *Forensic Science International* 74:63–77.

Bouvier, M., & Ubelaker, D. H. (1977). A comparison of two methods for the microscopic determination of age at death. *American Journal of Physical Anthropology* 46:391–394.

Cho, H., Stout, S. D., Madsen, R. W., & Streeter, M. A. (2002). Population-specific histological age-estimating method: a model for known African-American and European-American skeletal remains. *Journal of Forensic Sciences* 47:12–18.

Clarke, D. F. (1987). Histological and radiographic variation in the parietal bone in a cadaveric population. Master's thesis, Department of Anatomy, University of Queensland.

Cool, S. M., Hendrikz, J. K., & Wood, W. B. (1995). Microscopic age changes in the human occipital bone. *Journal of Forensic Sciences* 40:789–796.

Currey, J. D. (1964). Some effects of ageing in human Haversian systems. *Journal of Anatomy* 98:69–75.

Curtis, J. M. (2003). Estimation of age at death from the microscopic appearance of the frontal bone. Master's thesis, Department of Biology, University of Indianapolis.

Dominok, G. W. (1959). Zur alters- und geschlechtsbestimmung aus der morphlologie der menschlichen schädelkalotte. *Zentralblatt fur Allgemeine Pathologie u. Pathologische Anatomie* 100:54–64.

Ericksen, M. F. (1991). Histological estimation of age at death using the anterior cortex of the femur. *American Journal of Physical Anthropology* 84:171–179.

Evans, F. G. (1977). Age changes in mechanical properties and histology of human compact bone. *Yearbook of Physical Anthropology* 20:57–72.

Hauser, R., Barres, D., Durigon, M., & Derobert, L. (1980). Identification par l'histomorphometrie du femur et du tibia. *Acta Medicinae Legalis et Socialis* 30:91–97.

Hershkovitz, I., Greenwald, C., Rothchild, B., Latimer, B., Dutour, O., Jellema, L., & Wish-Baratz, S. (1999). Hyperostosis frontalis interna: An anthropological perspective. *American Journal of Physical Anthropology* 109:303–325.

Iwamoto, S., & Konishi, M. (1982). Study on the age-related changes of the compact bone and the age estimation: 3. Determination of the age limitation. *Medical Journal Kinki University* 7:33–40.

Iwamoto, S., Oonuki, E., & Konishi, M. (1978). Study on the age-related changes of the compact bone and the age estimation. 2. On the humerus. *Acta Medica Kinki University* 3:203–208.

Jowsey, J. (1966). Studies of Haversian systems in man and some animals. *Journal of Anatomy* 100:857–864.

Judd, L. (2002). Cranial vault thickness variation in Euroamericans. Master's thesis, Department of Biology, University of Indianapolis.

Kerley, E. R. (1965). The microscopic determination of age in human bone. *American Journal of Physical Anthropology* 23:149–164.

Kerley, E. R., & Ubelaker, D. H. (1978). Revisions in the microscopic method of estimating age at death in human cortical bone. *American Journal of Physical Anthropology* 49:545–546.

Kimura, K. (1992). Estimation of age at death from second metacarpals. *Zeitschrift feur Morphologie und Anthropologie* 79:169–181.

Klepinger, L. L., & Giles, E. (1998). Clarification or confusion: statistical interpretation in forensic anthropology. In K. J. Reichs (Ed.), *Forensic osteology: Advances in the identification of human remains* (2nd ed.), pp. 427–440. Springfield, IL: Charles C Thomas.

Lippert, H., & Käfer, H. (1974). Biomechanik des schädeldachs teil II dicken der knochenschichten. *Exerpta Medica-Forensic Science Abstracts Sect 49*:329–339.

Narasaki, S. (1990). Estimation of age at death by femoral osteon remodeling: Application of Thompson's core technique to modern Japanese. *J. Anthrop. Soc. Nippon. 98*:29–38.

Nawrocki, S. P. (1990). Cranial vault thickness in Homo. Master's thesis, Department of Anthropology, State University of New York at Binghamton.

Nawrocki, S. P. (1998). Regression formulae for estimating age at death from cranial suture closure. In K. J. Reichs (Ed.), *Forensic osteology: Advances in the identification of human remains* (2nd ed.), pp. 276–292. Springfield, IL: Charles C Thomas.

Osborne, D. L., & Curtis, J. (2005). A protocol for the staining of cement lines in adult human bone using toluidine blue. *The Journal of Histotechnology 28*:73–79.

Parfitt, A. M., Drezner, M. K., Glorieux, F. H., Kanis, J. H., Malluche, H., Meunier, P. J., Ott, S. M., & Recker, R. R. (1987). Bone histomorphometry: Standardization of nomenclature, symbols, and units. *Journal of Bone and Mineral Research 2*:595–610.

Pfeiffer, S. (1998). Variability in osteon size in recent human populations. *American Journal of Physical Anthropology 106*:219–227.

Robling, A. G., & Stout, S. D. (2000). Histomorphometry of human cortical bone: Applications to age estimation. In M. A. Katzenberg & S. R. Saunders (Eds.), *Biological anthropology of the human skeleton,* pp. 187–213. New York: Wiley-Liss.

Samson, C., & Branigan, K. (1987). A new method of estimating age at death from fragmentary and weathered bone. In A. Boddington A., A. N. Garland, & R. C. Janaway (Eds.), *Death, decay, and reconstruction: approaches to archaeology and forensic science,* pp. 101–108. Manchester: Manchester University Press.

Scheuer, L., & Black, S. (2000). *Developmental juvenile osteology.* San Diego: Academic Press.

Singh, I. J., & Gunberg, D. L. (1970). Estimation of age at death in human males from quantitative histology of bone fragments. *American Journal of Physical Anthropology 33*:373–382.

Stout, S. D., & Paine, R. R. (1992). Brief communication: Histological age estimation using rib and clavicle. *American Journal of Physical Anthropology 87*:111–115.

Stout, S. D., Porro, M. A., & Perotti, B. (1996). Brief communication: A test and correction of the clavicle method of Stout and Paine for histological age estimation of skeletal remains. *American Journal of Physical Anthropology 100*:139–142.

Stout, S. D., & Stanley, S. C. (1991). Percent osteon bone versus osteon counts: the variable of choice for estimating age at death. *American Journal of Physical Anthropology 86*:515–519.

Thompson, D. D. (1979). The core technique in the determination of age at death in skeletons. *Journal of Forensic Sciences 24*:902–915.

Thompson, D. D., & Galvin, C. A. (1983). Estimation of age at death by tibial osteon remodeling in an autopsy series. *Forensic Science International 22*:203–211.

Watanabe, Y., Konishi, M., Shimada, M., Ohara, H., & Iwamoto, S. (1998). Estimation of age from the femur of Japanese cadavers. *Forensic Science International 98*:55–65.

Wilkinson, L. (1992). SYSTAT for MacIntosh, V 5.2.1, Evanston, IL.

Yoshino, M., Imaizumi, K., Miyasaka, S., & Seta, S. (1994). Histological estimation of age at death using microradiographs of humeral compact bone. *Forensic Science International 64*:191–198.

Chapter 15

HISTOLOGICAL AGE
ESTIMATION IN SUBADULTS

Margaret Streeter

INTRODUCTION

Histological estimates of age at death in adult ribs rely on the quantification of remodeling, the accumulation of secondary osteons that occurs throughout life (Stout and Paine, 1992; Cho et al., 2002). Subadult rib cortices, on the other hand, are primarily under the influence of growth and modeling while the effects of remodeling are less evident until late in the first decade of life. Therefore, histological age estimation in the subadult rib cortex is based on the qualitative identification of the systematic changes associated with growth. Matching the presence and location of histological characteristics with the pattern described for one of the rib age phases provides a quick and easily replicable method of age estimation (Table 15.1).

The general developmental pattern in subadult ribs proceeds as follows. Ribs are initially formed of woven bone (Figure 15.1) which in a cortical cross-section presents a distinctive woven or tweed pattern under polarized light. In tubular bones such as the rib, modeling functions in conjunction with growth to transform the size and shape of the rib cage (Frost, 1958). Modeling drift (also called cortical drift), the deposition of lamellar bone on selective rib surfaces and the resorption of bone on other surfaces (Figure 15.2), acts to enlarge the rib cage and move the rib cortices through tissue space to achieve adult proportions. Through modeling, the woven bone is ultimately replaced by primary lamellar bone (Figure 15.3a) that is deposited in circumferential layers at periosteal and endosteal surfaces. The primary lamellae are often

232

TABLE 15.1
SUMMARY OF RIB PHASES

Phase	Primary Lamellar Bone	Remodeling	Woven Bone	Cutaneous Cortex	Pleural Cortex
Phase I– (Less than 5 yrs)	Rare	Rare	Most of both cortices	Thinner, mostly woven many primary vascular canals	Thicker, mostly woven bone, primary lamellae forms initially endosteally
Phase II– (5–9 yrs)	Pleural cortex	Large drifting osteons initially on pleural cortex originating at periosteum	Some areas on cutaneous cortex, rare on pleural cortex	Thinner, mostly intracortical woven bone, fewer primary vascular canals	Thicker, largely primary lamellar bone, few initial drifting osteons and many Volkmann's canals
Phase III– (10–17 yrs)	Both cortices intracortically, periosteally on cutaneous cortex	Drifting osteons on both cortices	Thin rind on cutaneous periosteal surface	Thinner, mostly lamellar bone with some remodeling, periosteal lamellar or woven bone, large resorptive bays (drifting osteons)	Thicker, denser remodeling, some areas of primary lamellar bone
Phase IV– (18–21 yrs)	Both cortices periosteally	Both cortices, fewer drifting osteons more Type 1 osteons	Rare	Thinner, dense remodeling osteons 2 to 3 rows deep	Thicker, dense remodeling osteons 3 to 4 rows deep, rare areas of primary lamellar bone

FIGURE 15.1
WOVEN BONE IN THE CUTANEOUS CORTEX OF A RIB FROM A 2-YEAR-OLD
(100X POLARIZED)

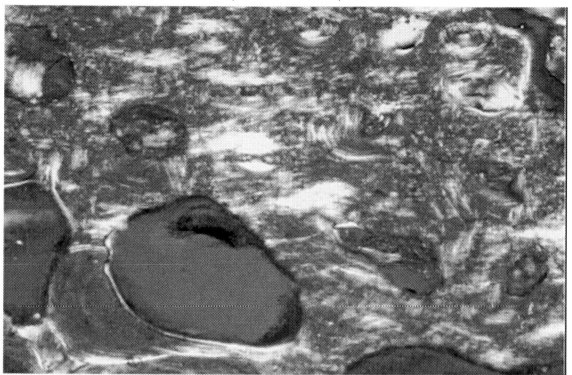

interrupted by primary vascular canals, (Figure 15.3b) blood vessels that were originally located on the bone surfaces but have subsequently been incorporated into the cortex as lamellar bone was deposited around them. Gradually remodeling begins to replace the circumferential lamellar bone with secondary osteons formed by the deposition of concentric lamellae (Figure 15.3c). Although remodeling has been shown to begin in prenatal life (Burton et al., 1989; Frost, 1963) osteon numbers do not correlate well with age due to the removal of remodeled areas by cortical drift.

The concentric arrangement of lamellar bone seen in the common or Type I osteon is created through the tethered resorption of previously existing bone followed by deposition of concentric lamellar bone around a central Haversian canal. Type I osteons are more typical of adult bones but in subadults remodeling usually takes the form of drifting osteons (Figure 15.4). Drifting osteons are similar to Type I osteons but they are more elongated rather than circular in cross-section and they have eccentric Haversian canals (Frost,

FIGURE 15.2
DIAGRAM SHOWING THE DEVELOPMENTAL TREND IN THE SUBADULT RIB CORTI-
CAL MORPHOLOGY. NOTE THE RESORPTION (R) ON THE PLEURAL PERIOSTEAL
AND CUTANEOUS ENDOSTEAL SURFACES, AND FORMATION (F) ON THE PLEURAL
ENDOSTEAL AND CUTANEOUS PERIOSTEAL SURFACES THAT ACTS TO MOVE THE
CORTEX THROUGH SPACE AS MODELING DRIFT WORKS WITH GROWTH. ALSO,
REMODELING IN THE FORM OF DRIFTING OSTEONS BEGINS FIRST ON THE THICK-
ER PLEURAL CORTEX AS DRIFTING OSTEONS TRAVEL FROM THE PERIOSTEUM
TOWARD THE ENDOSTEUM. THE THINNER CUTANEOUS CORTEX HAS A VERY
POROUS APPEARANCE DUE TO THE PRESENCE OF MANY LARGE RESORPTIVE BAYS
AND RETAINS AREAS OF WOVEN BONE LONGER THAN PLEURAL CORTEX

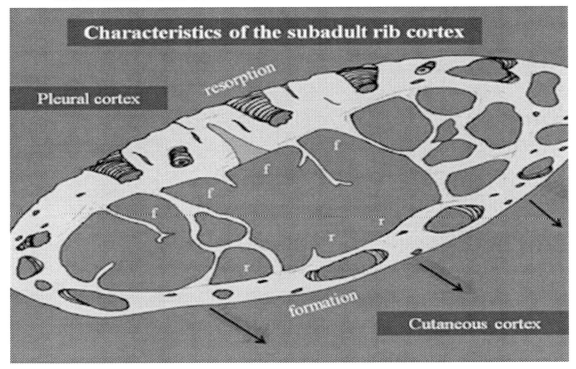

1963; Sedlin and Frost, 1963; Epker and Frost, 1965; Lacroix, 1971; Coutelier,
1976; Burton et al., 1989, Frost, 1989; Robling and Stout, 1998).

METHODOLOGY

The histological estimation of age in the subadult rib utilizes a cross-section
taken from the middle third of the fifth, sixth or seventh rib. Cortical bone
samples used to develop this method were taken at autopsy from 72 individ-

FIGURE 15.3
RIB CORTEX COMPOSED OF PRIMARY LAMELLAR BONE (A) WITH PRIMARY
VASCULAR CANALS (B) AND OSTEONS (C). NOTE THE FLOW OF LAMELLAE
AROUND THE PRIMARY CANALS AND THE INTERRUPTION OF THE LAMELLAE
BY THE SECONDARILY REMODELED OSTEONS (200X POLARIZED)

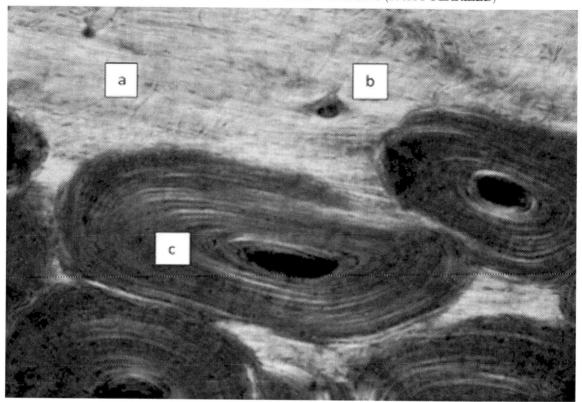

uals (45 males and 27 females), ranging from 2 to 21 years of age (mean age of 14.1 ± 5.2 years). Rib samples were provided by Missouri medical examiners obtained at autopsy from traumatic deaths and were judged to be metabolically normal. Of the 72 rib samples, 50 were reported by medical examiners personnel to be from individuals of European ancestry, 14 of African ancestry, 5 of Asian ancestry, and 3 were recorded as mixed or unknown ancestry. The defleshed bone sections were cut and polished to a thickness of approximately 80 microns (μm) using the method developed by Frost (1958). The resulting bone wafers were then mounted onto glass slides using standard histological methods (Stout and Paine, 1992; Streeter, 2005). The microscopic sections were scanned using a light microscope that was fitted with a pair of 10X widefield oculars and 4X, 10X, or 20X objectives. However any mag-

FIGURE 15.4
DRIFTING OSTEON (ARROW) SURROUNDED BY UNREMODELED
PRIMARY LAMELLAR BONE (100X POLARIZED)

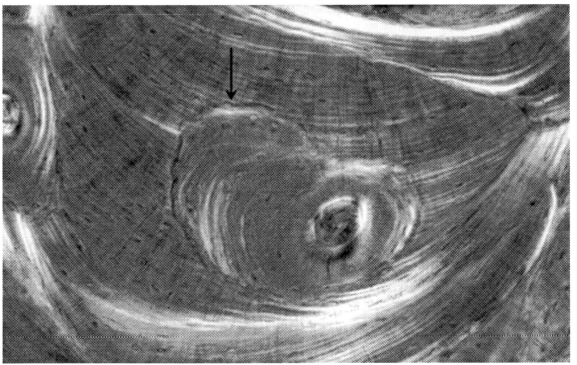

nifications that ensure accurate identification of the histological features in question are suitable, although a polarizer is necessary to detect woven bone.

Initial scanning of the rib cortex at a low magnification (e.g., 2X or 4X) facilitates the identification of the thicker pleural cortex and the thinner and more porous cutaneous cortex (Figure 15.2). The location of the costal grove on the inferior surface of the pleural cortex can also be used to differentiate between the two cortices. Higher power objectives should be used as needed for identification of histological structures such as primary vascular canals, Volkmann's canals and secondary osteons.

Phase I (Less than 5 Years)

In individuals less than two years of age the rib cortex is composed of the original woven bone and the marrow cavity is not yet well defined (Figure 15.5). Lamellar bone is rare on the cutaneous cortex in this first rib phase and evidence of cortical drift initially begins to appear on the pleural cortex as

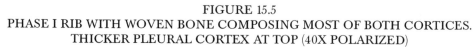

FIGURE 15.5
PHASE I RIB WITH WOVEN BONE COMPOSING MOST OF BOTH CORTICES.
THICKER PLEURAL CORTEX AT TOP (40X POLARIZED)

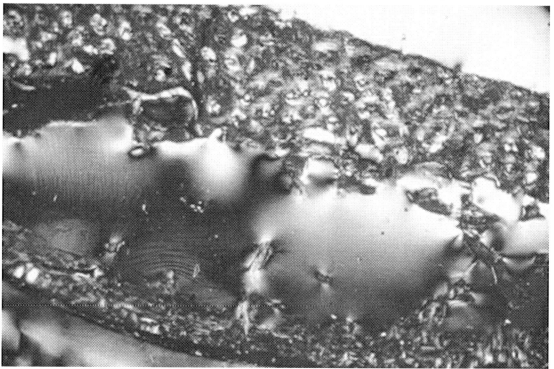

new unremodeled primary lamellae. This earliest lamellar bone is deposited endosteally on the pleural cortex and resorption is evident in the characteristic scalloped surface on the periosteal surface of that cortex. Conversely, woven bone is often retained throughout the cutaneous cortex with lamellar bone deposition appearing on the periosteal surface and resorption on the endosteal surface.

Phase II (5 to 10 Years)

The first indication of remodeling appears as drifting osteons that form on the pleural cortex. These osteons are typically seen to be traveling, or drifting, in more or less parallel columns from the periosteal surface toward the endosteum (Figure 15.6a). Frequently the drifting osteons are still in the process of forming, exhibiting a smooth formation front on the periosteal side of the wide resorptive bay and a resorption front on the endosteal side of the

FIGURE 15.6
DRIFTING OSTEONS TRAVELING FROM PERIOSTEUM OF PLEURAL CORTEX
(LEFT) TOWARD THE ENDOSTEUM (UPPER RIGHT). NOTE THE FORMING
DRFITING OSTEON (A) IN THE MIDDLE, WITH THE TAIL OF CONCENTRIC
LAMELLAE AND A SMOOTH DEPOSITION SURFACE (B) WHILE ON THE
OPPOSITE SIDE OF THE RESORPTIVE BAY IS THE LEADING EDGE OF
RESORPTION (C) WITH A SCALLOPED EDGE (100X POLARIZED)

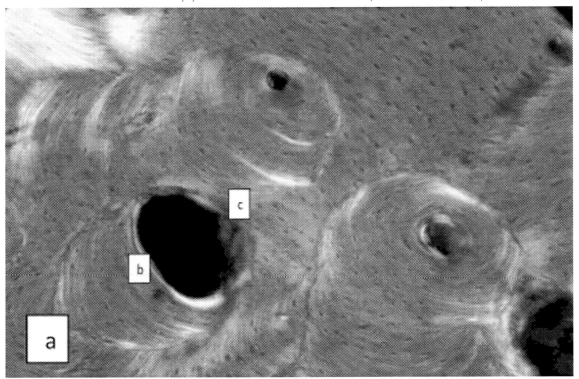

bay (Figure 15.6b). The primary lamellar bone located on the pleural cortex contains many Volkmann's canals (Figure 15.7a). The thinner cutaneous cortex is characterized by very little remodeling, areas of woven bone, primary vascular canals, and many large resorptive bays that give the cortex a very porous appearance (Figure 15.7b).

Phase III (11–17 Years)

In this third rib phase evidence of remodeling in the form of drifting osteons becomes widespread on both cortices though there are still wide expanses of unremodeled primary lamellae. On the pleural cortex osteon accumulations are often two to three rows deep from near the periosteum

FIGURE 15.7
VOLKMANN'S CANAL (A) ON THE PLEURAL CORTEX CONSISTING OF
UNREMODELED PRIMARY LAMELLAR BONE (B) (100X POLARIZED)

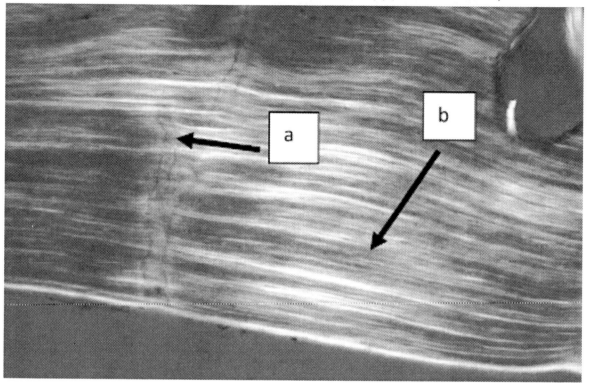

(Figure 15.8a) and areas of intracortical primary lamellar bone often remain. The cutaneous cortex is less densely remodeled than the pleural cortex. The cutaneous cortex is characterized by a thin rind of lamellar or woven bone deposited periosteally (Figure 15.8b).

Phase IV (18–22 years)

The histomorphology of the two rib cortices are more similar to each other and resembles the adult pattern. Remodeling is extensive, there are fewer drifting osteons and two to four rows of Type I osteons. Normally, woven bone is not seen in this last phase and unremodeled lamellar bone only occurs in isolated patches (Figure 15.9).

The estimation of age in the subadult rib relies on the recognition of age associated developmental trends including the location and orientation of histomorphological features in the cortex. Unlike histological aging methods

FIGURE 15.8
PHASE III SHOWING THE CUTANEOUS CORTEX WITH OSTEONS TWO TO
THREE ROWS DEEP (A) AND UNREMODELED PRIMARY LAMELLAR BONE (B)
THAT HAS BEEN DEPOSITED AT THE PERIOSTEUM (100X POLARIZED)

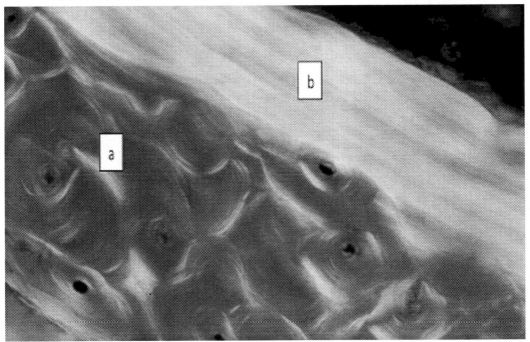

that require osteon counts, this qualitative method is less time intensive and does not require a specialized eyepiece grid or extensive histomorphometric training. Easily identified features in the bone microstructure such as formation or resorption, the presence of woven or lamellar bone, and remodeling by Type I and drifting osteons allows the classification of a rib into one of four phases associated with a specific age range.

REFERENCES

Burton, P., Nyssen-Behets, C., & Dhem, A. (1989). Haversian bone remodeling in human fetus. *Acta Anatomica 135*:171–175.

Cho, H., Stout, S. D., Madsen, R. W., & Streeter, M. (2002). Population-specific histological age-estimating methods. *Journal of Forensic Sciences 47*:12–18.

Coutelier, L. (1976). Le remaniement interne de l'os compact chez l' enfant. *Bulletin de l'association des anatomistes 60*:95–110.

Epker, B. N., & Frost, H. M. (1965). The direction of transverse drift of actively forming osteons in human rib cortex. *Journal of Bone and Joint Surgery 47S*:1211–1215.

FIGURE 15.9
PLEURAL CORTEX IN PHASE IV OF A 19-YEAR-OLD,
ENDOSTEUM AT TOP (200X POLARIZED)

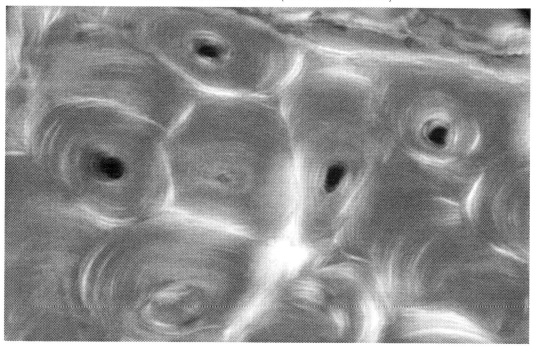

Frost, H. M. (1958). Preparation of thin undecalcified bone sections by rapid manual method. *Stain Technology 33*(6) 273–277.

Frost, H. M. (1963). Dynamics of bone remodeling. In H. M. Frost (Ed.), *Bone biodynamic,* pp. 315–333. Springfield, IL: Charles C Thomas.

Frost, H. M. 1985. The "New Bone": some anthropological potentials. *Yearbook of Physical Anthropology 28*:211–226.

Frost, H. M. (1989). The biology of fracture healing: An overview for clinicians. Part I. *Clinical Orthopedics and elated Research 248*:283–286.

Lacroix, P. (1971). The internal remodeling of bone. In G. H. Bourne (Ed.), *The biochemistry and physiology of bones,* pp. 119–143. New York: Academic Press.

Robling, A. G., & Stout, S. D. (1998). Morphology of the drifting osteon. *Cells Tissues Organs, 164*:192–204.

Sedlin, E. D., & Frost, H. M. (1963). Variations in rate of human osteon formation. *Canadian Journal of Biochemistry Physics 41*:19–22.

Stout, S. D., & Paine, R. R. (1992). Histological age estimation using rib and clavicle. *American Journal of Physical Anthropology 87*:111–115.

Streeter, M. (2005). *Manual for bone histology.* Unpublished Manuscript.

Chapter 16

MULTIFACTORIAL ESTIMATION OF AGE AT DEATH FROM THE HUMAN SKELETON

Natalie M. Uhl and Stephen P. Nawrocki

INTRODUCTION

An ever-present but seldom uttered surety of life is death, "only its time being doubtful" (Ascadi & Nemeskeri, 1970:24). Accurately estimating age at death has been the subject of decades of research, method development, and testing for human osteologists because age determination from the skeleton, whether for an individual or a population, is critical in analyzing and describing human skeletal remains. Despite an abundance of research and data, a single method for determining age at death from the human skeleton that is both accurate and precise and that appropriately combines multiple skeletal indicators continues to elude osteologists.

Some anthropologists (Brooks, 1955; Johnson, 1976; Lovejoy et al., 1985; Saunders et al., 1992) have attempted to develop methods to statistically combine aging methods to increase the accuracy of their predictions, in part because most anthropologists agree that "no one age indicator is adequate" (Brooks, 1955:588). These are generally referred to as "complex" or "multifactorial" aging methods. Despite this research, there is a general disagreement on the utility of multifactorial methods. Critics claim that the greater complexity of these methods does not generate age estimates that are any better than an experienced guess or a simple average of multiple indicators (Saunders et al., 1992).

The first attempt to combine two or more skeletal aging methods was Brooks (1955), who utilized Todd's studies of cranial suture closure and changes of the pubic symphyseal surface. She did not statistically combine these two methods, but applied both methods to each individual in her sample. The correlation between pubic age and known age was acceptable in most cases but the correlation between cranial suture closure and known age was very low.

Lovejoy et al. (1985) presented the *Multifactorial Summary Age* method, utilizing the pubic symphyseal face, iliac auricular surface, radiographs of the proximal femur, dental wear, and suture closure. Their review of skeletal aging methods recalls that most methods are fairly inaccurate and can be gravely affected by interobserver error. The Lovejoy et al. (1985) technique involves the seriation of specimens by age, thus requiring a skeletal assemblage, so its application to forensic anthropology is not appropriate.

Saunders et al. (1992) examined the pubic symphysis, iliac auricular surface, ectocranial sutures, and sternal rib ends on a known age historic cemetery sample and followed with a test of the Lovejoy et al. (1985) *Multifactorial Summary Age* method. Because each age indicator must be applied separately and the assemblage is archaeological and somewhat incomplete, the sample sizes differ, ranging from 27 to 49 individuals. The authors point out some of the incongruities in how skeletal aging methods are judged in the literature. Some anthropologists use inaccuracy, some include bias, and others use the correlation coefficient. Likewise, some authors report age ranges and some report means for each phase. In short, it is difficult to compare most aging methods because there is no standard for reporting results. Saunders and colleagues believe that the best way to assess aging indicators is the coefficient of determination (r^2), which quantifies the amount of variation in one variable that can be accounted for by the variance in another variable (i.e., the predictor variable) (Kachigan, 1982).

Overall, Saunders and colleagues found that their age estimates from a multifactorial approach were no more accurate than some of the single indicators (e.g., the auricular surface) or the simple averaging of all indicators. This study provides a fairly sound assessment of the multifactorial model but it also demonstrates some weaknesses. For example, the sample sizes (27 to 49 individuals) are small enough to pose a serious problem in the evaluation of aging methods and cannot account for a wide range of variation in skeletal form. In addition, the distribution of ages within the sample is not uniform. Despite the ineffectiveness of the Lovejoy et al. (1985) method, Saunders and colleagues do recommend the use of more than one age indicator in the estimation of skeletal age at death, though they also believe that each age indicator must be used alone and then the suite of age estimates should be eval-

FIGURE 16.1
DEMOGRAPHY OF THE STUDY SAMPLE

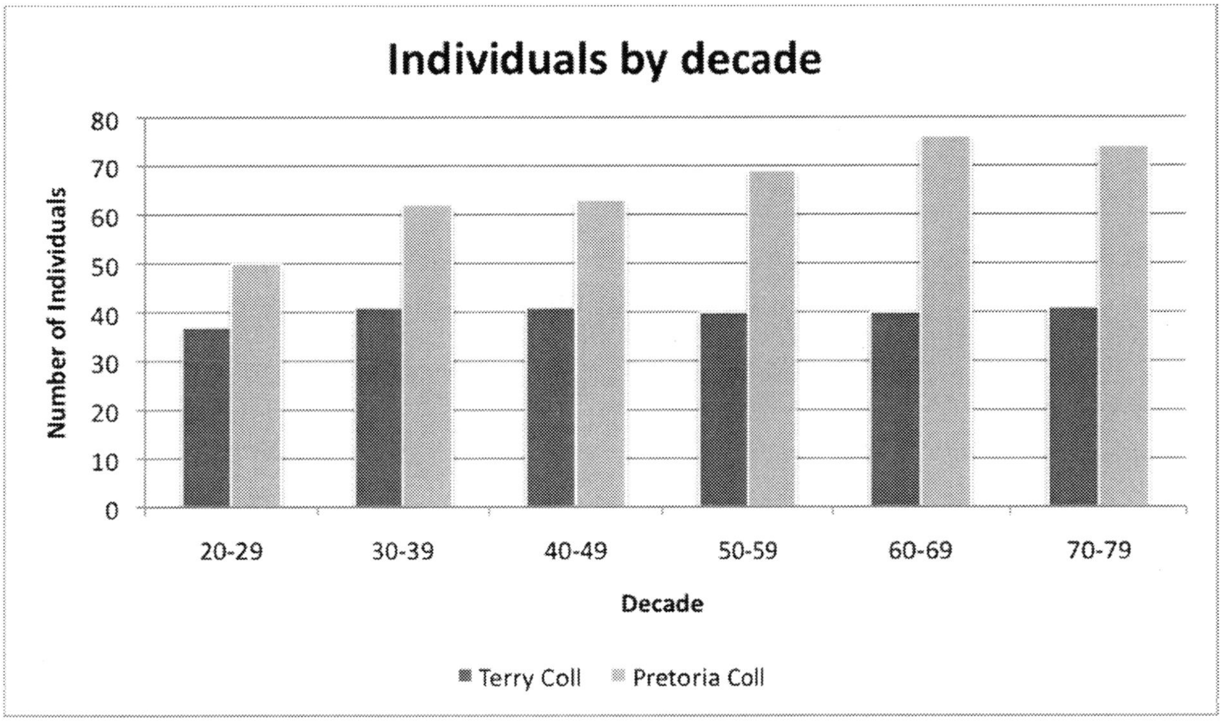

uated individually rather than statistically.

It is clear that the use of multiple age indicators for the determination of age at death is ideal, but a scientific, quantitative, and easily applied method for combining the data is lacking. A comprehensive approach to aging would simplify, and more importantly, standardize, age at death estimation from skeletal remains.

MATERIALS AND METHODS

The specimens used in this study are curated at one institution in the United States and one institution in South Africa. The Robert J. Terry Anatomical Collection is housed at the National Museum of Natural History, Smithsonian Institution, Washington, D.C. This collection of known individuals is cadaveric and was procured from the 1920s to the 1960s.

The Pretoria Bone Collection is curated by the Department of Anatomy, University of Pretoria, South Africa. It is a modern and growing collection composed of donated and unclaimed cadavers of known age, sex, and ancestry, dating from the mid-twentieth century to the present.

Data were collected for 240 individuals from the Terry Collection and 154 individuals from the Pretoria Bone Collection. Therefore, individuals of both European and African ancestry from the United States and South Africa constitute the present study sample. Figure 16.1 and Table 16.1 show the demographic distribution and the summary statistics for each collection and subgroup as well as for the entire study sample.

The sample was specifically constructed to form as even an age distribution among the subgroups as possible. An attempt was made to include five individuals from each subgroup per half-decade ranging from 20 to 79 years of age. Unfortunately, both collections have limitations and deficits, particularly for the youngest age groups, and especially for white females. For example, only one white female younger than 50 years was available from the Pretoria Bone Collection. As a result, groups lacking younger individuals have inflated mean ages.

The terms "black" and "white" are used throughout the remainder of this chapter and warrant an explanation here. The sample is comprised of individuals from two countries: the United States and South Africa. From the collections in both of these countries, two groups were studied: those of European ancestry (white) and those of African ancestry (black). Therefore, the study sample consists of Americans of European and African ancestry as well as Africans of European and African ancestry. The terms "black" and "white" are used as terms of convenience to represent individuals who share a Sub-Saharan African or Western European ancestry, respectively, but who now may be separated temporally and spatially.

Four areas of each skeleton were scored to assess age: the pubic symphysis, the iliac auricular surface, the sternal extremity of the ribs, and the sutures. Each specimen from the Terry Collection was scored on three separate occasions: once for the pelvis, once for the ribs, and once for the cranium. This strategy minimized potential bias resulting from knowing the other morphological age indicators during scoring. Separate scoring was not plausible for the postcrania of the Pretoria Collection, although the skulls from that collection were scored separately. All of the specimens were scored by the author with the exception of 54 crania from the Terry Collection, for which Nawrocki's (1998) original data on cranial suture closure was used.

The pubic symphysis was scored on a scale of 1 to 6 according to the Brooks and Suchey (1990) phase descriptions. Both left and right sides were scored, but the left side is used in this analysis. In the event that a left side was not present or scoreable (e.g., damaged or pathological), the right side was substituted.

Both left and right iliac auricular surfaces were scored according to the descriptions and phases from Osborne et al. (2004). This method assigns a score of 1 to 6 based on an evaluation of the joint surface and retroauricular area. The left auricular surface was used in the analysis, but if it was not present or scoreable, the right side was substituted.

Data were collected on ribs 4 through 7 from both the left and right sides, when present and undamaged. While the published standards are based on the right fourth rib, the fragility of the sternal extremities would severely restrict the sample if only right fourth ribs were included. If the right fourth rib was present, that score was used. If it was not present or scoreable then the left fourth rib score was used. If that was not present, then the right fifth rib score was used, and so on. Yoder et al. (2001) found no significant differences between the phase scores for the right fourth rib and any other rib 2-9.

Whites from both collections were scored and analyzed according to Îscan et al. (1984, 1985, 1991). Blacks from both the Terry and Pretoria Collections were scored according to Îscan et al. (1984, 1985, 1991), but the summary statistics from Oettlé (1998) were used in the analysis because Îscan et al. (1991) do not give complete data for Black individuals. It should be noted that the "95% confidence intervals" given by Îscan et al. and Oettlé were used despite their inappropriateness (Nawrocki, n.d.a), in order to assess their performance.

Cranial suture closure was scored according to Nawrocki (1998). For each individual, 27 vault and palatine landmarks were scored on a scale of 0 to 3 based on the amount of suture closure. These scores were summed for each cranium, producing a score that could range from 0 to 81 (SUMALL).

Before combining different skeletal indicators, the efficacy of each of the individual methods must be assessed because it will influence the performance of any multifactorial method. Because anthropologists do not typically agree on how to measure the effectiveness of aging methods, three common statistical approaches were used: inaccuracy, bias, and a calculation of the percentage of individuals correctly aged using previously published confidence intervals. For comparison, all three of these measurements were calculated for each of the multifactorial methods.

Inaccuracy is a measure of the absolute difference between estimated and actual age. Bias is a measure of the difference (positive or negative) between estimated and actual age for each individual. These measures are similar in that both are expressions of average estimation error. However, inaccuracy is the total, or overall, difference in age regardless of the direction of error, while bias indicates whether a method has a tendency to overage (positive bias) or underage (negative bias). Positive and negative bias values can offset each other in a sample, and so bias will nearly always be lower than inaccuracy. Inaccuracy includes an absolute value term so that it is always a positive number.

Following the analysis of the individual indicators three multifactorial procedures were tested: a simple average of the four point estimates, a range of spatial overlap of the four confidence intervals, and multiple linear regression. The simple average is a sum of the point estimates from each of the four methods divided by the number of methods to produce a target point estimate for each individual. Inaccuracy and bias for each of these "mean" age estimates was calculated for each collection and the entire sample, using the averaged point estimate as the predicted age. Because a true error range cannot be generated for this method, the overall inaccuracy (10.21 years) was substituted as a prediction interval, adding and subtracting it to the obtained average age for each individual to create an estimated age range. The number of individuals' ages falling into their estimated age range was then determined.

The second analysis utilizes published age ranges rather than the point or target estimates for each phase. The 95 percent prediction intervals for each method were spatially aligned and the "Total Minimum Range" (TMinR), from the highest minimum age to the lowest maximum age, was adopted as the estimated age range for each individual (Figure 16.2). The percentage of individuals falling into their calculated age range was then computed. While this method appears to be very objective, some unpredicted scenarios were encountered that made this method, at times, somewhat subjective. For example, some individuals had one indicator that did not overlap with the other three. In this situation, the three overlapping ranges were used and the fourth was excluded. The mathematical midpoint of the TMinR range was calculated for each individual by subtracting the highest minimum age from the lowest maximum age and dividing by two. This midpoint was then used as a target age estimate for the calculation of inaccuracy and bias statistics.

Next, the "Total Maximum Range" (TMaxR), using the spread from the lowest minimum age to the highest maximum age in the overlapping 95 percent ranges, was adopted as the estimated age range (Figure 16.3). The percentage of individuals falling into their calculated age ranges was then computed. As with the TMinR method, the midpoint of the range was calculated by subtracting the lowest minimum age from the highest maximum age and

FIGURE 16.2
ILLUSTRATION OF THE TOTAL MINIMUM RANGE (TMINR)

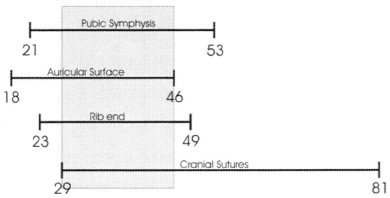

FIGURE 16.3
ILLUSTRATION OF THE TOTAL MAXIMUM RANGE (TMAXR)

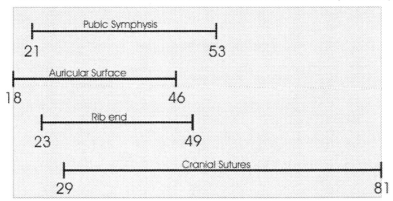

dividing by two. This midpoint was used as the target age estimate for the calculation of inaccuracy and bias statistics.

Using overlapping ranges solves the inherent problem in the simple averaging method by constructing a likely age range from the beginning. However, less obvious is how one should generate an actual point or target estimate for the decedent. The method of calculating the midpoints used here is not based on any theoretical principles and thus may not be particularly enlightening.

Lastly, a multiple linear regression equation for estimating age at death was calculated using all four variables. Theoretically, the use of several predictor variables (as opposed to only one in a simple regression) can reduce prediction error by accounting for more of the variance in the dependent variable (Kachigan, 1982). In an attempt to improve the performance of the regression equation, it was subjected to forward stepwise selection. This procedure limits the set of predictors only to those that contribute significantly to model, e.g., those that actually predict the variance in the dependent variable.

A regression equation was generated for the entire study sample and the percentages of individuals falling within the ± 1 and ± 2 standard error (se) intervals were calculated, along with inaccuracy and bias statistics.

RESULTS

Individual Indicators

Pubic Symphysis

As an individual indicator, the pubic symphysis had an overall inaccuracy of 12.05 years and a bias of -8.20 years (Table 16.2). When these statistics are broken down by ancestry/sex group and decade, they follow a typical pattern: inaccuracy is low for younger individuals and increases steadily with age, which can be expected for any aging indicator because of the so-called trajectory effect (variance in aging indicators increases with increasing age). Bias begins as a high positive number, approaches zero near middle age, and finally becomes a high negative number in old age. The pattern for bias indicates that the pubic symphysis is overaging younger individuals, both over- and underaging middle-aged individuals (averaging to nearly zero), and underaging older individuals. The published confidence intervals (Brooks and Suchey, 1990) correctly age 85 percent of the individuals in this sample (Table 16.3).

TABLE 16.2
INACCURACY AND BIAS FOR EACH INDICATOR BY COLLECTION AND OVERALL

Indicator	*Terry Collection*		*Pretoria Collection*		*Overall*	
	Inaccuracy	*Bias*	*Inaccuracy*	*Bias*	*Inaccuracy*	*Bias*
Public Symphysis	11.78	-6.38	12.44	-10.26	12.05	-8.20
Auricular Surface	12.39	-4.42	11.81	-5.13	12.15	-4.76
Sternal Rib Ends	10.96	-2.71	16.37	-12.13	13.10	-6.39
Cranial Sutures	15.99	14.07	10.71	8.76	15.24	9.98

TABLE 16.3
PERCENTAGES OF INDIVIDUALS WHOSE ACTUAL AGES FALL WITHIN
THE PUBLISHED 95% PREDICTION INTERVALS FOR EACH INDICATOR

	Terry	*Pretoria*	*Total*
Public Symphysis	85% (n = 205)	84% (n = 130)	85% (n = 335)
Auricular Surface	90% (n = 217)	96% (n = 149)	93% (n = 366)
Sternal Rib Ends	33% (n = 81)	15% (n = 23)	26% (n = 104)
Cranial Sutures	86% (n = 207)	84% (n = 130)	86% (n = 337)

The inaccuracy and bias values for Pretoria Whites are rather high compared to other subgroups. These high values are probably a result of uneven sampling; with fewer individuals in the younger age categories, older individuals have a disproportionate influence on mean inaccuracy, increasing it with their greater errors. In addition, with fewer younger individuals there are fewer positive bias values to offset the negative values in the older age range, producing a higher (negative) bias.

Iliac Auricular Surface

Inaccuracy and bias statistics for the auricular surface are given in Table 16.2. This method was almost on par with the pubic symphysis, with an inaccuracy of 12.15 years and a bias of -4.76 years. For the most part, inaccuracy and bias follow the expected patterns; however, for some groups, inaccuracy values start rather high, drop slightly, and then increase again. Bias follows this pattern for some groups (e.g., Terry black males), but in general, bias begins as a high positive number, approaches zero at middle age, and then becomes a high negative number. When the 95 percent prediction intervals are used (Osborne et al., 2004), 93 percent (366 of 394) of individuals in this sample fell into their predicted ranges (Table 16.3).

Sternal Ribs

Inaccuracy and bias statistics for the sternal extremity of the rib are given in Table 16.2. In terms of inaccuracy and bias the rib method performed better than any other individual method for the Terry Collection and worse than any other individual method for the Pretoria Collection. Because different standards have been published for different subgroups, the 95 percent ranges vary between ancestries and sexes. Not surprisingly, only 26 percent (104 of 394) of the individuals fell into these very narrowly-constructed age ranges (Table 16.3).

Cranial Sutures

Overall, the cranial suture equation had greater inaccuracy and bias values than the other individual skeletal indicators (Table 16.2). In addition, the pattern of error is a bit different, having larger errors in the earlier years compared to later years. This pattern may be due in part to the lower mean age of the current sample (51.4 years) compared to Nawrocki's (1998) sample (53.7 years), on which the equations are based. Nawrocki included individuals as old as 85, whereas the present study sample includes individuals only as old as 79.

Table 16.3 gives the percentage of individuals by decade that fell into the ± 2 se intervals predicted by their cranial suture. The age for each individual was estimated using a general equation (Nawrocki, 1998). The results show that the ± 2 se interval correctly aged 86 percent and 84 percent of individuals from the Terry Collection and Pretoria Collection respectively.

Inaccuracy is lowest for the pubic symphysis and highest for the cranial sutures, although all four methods perform similarly. Bias is negative for all but the sutures, indicating that the latter method tends to overestimate age at death while the other indicators tend to underestimate it. Bias is lowest (closest to zero) for the auricular surface and highest for the sutures.

When the percentage of individuals whose actual ages fell within the published confidence interval is considered, the pubic symphysis, auricular surface, and cranial sutures all had comparable success. The sternal rib ends, however, produced dismal results, no doubt due to the unreasonably narrow and incorrectly constructed "confidence intervals" provided in the original publications. However, the method's difficulty in predicting age for the Pretoria Collection—evidenced by the inaccuracy and bias statistics given previously—suggests that the method has other flaws. Overall, the iliac auricular surface was the most successful at correctly aging individuals.

TABLE 16.4
INACCURACY, BIAS, AND PERCENTAGES OF INDIVIDUALS WHOSE ACTUAL AGES
FALL INTO THE ± 1 AND ± 2 SE RANGES FOR THE SIMPLE AVERAGE METHOD

	Inaccuracy	*Bias*	*1 se*	*2 se*
Terry	9.69	-0.77	57% (n = 139)	94% (n = 228)
Pretoria	10.77	-4.67	51% (n = 79)	91% (n = 141)
Total	10.21	-2.31	55% (n = 218)	94% (n = 369)

Complex Methods

Simple Average

The effectiveness of this method was measured using inaccuracy and bias statistics (Table 16.4). For each collection, and for the entire sample, this method had lower inaccuracy and bias values than any of the individual methods. The bias evinced by the simple average method shows the typical trend—a high positive number for younger individuals, approaching zero at middle age, and finally becoming a large negative number in old age.

In order to further compare this method to the individual indicators, an approximation of a 95 percent prediction interval was constructed using the overall inaccuracy (10.21 years) as a substitute for the standard deviation. The percentage of individuals' actual ages falling into the ± 1 se and ± 2 se ranges were calculated (Table 16.4). Perhaps predictably, only 56 percent of the Terry individuals and 51 percent of the Pretoria individuals were correctly aged using the ±1 se range, on the other hand the ± 2 se range correctly aged 94 percent and 91 percent of Terry and Pretoria individuals respectively.

The simple average is appealing as a straightforward method for generating a target age for an unidentified skeleton, because it tends to "average-out" any indicators that are unusual or atypical for a particular individual. However, one could also argue that simple averaging should not work, because it takes the best indicator and "dilutes" it with the broader error ranges of the less-effective indicators. Another problem with averaging is that it is not possible to generate a statiscally valid error range for a given estimate.

TABLE 16.5
INACCURACY, BIAS, AND PERCENTAGES OF INDIVIDUALS WHOSE
ACTUAL AGES FALL INTO THE TOTAL MINIMUM RANGE (TMINR)

	Inaccuracy	*Bias*	*% correct*
Terry	9.44	-2.66	61% (n = 147)
Pretoria	9.38	-5.41	63% (n = 97)
Total	9.41	-3.74	62% (n = 244)

Overlapping Age Ranges

A common way anthropologists arrive at a final age range estimate is to look at the overlapping ranges of the available individual indicators. While this method is not guided by a particular statistical methodology, it is often employed as a simple way to combine and document age estimates and therefore deserves further investigation.

The first method incorporated the age range stretching from the highest minimum estimate to the lowest maximum estimate and is referred to as the Total Minimum Range (TMinR). As with the other methods, evaluation included a calculation of the percentage of individuals' actual ages falling within the range, as well as inaccuracy and bias statistics (Table 16.5). The percentage of individuals' actual ages falling within the range was 62 percent overall, which is lower than any of the individual indicators but quite high considering that TMinR will always be narrower than any correctly constructed 95 percent prediction interval for the individual indicators. The product of this analysis is the opposite of the simple average – a range is calculated, but no point estimate is generated. Inaccuracy and bias statistics were calculated from the mathematical midpoint of each individual's range. Inaccuracy is slightly lower than for the simple average method; however, bias indicates that it underages individuals by about 1.5 years more than the simple average method.

Next, the Total Maximum Range (TMaxR), defined as the lowest minimum estimate to the highest maximum estimate, was calculated for each individual. This method was evaluated in exactly the same fashion as the TMinR. Every individual in both collections was correctly aged using this method. However, this method has greater inaccuracy than the TMinR and simple

TABLE 16.6
REGRESSION EQUATION COMBINING THE AGING INDICATORS

PS Phase*(4.983) + AS Phase*(2.698) + Rib Phase*(2.639) + CS SUMALL*(0.075) - 0.029

(Adj. r^2 = 0.526; inaccuracy, 9.53; bias, 0.01; se = 10.99)

TABLE 16.7
INACCURACY, BIAS, AND PERCENTAGES OF INDIVIDUALS WHOSE ACTUAL AGES
FALL INTO THE ± 1 SE AND ± 2 SE INTERVALS FOR THE REGRESSION EQUATION

	Inaccuracy	*Bias*	*1 se*	*2 se*
Terry	9.50	1.23	66% (n = 159)	94% (n = 227)
Pretoria	9.61	-2.09	65% (n = 100)	96% (n = 149)
Total	9.53	0.01	66% (n = 259)	95% (n = 376)

averaging methods. Such large ranges (sometimes from 18 to 90 years!) are created that the method becomes impractical and meaningless. The inaccuracy values reflect these wide ranges as they were calculated from the midpoint of each range. A large range creates higher inaccuracy (regardless of the method's real accuracy) because that midpoint falls at around the mid-50s for every individual.

Linear Regression

The final complex method investigated was linear regression. The equation, which includes all four individual indicators, is given in Table 16.6 and applies to all groups in the study. While all four indicators contribute to the equation (verified with forward stepwise selection), the coefficient of each individual indicator partly reflects its relative inaccuracy (e.g., the pubic symphysis has the lowest inaccuracy and therefore has the largest weight in the regression equation).

As with the previous methods, the regression was assessed by calculating the percentage of individuals' actual ages falling within ± 1 and ± 2 se intervals (Table 16.7). The percentages falling within ± 1 se are comparable to those obtained for the simple average and TMinR methods. The ± 2 se percentages are very similar to those calculated for most of the individual indicators, around 95 percent for each collection and overall. The inaccuracy and bias statistics are given in Table 16.7. The method seems to work very well for all groups, although the inaccuracy and bias are slightly lower for the Terry sample compared to the Pretoria sample.

DISCUSSION

The purpose of this study was to reduce the error in determining adult age at death by investigating different ways of combining age estimates from several indicators. For comparison, basic statistics were calculated for each individual age indicator. Subsequent analysis of several multifactorial methods ensued, including a simple average of all four individual indicators, consideration of the overlapping ranges of the individual age estimates, and linear regression.

Individual Indicators

Confidence Interval Classification

Four individual indicators were investigated in this study. When published confidence intervals were applied to the present study sample (Table 16.3), the iliac auricular surface phase ranges were the most effective, including the correct age for 96 percent (378 of 394) of the sample. The pubic symphysis and the ± 2 se interval for the cranial sutures equation were comparable at 85 percent (335 of 394) and 86 percent (336 of 394), respectively. The sternal extremities of the ribs, however, had meager success, with only 26 percent (104 of 394) of individuals' documented ages falling within the predicted ranges. These results do not necessarily reflect the method *per se,* but they do demonstrate a serious problem with the constructed age ranges for this method. Some ranges are as narrow as two years and cannot possibly account for the amount of human variation in this study sample. The rib method may include too many phases—perhaps some of them could be combined to produce more inclusive phase categories.

Inaccuracy and Bias Statistics

Inaccuracy and bias statistics are useful measures for analyzing, testing, and comparing aging methods and were calculated for each of the four individual indicators (Table 16.2). For the overall sample, the pubic symphysis had the lowest inaccuracy of 12.05 years, while the auricular surface had the lowest bias (closest to zero) of -4.76 years. While the sternal extremities of the ribs had a rather high overall inaccuracy (13.10 years), they had the lowest inaccuracy and bias for the Terry Collection at 10.96 years and -2.71 years, respectively. The auricular surface had the lowest inaccuracy and bias for the Pretoria Collection at 11.81 years and -5.13 years, respectively.

While all three of the phase methods had comparable inaccuracy and bias values, the cranial suture method had an inaccuracy of 15.24 years and a bias of 9.98 years. It is notable that for poorly distributed subgroup samples (lacking younger individuals, such as Pretoria white females), the inaccuracy and bias increase for the phase methods. The phase methods tend to be less accurate and grossly underage older individuals due to the trajectory effect (an increase in variation with age). However, the cranial suture equation behaves counter-intuitively. The inaccuracy and bias for the cranial suture equation actually decreases dramatically with increasing age in these subgroups, probably because the phase methods were developed on younger samples while the cranial suture method was developed on a slightly older sample and its upper limit is not artificially truncated.

Complex Methods

Simple Average

This method combined the four individual indicators by simply taking the average of the four age estimates and was evaluated via inaccuracy and bias statistics and percent of individuals correctly aged. The inaccuracy and bias statistics for each collection and the entire sample were lower than any of the individual indicators (Table 16.4) at 10.21 years and -2.31 years, respectively. Despite the fact that some indicators are less accurate than others, they are more effective at predicting age when combined. It should be noted that this method does not weigh the individual indicators as linear regression does. The biggest obstacle presented by this method is the construction of a proper error interval. The average only gives a target age estimate and does not provide any data with which to construct an error interval. As a rough substitute, the inaccuracy (10.21 years) was used to construct ± 1 and ± 2 se intervals for subsequent analyses. The ± 1 se interval correctly included 55 percent (218 of 394) of individuals' ages, while the ± 2 se interval correctly included 94 percent (369 of 394) of individuals. In this respect, the simple average performs better than any of the four individual indicators.

Overlapping Age Ranges

Many practicing anthropologists determine a final age range by looking at the spatial overlap of the prediction intervals of several aging indicators. This method is not rooted in rigorous statistical methodology but its simplicity is intuitively appealing. The dilemma presented by this method is the opposite of that presented by the simple average method: an age range is easily established but there is no standard for constructing a single point or target estimate, which also makes it impossible to calculate inaccuracy and bias statistics. To remedy this, the mathematical midpoint of the established range for each individual was calculated and used as a surrogate point estimate for age.

The first test combined the smaller age range, referred to as the Total Minimum Range (TMinR), which covered the interval between the highest minimum estimate and the lowest maximum estimate of the four individual indicators. The overall inaccuracy and bias statistics (Table 16.5) were lower than any of the preceding methods, including the simple average. It is notable that this method is the first to have an inaccuracy below 10 years for each collection, working almost equally well for each. Bias values indicate that TMinR tends to underage individuals at a slightly higher rate than the simple average method.

Next, the percentage of individuals falling into their predicted age ranges was calculated. The TMinR method correctly aged 62 percent (244 of 394) of individuals, slightly more than for the other methods' ± 1 se intervals. This percentage is quite high considering that the resulting ranges are relatively narrow, some being only two years wide (e.g., 23 to 25 years). These ranges are much narrower than properly constructed 95 percent prediction intervals.

The second overlapping range method comprised the interval between the lowest minimum estimate and the highest maximum estimate of the four individual indicators; this is referred to as the Total Maximum Range (TMaxR). Inaccuracy was higher than any of the other complex methods but was comparable to the three individual phase methods, a byproduct of the very wide age ranges produced by this method. Many of the ranges encompassed the entire range of ages in the study sample (e.g., 18 to 80 years). Because the mid-point of the range was substituted as the point estimate, this method's point estimates were all middle-aged, causing a high inaccuracy (12.43 years) but balancing out the bias reasonably well (3.51 years).

The percentage of individuals' actual ages falling into their predicted ranges was 100%. While these results may seem promising, one must consider the balance between accuracy and precision. While the method is accurate (despite the inaccuracy statistic)–it always produces a range that encompasses the true age of the individual–it is so imprecise that it is meaningless and ineffective.

Linear Regression

The final complex method tested in this study was linear regression. Linear regression acts similarly to the simple average method except that the independent variables (aging indicators) do not contribute equally and valid error ranges are produced. While these advantages alone make it a very appealing method, it is also very easy to apply.

The regression equation was generated for the entire sample (Table 16.6). A forward stepwise regression retained all four indicators in the equation; however, each indicator is weighted according to its individual contribution, as reflected by the regression coefficient. The pubic symphysis has the highest weight, while the cranial sutures had a very low weight, which may reflect effectiveness or could be a remnant of the larger scoring scale (0 to 81), as opposed to the scales of 1 to 6 or 1 to 8 for the phase methods.

In contrast to the other complex methods, linear regression produces both a valid point estimate and a proper error range. The point estimate was used to calculate inaccuracy and bias statistics (Table 16.7). The overall inaccuracy was almost identical to that calculated for the TMinR method. This equation seems to produce slightly better results for Blacks, possibly due to sampling error, as the largest differences are seen in the youngest decade and White males and females were lacking in this category. Because of the nature of regression, bias is automatically balanced out to nearly zero for all equations.

The percentages of individuals' actual ages falling into their predicted ± 1 se and ± 2 se intervals were calculated (Table 16.7). The ± 1 se interval correctly aged 66 percent (259 of 394) of individuals. Theoretically, the ± 2 se interval should include 95 percent of the population, and the results were exactly as expected (376 of 394).

While regression equations are slightly more sophisticated than a simple average they are essentially as easy to use with the added advantage of properly weighted variables, and the generation of both a valid point estimate and true error range. An inherent disadvantage in the use of linear regression equations is that all four indicators must be present and scoreable. Additionally, the progression of skeletal aging is probably not linear, but regression forces it into a linear model.

CONCLUSIONS

The aging indicators investigated in this study were all more effective when combined than when used as individual indicators. With the exception of the totally ineffective TMaxR method, the complex methods all decreased over-all inaccuracy by at least two years. The regression equation had the lowest inaccuracy (9.53 years), but all of the complex methods' inaccuracies hovered around 9.5 or 10 years.

While most anthropologists would tend to believe that combining the age estimates from different indicators would improve the accuracy of their final age assessments, how one should combine these indicators is not always clear. This study presents several easy, applicable methods of combining aging indicators to arrive at a final, calculated point estimate and error range. The simplest of these methods is to average the target estimates obtained from the available individual aging indicators. Averaging improves the accuracy of age estimation and is intuitively obvious in its approach. However, this method does not produce the all-important prediction interval that an anthropologist must offer as a statement of the uncertainty for the methods used. A more accurate and statistically valid method is linear regression, which produces both a target estimate and a prediction interval for the decedent.

This study used only four of many possible individual aging indicators and only included individuals with all four indicators intact and undamaged. Because anthropologists often handle incomplete, fragmentary, and/or damaged human remains, methods combining fewer and different aging indicators are needed. Because the effectiveness of a complex method is limited by the quality of the methods it combines, continued refinement of individual methods can lead to continued improvements, as can other statistical methods such as transition analysis (see Konigsberg, 2000 or Boldsen et al., 2002). Furthermore, the use of geographically diverse skeletal samples in this study indicates that methods originally developed in the United States appear to be applicable to the South African sample as well.

ACKNOWLEDGMENTS

This research was funded in part by a grant from the University of Indianapolis. Many thanks to Dr. David Hunt for access to the R. J. Terry Collection, and Dr. Ericka L'Abbe and Marius Loots for access to the Pretoria Bone Collection and many other arrangements while in South Africa.

REFERENCES

Ascadi, G. Y., & Nemeskeri, J. (1970). *Human lifespan and mortality.* Akademiai Kiada, Budapest.

Boldsen, J. L., Milner, G. A., Konigsberg, L. W., & Wood, J. W. (2002). Transition analysis: A new method for estimating age from skeletons. In R. D. Hoppa & J. W. Vaupel (Eds.), *Paleodemography: Age distributions from skeletal samples,* pp. 73–106. Cambridge University Press, Cambridge.

Brooks, S. T. (1955). Skeletal age at death: The reliability of cranial and pubic age indicators. *American Journal of Physical Anthropology 13:*567–589.

Brooks, S. T., & Suchey, J. M. (1990). Skeletal age determination based on the *os pubis:* A comparison of the Acsádi-Nemeskéri and Suchey-Brooks methods. *Human Evolution 5:*227–238.

Îscan, M. Y. (1991). The aging process in the rib: An analysis of sex- and ancestry-related morphological variation. *American Journal of Human Biology 3:*617–623.

Îscan, M. Y., Loth, S. R., & Wright, R. K. (1984). Metamorphosis at the sternal rib end: A new method to estimate age at death in white males. *American Journal of Physical Anthropology 65:*147–156.

Îscan, M. Y., Loth, S. R., & Wright, R. K. (1985). Age estimation from the rib by phase analysis: White females. *Journal of Forensic Sciences 30:*853–863.

Johnson, J. S. (1976). A comparison of age estimation using discriminant function analysis with some other age estimations of unknown skulls. *Journal of Anatomy 121:*475–484.

Kachigan, S. K. (1982). *Multivariate statistical analysis: A conceptual introduction.* New York: Radius Press.

Konigsberg, L. W. (2000). Nphases program. http://konig.la.utk.edu/nphases2.htm.

Lovejoy, C. O., Meindl, R. S., Mensforth, R. P., & Barton, T. J. (1985). Multifactorial determination of skeletal age at death: A method and blind tests of its accuracy. *American Journal of Physical Anthropology 68:*1–14.

Nawrocki, S. P. (1998). Regression formulae for the estimation of age from cranial suture closure. In K. Reichs (Ed.), *Forensic osteology: Advances in the identification of human remains* (2nd ed.), pp. 276–292. Springfield, IL: Charles C Thomas

Nawrocki, S. P. n.d.a. Prediction intervals for estimates of age at death from the sternal extremity of the rib. Manuscript in preparation.

Oettlé, A. C. (1998). Age estimation from sternal ends of ribs by phase analysis in South African Blacks. MSc. Thesis, University of Pretoria, South Africa.

Osborne, D. L., Simmons, T. L., & Nawrocki, S. P. (2004). Reconsidering the auricular surface as an indicator of age at death. *Journal of Forensic Sciences 49:*905–911.

Saunders, S. R., Fitzgerald, C., Rogers, T., Dudar, C., & McKillop, H. (1992). A test of several methods of skeletal age estimation using a documented archaeological sample. *Canadian Society of Forensic Sciences Journal 25*(2):97–118.

Yoder, C., Ubelaker, D. H., & Powell, J. F. (2001). Examination of variation in sternal rib end morphology relevant to age assessment. *Journal of Forensic Sciences 46*(2):223–227.

Chapter 17

A TEST OF THE FORENSIC APPLICATION OF TRANSITION ANALYSIS WITH THE PUBIC SYMPHYSIS

CAROLYN V. HURST

INTRODUCTION

Determining age at death in medicolegal investigations is a major component of the identification process. The pubic symphysis is often used in age at death estimation because it undergoes predictable developmental and degenerative changes that correlate well with chronological age. Since T. Wingate Todd's first pubic symphyseal age at death estimation method in 1920, there have been a number of aging methods established based on these osseous transformations. A more recent development is the ADBOU Age Estimation computer software program, a statistically based age estimation program which utilizes a component scoring system and prior age at death distributions from reference samples to inform its estimates based on the observable characteristics of the pubic symphysis of an unknown individual (Boldsen et al., 2002). This method was originally developed for bioarchaeological investigations where available skeletal components, including cranial sutures, the iliac auricular surface, the pubic symphysis, or any combination of these could be used for age estimations in archaeological populations. However, forensic applicability is suggested to attain age estimates of unknown individuals in medicolegal contexts based on appropriate reference samples from contemporary populations.

BACKGROUND

The pubic symphysis of the *os coxa* is frequently used as a skeletal indicator of age because it undergoes fairly standard development and degeneration that correlates well with age (Gilbert and McKern, 1973; Katz and Suchey, 1986; Brooks and Suchey, 1990; Moore-Jansen et al., 1994). The utility of using the pubic symphysis was first recognized by Todd (1920) who divided these developmental and degenerative patterns into ten stages, each progressing in age from 18 to 50+ years. Unfortunately, the skeletal collection that was the basis for the Todd method included samples with inaccurate or unverified ages and the majority of the collection consisted of individual who were 40 years or older. Thus, the correlation of ages with particular symphyseal morphologies was not precise and the < 40 age category was underrepresented limiting the range of morphological variation.

In an effort to improve upon this method, McKern and Stewart (1957) examined the pubic symphysis using a sample of Americans killed in the Korean War to create a component system to estimate age at death. In this method, the pubic symphysis is evaluated for the development of the dorsal plateau, the ventral rampart, and the symphyseal rim. These three characteristics are scored independently and subsequently summed for comparison to a reference table to determine the age. However, the use of soldiers killed in the Korean War for a reference sample is problematic because young adult white males dominate the sample. Unfortunately, the bias of the reference sample makes this technique of little use for the aging of individuals that do not fit this demographic.

Realizing that developmental schedules and morphological changes manifested in the pubis are different in the sexes, Gilbert and McKern (1973) recognized that a separate standard was necessary for females. Thus a component technique, analogous to McKern and Stewart's (1957) method for aging, was developed from a sample of 103 females (Gilbert and McKern, 1973). Unfortunately, this system lost favor when a study by Suchey (1979) revealed that the technique was highly unreliable and yielded inaccurate estimates in 49 percent of cases tested (Suchey, 1979; White and Folkens, 2005).

To remedy the issues of problematic reference samples, a new aging technique utilized an extensive autopsy sample of 1012 individuals (739 males and 273 females) from the Los Angeles County Medical Examiner's Office (Katz and Suchey, 1986). The pubic morphological variation of this large sample was examined and subjected to statistical analysis by Katz to create what is now known as the Suchey-Brooks Method (Brooks, 1990). This technique revised Todd's (1921) system by collapsing his ten stages into six and creating broader age ranges (Katz and Suchey, 1986). The extensive sample also allowed for the creation of separate male and female standards to increase the precision of the technique. To supplement the descriptions of the pubic symphysis at particular developmental or degenerative stages, France Casting (2007) created a set of casts that provide early and late examples of each phase to aid in the proper assessment of age. While these techniques have become standard practice in physical anthropology, new methods are often devised to improve upon traditional approaches. The use of transition analysis in the ADBOU Age Estimation program is one such method. Although originally developed for bioarchaeological applications, the ADBOU Age Estimation program has the potential to usher in a new era of forensic age at death estimation.

TRANSITION ANALYSIS AND THE ADBOU AGE ESTIMATION PROGRAM

The ADBOU Age Estimation program (ADBOU refers to the University of Southern Denmark's Institute of Forensic Medicine, Department of Anthropology) is an adult skeletal aging technique based on a unique component system that bases its estimates on the most likely age that a skeletal feature will transition from one stage to the next. A common problem in age at death estimations is age mimicry, the bias of age estimations towards the composition of the reference sample. To avoid this issue, ADBOU Age Estimation program uses prior age at death distributions from reference populations that are more representative of mortality patterns of a given population, rather than the bones included in the sample. The ADBOU Age Estimation program utilizes five features from the pubic symphysis, nine features from the iliac auricular surface, and five cranial suture segments to obtain its age prediction. The software also allows the practitioner to separately score the right and left sides of the pubic symphysis and auricular surface and assign intermediate scores between phases if necessary. This information is then used to calculate maximum likelihood point age estimates and confidence intervals. The basic procedure is as follows:

1. Score the various features of the skeletal site according to provided guidelines.
2. Input values into the ADBOU Age Estimation Program.

TABLE 17.1
SCORING CATEGORIES FOR SYMPHYSEAL RELIEF

SYMPHYSEAL RELIEF
1. Sharp billowing
2. Soft, deep billowing
3. Soft, shallow billowing
4. Residual billowing
5. Flat
6. Irregular

TABLE 17.2
SCORING CATEGORIES FOR THE SUPERIOR APEX

SUPERIOR APEX
1. No protuberance
2. Early protuberance
3. Late protuberance
4. Integrated

TABLE 17.3
SCORING CATEGORIES FOR THE SYMPHYSEAL MARGIN

VENTRAL SYMPHYSEAL RELIEF
1. Serrated
2. Beveling
3. Rampart Formation
4. Rampart completion I
5. Rampart completion II
6. Rim
7. Breakdown

TABLE 17.4
SCORING CATEGORIES FOR THE DORSAL SYMPHYSEAL MARGIN

DORSAL SYMPHYSEAL MARGIN
1. Serrated
2. Flattening incomplete
3. Flattening complete
4. Rim
5. Breakdown

TABLE 17.5
SCORING CATEGORIES FOR THE SYMPHYSEAL TEXTURE

SYMPHYSEAL TEXTURE
1. Smooth (fine grained)
2. Coarse grained
3. Microporosity
4. Macroporosity

    3. Enter "Sex," "Race," and "Hazard" information.

       Note: "Hazard" refers to either an archaeological or forensic context.

    4. Calculate the age range.

Although Transition Analysis allows for separate scoring of the pubic bones, iliac auricular surface, and cranial sutures to estimate the age at death, this pilot study focuses on its utility in estimating ages solely from the pubic symphysis. To obtain an estimate from the pubic symphysis, five different aspects must first be evaluated and scored (Tables 17.1–17.5) (Boldsen et al., 2002).

To aid in the proper scoring of these features, descriptions of each stage are provided by Boldsen et al. (2002). The right and left pubic bones are scored independently for each feature, and if a particular aspect is between stages it is to be marked as such (Boldsen et al., 2002). For example, if the superior apex is between "late protuberance" and "integrated" it should be scored as a 3–4. These two features are unique to pubic bone aging techniques and help account for variation that may occur between the left and right pubic symphyses and any difficulties in assigning a particular phase. Once these scores have been determined, they are entered into the ADBOU Age Estimation computer program. The program calculates age estimates using an informative prior age at death distribution based on "sex," "race" (only black or white are available at this point) and whether the remains are from an "archaeological" or "forensic" context (Boldsen et al., 2002). In this program, the "forensic" population is defined by the 1996 Center for Disease Control and Prevention (CDC) homicide data. Although this distribution is labeled "forensic," a personal communication with Milner (April 9, 2007) revealed that this distribution is actually only appropriate for use with homicide victims, not all medicolegal cases. This reference sample provides a representative target population that provides the actual age distribution of individuals who died in homicide-related events. Prior age at death distributions are used in the function to calculate the most likely age of the individual in question, thus taking into account both skeletal features and mortality characteristics of the population. For instance, the bioarchaeological sample age distribution has higher rates of death in women of childbearing age, while the forensic sample has a higher frequency of young adult males, since this is the demographic most represented in the homicide data.

MATERIALS AND METHODS

This pilot research focuses on evaluating the pubic symphyseal age estimates obtained from the ADBOU Age Estimation software compared to methods commonly used in the contexts of forensic anthropology. The sample consists of 60 pubic symphyses (46 male and 14 female) of known age from the Pima County Forensic Science Center (FSC) in Tucson, Arizona (Figure 17.1). Fifty-six of the 60 pubic symphyses were from the Walter H. Birkby Reference Collection housed at the FSC. An additional 4 male pubic symphyses were analyzed during routine forensic anthropological examination and their ages became known upon positive identification. The male sample ranges from ages 11 to 72 with an emphasis on the 11–20 age span (39%). The female sample ranges in age from 12 to 69 with a fairly even distribution.

Each individual of the male sample was evaluated using 4 different methods: Todd (1921), McKern and Stewart (1957), Suchey-Brooks (Brooks and Suchey, 1990), and ADBOU Age Estimation Program (Boldsen et al., 2002).

FIGURE 17.1
AGE DISTRIBUTION OF SAMPLE BY SEX

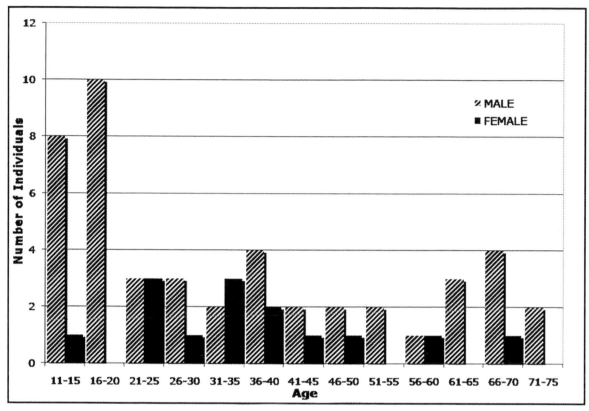

For the female sample, only the Suchey-Brooks (1990) and ADBOU methods were compared because other techniques have not proven their utility in providing accurate age estimations for females. Each pubic symphysis was scored according to the relevant guidelines of the specific aging method. The Suchey-Brooks male and female age determination casts were utilized in concert with the written definitions.

Once the ages of all pubic symphyses had been estimated, they were compared to the known age of the individual. Classification accuracy was used to evaluate the performance of each of the methods and is defined as the percent of correctly classified individuals into a given confidence interval. Values that were encompassed within the confidence intervals of ADBOU, Suchey-Brooks (1990), and McKern and Stewart (1957), and those that were within the given age range of Todd (1921) were classified as correct age estimates.

TABLE 17.6
ACCURACY OF TESTED PUBIC SYMPHYSIS AGING TECHNIQUES

	MALE N=46		FEMALE N=14		TOTAL N=60	
CORRECT	N	%	N	%	N	%
Todd	10	21.74	--	--	10	21.74
McKern-Stewart	12	26.09	--	--	12	26.09
Suchey-Brooks	29	63.04	9	64.29	38	63.33
Milner-Boldsen	24	52.17	9	64.29	33	55.00

RESULTS

For the sample of male pubic bones, the Suchey-Brooks method had the highest percent correct, accurately estimating the ages of 29 of the 46 analyzed. Using ADBOU, 24 were correctly estimated, while the other methods, McKern and Stewart and Todd, fell short correctly identifying only 12 and 10, respectively (Table 17.6). There were 9 individuals that none of the methods identified correctly. This could be indicative of unexpected variation or intraobserver error. For the female estimates, the Suchey-Brooks and Boldsen et al. methods both correctly estimated the ages for 9 of the 14 samples, with 4 individuals that were incorrectly assessed by both.

DISCUSSION

While it seems the Suchey-Brooks method is the most accurate, several points should be considered. The sample size and age distributions were less than ideal for testing purposes. The skew of the male sample towards 11 to 20-year-olds is an unlikely age at death distribution for a medicolegal context. Not only are people of this age range less likely to die in contexts of medicolegal import, but they also have a suite of features beyond the pubic symphysis to help in age determination. Boldsen and colleagues (2002) began work with transition analysis to address the problem of accurately estimating the ages of adults, because variation increases with age and since there are already a number of accurate methods for determining juvenile age at death. For this reason, the ADBOU Age Estimation program has an artificial age range from 15 to 110 (Milner, personal communication, April 9, 2007). This means that it is unable to estimate any age less than 15, making it impossible to correctly identify the ages of four of the individuals in the sample. With this being said, the other aging methods have the same limitations. The lowest possible estimate for Todd is 18 years, McKern and Stewart is 16.8 years, and Suchey-Brooks is 16.4 years (Brooks and Suchey, 1990; McKern and Stewart, 1957; Todd, 1921).

Another consideration is the appropriateness of the prior distributions that are used to aid in the calculation of the age estimates. The ADBOU Age Estimation program provides the user with three different fields that have prior age at death distributions that may be correlated to help calculate a more accurate age. These include "sex" (male or female), "race" (black or white), and "context" (archaeological or forensic). However, Milner warns that in cases of unknown affinity to use the white "race" category as this reference sample is larger and therefore, more robust (personal communication, January 19, 2008). Although it was possible to include sex as a delimiting factor in this particular study, "race" could not be included because the samples from FSC did not have this information documented. The forensic prior distribution was calculated from the 1996 CDC homicide data, which may not be an accurate analogue for the sample populations. Also, the use of the term "forensic" for homicide data was inaccurate because many forensic cases are not homicide related. In fact, the majority of the exams at FSC were related to unidentified remains with no signs of perimortem trauma (B. Anderson, personal communication, April 2, 2007). Milner (personal communication, April 9, 2007) addressed this misnomer and admitted that the "forensic" distribution should be labeled as a "homicide" distribution to avoid confusion and should only be used for actual homicide victims. He also mentioned that in a later version of the program, a prior distribution for a modern population from a developed nation, either a population from Western Europe or the United States, will likely be included. This type of informed prior distribution would have been the most appropriate for the sample populations analyzed.

An age estimation technique should not only be accurate, it should also be efficient and simple to utilize. The Suchey-Brooks (1990) method is modeled after, and considered by its authors to be, a "modified Todd Method" that collapses his ten phases into six (Brooks and Suchey, 1990:229). Both employ the gestalt concept of pubic symphysis assessment where the symphyseal face of the pubic symphysis is evaluated as a whole and the overall pattern is considered. McKern and Stewart (1957) and Boldsen et al. (2002) alternatively use a method where component parts are scored independently. The latter approach is far more time-consuming because one must locate, evaluate, and score each characteristic. Although experience decreases the time necessary for this process, it is not usually as fast as the gestalt techniques. In this study, the most efficient and user-friendly method was Suchey-Brooks. The casts made it easier to match an unknown pubic bone to a particular phase. This choice could be further validated by the provided descriptions. The phase descriptions of Todd tended to be general or difficult to interpret, while the McKern and Stewart descriptions are useful, but are subjective to developmental changes with little attention to degeneration due to the young reference sample. With the Boldsen et al. (2002) method, some of the definitions were difficult to understand with unfamiliar terminology and lack of visual aids to illustrate the author's descriptions.

CONCLUSIONS

Methods of aging the pubic symphysis have greatly progressed since Todd first created a technique to evaluate the changes he had observed. Since then, Todd's (1921) method has largely been replaced by Suchey-Brooks (1990) and new methods, like transition analysis, will continue to contribute and improve the field. In this pilot study, Suchey-Brooks (1990) proved to be the most accurate, easiest to learn, and most efficient technique. The ADBOU age estimation program, although still in its developing stages, demonstrated its utility in forensic applications with a strong performance.

Boldsen and colleagues' (2002) transition analysis provides a fairly accurate method for determining age from various features of the pubic symphysis. Its ability to score the left and right pubic bones independently to obtain an overall estimate is valuable when other methods place them in two different stages leaving the omnibus estimation to the evaluator. Also, the inclusion of aging methods for the iliac auricular surface and cranial sutures can help validate pubic ages or can be utilized in cases where pubic bones are not recovered or are unable to be scored. It should also be noted that in Boldsen et al. (2002), the best quality of age estimates was obtained by combining information from the pubic symphysis, auricular surface, and cranial sutures, but the accuracy was only slightly higher than estimates from the pubic symphysis alone. Including these other skeletal features may improve the estimation ability of transition analysis and should be tested in future research. Transition analysis has obvious utility in forensic applications, and with continued improvements, like the addition of more representative populations, it may prove to be a valuable tool in forensic age estimations.

ACKNOWLEDGMENTS

The author would like to acknowledge the Pima County Forensic Science Center and the University of Arizona for providing the opportunity to conduct this research project. Additionally, a heartfelt thank you to Dr. Bruce Anderson, Dr. Walter Birkby, and Dr. Todd Fenton for their support and guidance in this and many other endeavors.

REFERENCES

Boldsen, J. L., Milner, G. R., Konigsberg, L. W., & Wood, J. W. (2002). Transition analysis: A new method for estimating age from skeletons. In R. D. Hoppa & J. W. Vaupel (Eds.), *Paleodemography: Age distribution from skeletal samples,* pp. 73–106. Cambridge: Cambridge University Press.

Brooks, S., & Suchey, J. M. (1990). Skeletal age determination based on the os pubis: A comparison of the Acsádi-Nemeskéri and Suchey-Brooks methods. *Human Evolution 5:*227-238.

France Casting. (2007). Suchey-Brooks male age determination #SA001. Suchey-Brooks female age determination #SA002. Electronic document: www.francecast.com.

Gilbert, B. M., & McKern, T. W. (1973). A method for aging the female *os pubis. American Journal of Physical Anthropology 38:*31–38.

Katz, D., Suchey, J. M. (1986). Age determination of the male *os pubis. American Journal of Physical Anthropology 69:*427–435.

McKern, T. W., & Stewart, T. D. (1957). Skeletal age changes in young American males. Natick, Massachusetts: Quartermaster Research and Development Command Technical Report EP-45.

Milner, G. R., & Boldsen, J. L. (2007). Transition analysis: various images. Powerpoint Presentation. Penn State Department of Anthropology.

Moore-Jansen, P. H., Ousley, S. D., & Jantz, R. L. (1994). Data collection procedures for forensic skeletal material. Report of Investigations 48, University of Tennessee, Anthropology Department, Knoxville, TN.

Suchey, J. M. (1979). Problems in the aging of females using the *os pubis. American Journal of Physical Anthropology 51:*467–470.

Todd, T. W. (1920). Age changes in the pubic bone: I. The male white pubis. *American Journal of Physical Anthropology 3:*285–334.

Todd, T. W. (1921). Age changes in the pubic bone. *American Journal of Physical Anthropology 4:*1–70.

White, T. D., & Folkens, P. A. (2005). *The human bone manual.* Burlington, Massachusetts: Elsevier Academic Press.

INDEX